Modernism and the Spirit of the City

The modernist architecture that swept the world in the first half of the twentieth century was praised by its advocates and attacked by its critics for its rationalist and functionalist character, grounded on the dictates of the engineer and the technologist. *Modernism and the Spirit of the City* challenges this simple reading, and investigates the complex cultural, social, and religious imperatives that lay below the smooth, white surfaces of the new architecture.

Over a historical span that runs from the 1890s to the 1950s, ten distinguished scholars address those issues of aesthetics, poetics, spirituality, national identity, and commerce that were interwoven in the search for the ultimate goal of modernist architecture and urban design: paradise on earth. The first part of the book is devoted to strategies employed to define the 'spirit' of the city; the second considers the architectural intervention in the city and its aesthetic resonance; the third, the role of architecture and urban design as a site of spiritual speculation and reassurance in a robustly agnostic age.

This selection of ground-breaking essays offers a significant and long overdue reassessment of the aims and intentions of European architecture and urbanism in the early twentieth century. On the basis of British, French, and German examples, it argues that myth, history and spirituality, on one hand, and instrumental reason, order, and functionalism, on the other, need not be understood as mutually hostile, but as essential complements to each other.

Modernism and the Spirit of the City

Edited by Iain Boyd Whyte

Routledge
Taylor & Francis Group

LONDON AND NEW YORK

First published 2003 by Routledge
11 New Fetter Lane, London EC4P 4EE

Simultaneously published in the USA and Canada
by Routledge
29 West 35th Street, New York, NY 10001

Routledge is an imprint of the Taylor & Francis Group

Typeset in ITC Charter by Wearset Ltd, Boldon, Tyne and Wear
Printed and bound in Great Britain by TJ International Ltd, Padstow

British Library Cataloguing in Publication Data
A catalogue record for this book is available from the British Library

Library of Congress Cataloging in Publication Data
Modernism and the spirit of the city / edited by Iain Boyd Whyte.
   p. cm.
   Includes bibliographical references and index.
   1. City planning–Europe–History–20th century–Congresses.
   2. Modern movement (Architecture)–Europe–Congresses.
   3. City and town life–Europe–History–20th century–Congresses.
   I. Whyte, Iain Boyd, 1947–
   NA9010.M63 2002
   711'.4'0940904–dc21

   2002155376

ISBN 0-415-25840-5 (hbk)
ISBN 0-415-25841-3 (pbk)

Contents

Notes on contributors

Helge David has an MA from the University of Bonn and has published the writings of the architect August Endell as *Vom Sehen: Texte 1896–1925: Über Architektur, Formkunst und 'Die Schönheit der grossen Stadt'*, Basel/Boston: Birkhäuser, 1995. His doctoral dissertation on Endell is nearing completion, and he currently works as a freelance art historian and author.

David Frisby is Professor of Sociology at the University of Glasgow. His recent publications include *Cityscapes of Modernity*, Cambridge, Polity Press, 2001; *Fragments of Modernity*, Cambridge, Polity Press, 1985; *Georg Simmel* (revised edition), London, Routledge, 2002; and *Simmel and Since*, London, Routledge, 1992. He is editor of Georg Simmel's *Philosophy of Money: Expanded Edition*, London, Routledge, 2003, and co-editor (with Mike Featherstone) of *Simmel on Culture*, London, Sage, 1997. Forthcoming publications include (with Iain Boyd Whyte) *The Metropolitan Project: Berlin and Vienna 1880–1940*, Berkeley, CA, University of California Press; and *Metropolitan Architecture and Modernity: Otto Wagner's Vienna*, Minneapolis, University of Minnesota Press.

Karen Lang is Assistant Professor of modern European art history at the University of Southern California. In addition to essays on the German monument and national identity, she has written on the Kantian sublime, the late eighteenth-century cult of ruins, and Alexander Pope's garden and grotto. She has been the recipient of postdoctoral fellowships from the Getty Grant Program and the Clark Art Institute, and is currently completing a book on the early years of German art history, to be published by Cornell University Press.

Helen Shiner is completing a doctorate at the Courtauld Institute of Art on the patronage of architectural sculpture in Germany, 1890–1933. She has published on the sculptors Ernst Barlach, Moïssy Kogan and Winifred Turner. Most recently, her article on the Model Factory designed by Walter

Gropius and Adolf Meyer for the 1914 Werkbund Exhibition in Cologne was published in Stephen Newton and Brandon Taylor (eds) *Painting, Sculpture and the Spiritual Dimension: The Kingston and Winchester Papers*, London, Oneiros Books, 2003.

Rudolf Stegers studied German and French philology at the Universities of Münster and Berlin. He is a freelance architectural critic based in Berlin, author of a monograph on the architect Rudolf Schwarz, and curator of the exhibition *Glück Stadt Raum in Europa 1945 bis 2000* (*Happiness City Space in Europe 1945–2000*), held at the Academy of Arts, Berlin, in 2002. He is presently writing a book on sacred architecture in Europe after 1970.

Rob Stone lectures on architecture and aural culture at Goldsmiths College, London, and is the author of many articles treating the relationships between the poetics of modernist architecture and the emergence of the various cultures of mass suburbanisation. His current project is a book entitled *Auditions: Architecture and Aurality*.

Volker M. Welter is Associate Professor at the Department of History of Art and Architecture at the University of California, Santa Barbara. His main research interests are the history, theory, and historiography of modern and contemporary architecture; nineteenth- and twentieth-century urbanism; the architectural history of Zionism; and architectural representations of public space. He is author of *Biopolis: Patrick Geddes and the City of Life*, Cambridge, MA, MIT Press, 2002; co-editor of *The City after Patrick Geddes*, Bern, Peter Lang, 2000; and is currently completing a book on Ernst L. Freud (1892–1970), the architect son of Sigmund Freud.

Dagmar Motycka Weston is an architect and historian, who teaches at the University of Edinburgh. She is interested in the ways in which the history and philosophy of architecture can fruitfully inform contemporary design. Her current research is focused on modernity, and on the interrelated themes of art and architecture in the early twentieth century. She has published on Surrealist Paris and on Giorgio de Chirico, and is completing a book on Le Corbusier and the problem of space.

Rhodri Windsor Liscombe currently chairs the Department of Art History and the Interdisciplinary Graduate Program at the University of British Columbia. A graduate of the Courtauld Institute of Art, he previously taught at London and McGill Universities. His major publications include *William Wilkins 1778–1839*, Cambridge, Cambridge University Press, 1980

– revisited in *The Age of Wilkins: The Architecture of Improvement* (with David Watkin), Cambridge, Fitzwilliam Museum, 2000; *Francis Rattenbury and British Columbia: Architecture and Challenge in the Imperial Age* (with Anthony Barrett), Vancouver, University of British Columbia Press, 1983, *'Altogether American': Robert Mills, Architect and Engineer*, New York, Oxford University Press, 1994; and *'The New Spirit': Modern Architecture in Vancouver 1938–1963*, Montreal, Canadian Centre for Architecture, 1997. His current research centres on intersections between Modern Movement architecture and late British Imperialism and has been awarded a J. S. Guggenheim Fellowship.

Iain Boyd Whyte is Professor of Architectural History at the University of Edinburgh, a former Fellow of the Alexander von Humboldt-Stiftung and Getty Scholar. He was co-curator of the Council of Europe exhibition *Art and Power*, shown in London, Barcelona and Berlin in 1996/7, and is a former Trustee of the National Galleries of Scotland. His research has focused on early Modernism in Germany, Austria and the Netherlands, and his books include *Bruno Taut and the Architecture of Activism*, Cambridge, Cambridge University Press, 1982; *The Crystal Chain Letters: Architectural Fantasies by Bruno Taut and his Circle*, Cambridge, MA, MIT Press, 1985; *Emil Hoppe, Marcel Kammerer, Otto Schönthal: Three Architects from the Master Class of Otto Wagner*, Cambridge, MA, MIT Press, 1989; and *Hendrik Petrus Berlage on Style 1886–1909*, Santa Monica: Getty Center for the History of Art and the Humanities, 1996. Forthcoming publications include (with David Frisby) *The Metropolitan Project: Berlin and Vienna 1880–1940*, Berkeley, CA, University of California Press.

Introduction

Iain Boyd Whyte

> The modern mind has not made up its mind whether it should be Christian or Pagan. It sees with one eye of faith and the other of reason. Hence its vision is necessarily dim in comparison with either Greek or biblical thinking.
>
> (Karl Löwith)[1]

The chapters that follow are drawn from two symposia, one held at the Whitney Humanities Center, Yale University, in March 1999, the second the following spring in Edinburgh, under the aegis of the Association of Art Historians Annual Conference, 'Body and Soul'. The two symposia were elements of a research project funded by the Getty Grant Program.

Entitled 'City and Spirit in Modernity', the aim of this project was to challenge the banal reductionism of the postmodernist critique, which admits only a stern Calvinism and a mechanistic imperative to the mind of modernism. A purely scientific or sociological account of early twentieth-century architectural modernism, grounded on such noble concepts as truth, rationality, objectivity or method, fails to capture the core of architecture and, paradoxically, diminishes it.

Prologue

In common with every other expression of cultural modernism, modernist architecture denies easy definition. As Karl Marx famously noted in the mid-nineteenth century: 'In our days everything is pregnant with its contrary.'[2] The juxtaposition in Le Corbusier's *Vers une Architecture* of the Parthenon and a Delage sports car is a paradigmatic example, and the notion of a timeless aesthetic of modernism is patently absurd. The attempt to join the temple and the machine is doomed in terms of a common-sense understanding of the machine. It is also doomed historiographically. For the religious and philosophical positions underpinning the Parthenon on one hand,

and the restless, progressivist search for an ever more efficient front brake on the other, are at total variance with each other.

According to the Greek view of life and the world, 'Everything moves in recurrences, like the eternal recurrence of sunrise and sunset, of summer and winter, of generation and corruption.'[3] Historical movement, analogous to the cycles of the cosmos or the seasons of nature, is a tale of unending repetition in which all change is understood as simply the same thing but in a new constellation. There is no notion of the particularity of the moment or of a progressive course of history. In his *History of the Peloponnesian War*, for example, Thucydides barely mentions the extraordinary cultural triumphs of Athens in the mid-fifth century BC. The newly built Parthenon is referred to simply as the home of the treasury, while the Propylaea and the other great buildings of Periclean Athens are alluded to only as expenses that had drained the resources available for war. The Greek historian does not reflect on possible future eventualities nor does he regard the present as a time for decision in which man must assume responsibility towards the future. The same holds true for the Greek builder.

In contrast, the designer of the modern motor car is engaged in a Darwinian struggle for supremacy and survival. The goal is not to refine endlessly the archetype on the cyclical, Stoic model, but to challenge it with ever newer and ever better solutions. The only goal here is progress. And the notion of progress implies a quite different, teleological scheme. It is a scheme grounded not in Antiquity, but in the eschatological pattern established by the Jewish and Christian religions, with their faith in the fulfilment of the world's history through 'final' events such as the coming of the Messiah or the Last Judgement. History is to be understood as a single, unified, future-directed progression. The possibility, indeed the inevitability of progress towards a final goal, is central to Judaeo-Christian thought, and is one that survives, albeit in modified forms, in the modern period. As Karl Löwith has argued, the central modern idea of progress is simply a secularised version of ideas that derived from medieval Christianity:

> The ideal of modern science of mastering the forces of nature and the idea of progress emerged neither in the classical world nor in the East, but in the West. But what enabled us to remake the world in the image of man? Is it perhaps that the belief in being created in the image of a Creator-God, the hope in a future kingdom of God, and the Christian command to spread the gospel to all nations for the sake of salvation have turned into a secular presumption that we have to transform the world into a better world?[4]

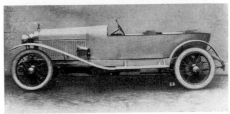

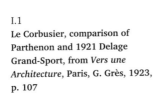

I.1
Le Corbusier, comparison of
Parthenon and 1921 Delage
Grand-Sport, from *Vers une
Architecture*, Paris, G. Grès, 1923,
p. 107

Conflating these two fundamentally opposing world views into one, Le
Corbusier offers the Parthenon in *Vers une Architecture* as:

> a product of selection applied to a standard ... When once a
> standard is established, competition comes at once and violently
> into play. It is a fight; in order to win you must do better than
> your rival *in every minute point*, in the run of the whole thing and
> in all the details. Thus we get the study of minute points pushed
> to its limits. Progress.[5]

Such a notion of progress would have been utterly incomprehensible to the
builders of the Parthenon.

The confusion between timeless, immutable goals and an unstable,
progressive process aiming at a distant resolution, whose character has not
been fully revealed, has not found an adequate response in the critical histories
of modernist architecture. In this, the historians have followed the lead of the
architects themselves, who in the late 1920s sought to enlist a Cartesian and
ultimately platonic faith in geometry to link the immutable values of Antiquity
to the unstable world of the machine and the engineer. The guiding spirit of
the first CIAM (Congrès Internationaux d'Architecture Moderne) conference
in 1928 was distinctly Cartesian, seeking to reduce enormously complex

questions into simple, tractable formulae. For Descartes, human knowledge found its measure in divine knowledge, and most directly approached divine truth when man thought with the precision and clarity of the mathematician or geometer. An inevitable consequence of this is a downgrading of the sensuous, of instinct and, inevitably, of the arts. This is the Cartesian paradox: 'Art is asked to become like thought, and yet it cannot become thought without ceasing to be sensuous – i.e. without ceasing to be art.'[6] In order to assert its Cartesian pedigree, the divine and the numinous were to be approached via geometry and reason, rather than instinct or inspiration. For this reason, Le Corbusier's battle plan at La Sarraz was reduced to 'six questions of technology and not expecting to engage with questions of architectural aesthetic'.[7]

The folly and one-sidedness of this approach rapidly became clear. Only seven years later, in 1935, Walter Gropius was complaining bitterly that the initial, idealist aims of the modern movement had been lost and submerged under the simplistic formulae of geometric functionalism. 'That is why', he wrote in *The New Architecture and the Bauhaus*:

> the movement must be purged from within if its original aims are to be saved from the straight-jacket of materialism and false slogans inspired by plagiarism or misconception. Catch-phrases like 'functionalism' (*die neue Sachlichkeit*) and 'fitness for purpose = beauty' have had the effect of deflecting appreciation into external channels or making it purely one-sided.[8]

At the point when Gropius was bemoaning the banality of the polemical position adopted by CIAM, the early historians of the modern movement were launching their own, one-sided account.

Nikolaus Pevsner, for example, looking back in 1966 to the writing in the mid-1930s of his *Pioneers of Modern Design*, recalled that:

> To me, what had been achieved in 1914 was *the* style of the century. Here was the one and only style which fitted all those aspects which mattered, aspects of economics and sociology, of materials and function. It seemed folly that anyone would wish to abandon it.[9]

For Pevsner, the progressive force of modernism had found its architectural apotheosis. History could now stand still, or revert to a Stoic model. With a comparable certainty, Sigfried Giedion endorsed the easy pragmatics of CIAM – of which he was secretary – in his magisterial account of modernism, *Space, Time, and Architecture*, which first saw light as the Charles Eliot Norton Lectures, delivered at Harvard in 1938–9. For him the issues that counted were those endorsed by CIAM: social analysis, materials, function. From this position, he damned the visionary and apparently irrational architecture of Expressionism as a hopeless dead end:

> Faustian outbursts against an inimical world and the cries of outraged humanity cannot create new levels of achievement. They remain transitory facts – however moving they may be – and not constituent ones … The Expressionist influence could not be a healthy one or perform any service for architecture.[10]

The heroic and highly partisan account offered by Pevsner and Giedion has been vigorously critiqued over the past forty years. Reyner Banham, writing at the end of the 1950s, leapt beyond the narrow constraints of the functionalist definition to study the 'irrationalist' contributions of Italian Futurism and German Expressionism. Sympathetic to the strategy of the high modernists in the late 1920s and early 1930s in combating either political hostility or simple indifference to their architecture, he was critical of the final result. As he wrote in *Theory and Design in the First Machine Age*:

> Under these circumstances it was better to advocate or defend the new architecture on logical and economic grounds than on grounds of aesthetics or symbolisms that might stir nothing but hostility. This may have been good tactics – the point remains arguable – but it was certainly misrepresentation. Emotion had played a much larger part than logic in the creation of the style.[11]

A more subtle and differentiated critique of the historiography of nineteenth- and twentieth-century architecture was offered by David Watkin in his *Architecture and Morality*, first published in the late 1970s. It is framed as a critique of three of the 'most persistent explanations of architecture', which Watkin identifies as framed 'in terms of (1) religion, sociology, or politics; (2) of the spirit of the age; and (3) of a rational or technological justification'.[12] Attacking the belief that 'architecture expresses social, moral and philosophical conditions', Watkin launches a tirade against Pugin, Viollet-le-Duc, Lethaby, Le Corbusier, Bruno Taut, Herbert Read, Lewis Mumford, Sigfried Giedion and Robert Furneaux Jordan, as prophets of an architecture linked to moral purpose. As he writes of Taut's *Modern Architecture*, 1929: 'Towards the end of the book we are shown the divine light of modern architecture illuminating the way from a Ruskinian Apocalypse to the Communist Utopia.'[13] Simply to denounce this tradition, as Watkin does, is to ignore the essential driving force of early twentieth-century architecture, namely the coalescence of religious and mystic belief with dreams of the harmonious social collective. His alternative is disappointingly vague: a return to 'the old world in which individual taste and imagination were regarded as important'.[14]

Paradoxically, neither Banham's account nor the traditionalist position of Watkin found favour with those postmodernist commentators and historians who sought to critique the modernist movement in the late 1970s and 1980s. In constructing their challenge to the historical edifice of modernism, the postmodernists were more than happy to recycle the old bricks and accept the Pevsnerian assurance that modernist architecture was all about materials and function. The social and architectural revolution that has dominated the twentieth century was presented by Heinrich Klotz as the 'victory of the square, the crate, the box – the multipurpose case as universal packaging',[15] and by Charles Jencks as a Protestant Reformation led by the likes of 'John Calvin Corbusier', 'Martin Luther Gropius', and 'John Knox van der Rohe'. Like the modernist historians before them, the postmodernists were content with the simple story and the rationalist account of the world.

Redemption

Even when it is unaware of the existence or implications of this position, or even actively hostile to the idea, the modern world is deeply indebted to and implicated in the Christian eschatology. Walter Benjamin insisted shortly before his death that 'Our image of happiness is indissolubly bound up with the image of redemption ... Like every generation that preceded us, we have been endowed with a weak messianic power.'[16] This lingering, messianic belief found widespread expression in the modernist impulse in architecture, with its insistent emphasis on progress and end goals and its biblical patterns of guilt and expectation. Colin Rowe points us exactly in this direction in *The Architecture of Good Intentions*, when he concludes: 'It is only this eminently dramatic and ultimately Hebraic conception of history in terms of architectural sin and architectural redemption which provides any real accommodation for the emotional preconditions of modern architecture's existence.'[17]

Modernist architecture picks up where the Bible stops, with the Revelation of St John the Divine and the ecstatic description of 'that great city, the holy Jerusalem, descending out of heaven from God',[18] symbolising the perfect harmony of heaven and earth. The challenge posed in the late nineteenth century by Darwinism and contemporary science to the Christian account of man's origins and expectations had enormous implications for the metaphor of the city as the seat of faith and worship. In the new atmosphere of religious scepticism, many of the spiritual and societal expectations that had previously been attached to the Godhead were refocused on the city itself, and on architecture as the vehicle for metaphysical speculation. Art and the human artefact assumed the functions of religion, and the artist those of the redemptor or Messiah. Matthew Arnold characterised this shift from faith to poesis in a famous paragraph first published in 1879:

> There is not a creed which is not shaken, not an accredited dogma which is not shown to be questionable, not a received tradition which does not threaten to dissolve. Our religion has materialised itself in the fact, in the supposed fact; it has attached its emotion to the fact, and now the fact is failing it. But for poetry the idea is everything; the rest is a world of illusion, of divine illusion. Poetry attaches its emotion to the idea: the idea *is* the fact. The strongest part of our religion to-day is its unconscious poetry.[19]

The spiritual vacuum left when the explicatory narratives of Christianity were revealed as baseless prompted any number of fragmentary systems, ranging from theosophy and dance to socialism and vegetarianism, to offer themselves as total, holistic solutions to the crisis of faith. Architecture was another. Its totalising claims were perfectly summed up by Le Corbusier in the Charter of Athens: 'Architecture holds the key to everything.'[20]

The identification of architecture as a site of spiritual reassurance and consolation accompanied the progress of modernist architecture from its gestation in the 1890s until its all-conquering climax in the 1950s. For the architects, however, the goal was less concerned with Christian redemption than with the man-made paradise. As Reinhart Koselleck notes: 'In the course of the unfolding of Descartes' *cogito ergo sum* as the self-guarantee of man who just freed himself from religious bonds, eschatology turns into utopia. The planning of history becomes just as important as the conquest of nature.'[21] Architecture became a vehicle for progress defined on the Judaeo-Christian model as a single, unified, beneficent, and future-directed force. Architecture would promote and enable a new culture that would be both collective and religious.

The collective

This pattern, which is fundamental to the understanding of the ideology of modernist architecture, is well illustrated by a text written by the Dutch architect Hendrik Petrus Berlage. As the key figure in early Dutch modernism, Berlage formed the essential link between the architecture of nineteenth-century Roman Catholic revivalism in the Netherlands, the fascination with the theosophical gnosis and with number mysticism that had gripped the Dutch architectural avant-garde in the 1890s, and the modernist sensibilities of De Stijl. Writing in 1908, Berlage specifically links the pared-down formal language of emerging modernism with a spiritually driven communitarianism:

> The *sachlich*, rational, and therefore clear construction can become the basis of the new art, but only when this principle has penetrated deeply enough and been applied widely enough will we stand at the door of a new art. And at the same moment the new, universal spirit (*Weltgefühl*) – the social equality of all men – will be revealed, a spirit whose ideals are located not in the beyond but here on earth, confronting all of us. In the final analysis, however, does this not represent a step nearer to the ultimate goal of all religions, a realization of the Christian idea? Or is it wrong to ascribe the entire Christian doctrine exactly to this principle of human equality – the first condition of an idealist endeavour? ... It would even seem that architecture will be the art of the twentieth century, a conviction that I also draw from the social and spiritual manifestations of the present. For with the growth of the workers' movement is evolving the art that man – the entire human race – can least do without; it is the art that is closest to him, and this is architecture ... The artists of the present are confronted by the wonderful task of making the formal preparations for the artistic advance, that is, for the great architectural style of this future community. They will gradually join together, even though they now have a sense of loneliness, a feeling characteristic of a religious interregnum. They are abused as bearers of ideas on the arts that stand beyond the broad masses, but which anticipate the coming age.[22]

A few years later, and much more directly, the architect Bruno Taut, writing in Berlin during World War I, insisted: 'Without faith there is no true culture, no art.'[23] The faith in question was a benign, utopian socialism, unaligned to the orthodoxies of the political parties. Taut proposed 'Christianity in a new form', which he defined as 'social commitment'.[24] This he described as follows:

> A feeling exists, or at least slumbers in all of us, that somehow we should help to improve the lot of mankind, that somehow one should struggle to achieve spiritual salvation for oneself and thus

for others, that one should feel a sense of solidarity with all men. Socialism in the non-political, supra-political sense is the simple, straightforward relationship between men, far removed from any form of domination. It straddles the divide between the warring classes and nations and binds mankind together.[25]

The Messiah

This 'straightforward relationship' was less straightforward, however, than Taut would have us believe, since the architect claimed a particular role in the secularised eschatology, as leader, priest, or Messiah. The prime source here was Friedrich Nietzsche. Hailing the 'death of God', and dismissing the priests of conventional Christianity, he turned to the artists as their successors. In his 1906 essay 'Bilse und ich', Thomas Mann noted: 'In Europe there is a school of intellectuals – the German cognitive poet Friedrich Nietzsche created it – in which it has become customary to merge the concept of the artist with that of the sage.'[26] Responding to Nietzsche's radical critique of nineteenth-century philistinism, positivism, and materialism, the first generation of the modernist avant-garde was massively attracted to the Nietzschean notion of a new, self-created élite composed of the strong, the vigorous and the talented. This élite, to paraphrase Nietzsche, would *be* something new, would *signify* something new and would *represent* new values. Unlike poetry or painting, however, architecture is a socially determined art, and the architects also responded to readings of Nietzsche that proposed social and political regeneration based on a modernist secular religiosity. Both intellectual élitism and utopian socialism sprouted from Nietzschean roots. Architecture formed a bridge between the two.

Paul Turner's research has shown that Le Corbusier read *Also sprach Zarathustra* in French translation in 1908 or 1909 while living in Paris. He also read Edouard Schuré's *Les Grands Initiés*, a paean to the great mystics in history, listed by Schuré as Rama, Krishna, Hermes, Moses, Orpheus, Pythagoras, Plato and Jesus. The fascination with the Messiah figure was further reinforced by Le Corbusier's reading, in the same period, of Ernest Renan's *Vie de Jésus*. Turner concludes:

> In some of these books . . . Jeanneret's annotations suggest that he had begun to identify with these figures and to think of himself as a kind of prophet too, in the realm of art and architecture. This discovery is of more than merely psychological interest to us, for it suggests a special conception of the role of

the architect – not as someone concerned with solving problems empirically in the world, but rather as someone intuiting universal truths, which he then reveals to the world.[27]

Le Corbusier's interest in Nietzschean vitalism can only have been reinforced by his five-month stint in Peter Behrens's atelier at Neubabelsberg, outside Berlin, which commenced in November 1910. Such was the intensity of Behrens's identification with Nietzsche earlier in the decade, that his design for the Hamburg Vestibule at the 1902 Turin Exhibition of Decorative Arts was dubbed 'the tomb of the unknown superman'. By happy coincidence, Behrens exhibited a book cover for *Also sprach Zarathustra* at the same exhibition, decorated with a powerful crystalline motif, the recurring symbol of purity and transcendence.[28]

And Behrens was not alone. Bruno Taut wrote to his brother Max, also an architect, in June 1904: 'I've read Nietzsche's Zarathustra over the last three months – a book of enormous and serious vitality.'[29] The image of the redemptive artist has manifest links to the romantic cult of genius as it had evolved in the nineteenth century. For Nietzsche, the artist was one who could go where others did not dare, and give form to ideas inaccessible to the dull-witted masses. He counts himself among the artists in *Die fröhliche Wissenschaft*, characterising them as superhuman figures who 'ascend the most hazardous paths with open eyes, and indifferent to all dangers . . . indefatigable wanderers on heights that we do not perceive as heights, but as our plains, our places of safety'.[30] A visual equivalent would be a painting from 1918 entitled 'The Path of Genius' by Wenzel August Hablik, who was linked to the visionary Berlin group the Crystal Chain. Hablik's artist/genius stands triumphantly on a rocky outcrop, viewing the crystal temples of a secular New Jerusalem, while mere mortals slump below, broken by their efforts to reach the transcendent truth. The experience of Hablik's 'genius' is clearly modelled on the biblical Revelation, which recounts:

> So in the Spirit he carried me away to a great high mountain, and showed me the holy city of Jerusalem coming down out of heaven from God. It shone with the glory of God; it had the radiance of some priceless jewel, like a jasper, clear as crystal.[31]

I.2
Wenzel Hablik, *The Path of Genius*, 1918, oil on canvas, Wenzel-Hablik Museum, Itzehoe

Temple and tower

As Karsten Harries has noted:

> The art most qualified to imitate the Heavenly City is architecture. Just as the church, the community of believers on earth, is but an image of the invisible church above, so the beauty of the physical church is but an image of the city in heaven.[32]

A favoured device of Romanticism, the image of the cathedral was summonsed with ever-increasing intensity towards the end of the nineteenth century to promote a wide spectrum of ideological and cultural positions. For the anarchist Pjotr Kropotkin, the cathedral was the lasting monument to mutual aid, social harmony and cooperative achievement. For Camille Pissarro, the cathedral embodied the *sensation vitale* that was the prerequisite for all great art. For Rainer Maria Rilke, writing in 1899, the cathedral symbolised a God that does not yet exist, but who will be brought into existence by the work of the artist: 'those who are solitary creators and make works of art are building Him'.[33]

> Wir bauen an dir mit zitternden Händen
> Und wir türmen Atom auf Atom.
> Aber wer kann dich vollenden,
> du Dom?[34]

> (We build you with trembling hands
> And pile up atom upon atom.
> But what human hand, Cathedral, can make you complete?)

In the first decade of the twentieth century, Wilhelm Worringer published his *Formprobleme der Gotik*, in which he argued for the immateriality and spirituality of Gothic architecture. In contrast to Greek architecture, which achieved its effects through and by means of the stone, the Gothic achieved its expressive power in spite of the stone. 'Spirit,' said Worringer, 'is the opposite of matter. To dematerialise stone is to spiritualise it.'[35] For Worringer, spiritual and spatial experiences were analogous, in that they were fed by the senses and resistant to abstraction and intellectualisation.

The soaring spire of the cathedral, apparently defying both material constraints and gravity, is the ultimate icon of the human spirit released from the burdens of daily life. Physical height, however, is not the sole preserve of spirituality, and can also act as a symbol of intellect. Indeed, the iconography of the tower embraces both religious longing and intellectual knowledge. Writing in the first half of the last century BC in *De rerum natura* (The Nature of the Universe), Lucretius assured his readers: 'But this is the greatest joy of all: to stand aloof in a quiet citadel, stoutly fortified by the teaching of the wise, and to gaze down from that elevation on others wandering aimlessly in a vain search for the way of life.'[36] The cult of the tower as a secular temple, appealing both to memories of faith and to encoding through knowledge, developed strongly in the eighteenth century, when, in the words of Antje von Graevenitz, temples became favoured as 'a mystical pendant to the Enlightenment'.[37] In the late nineteenth and early twentieth centuries, this ambivalent and thus potent coupling of intellect and spirit produced a series of schemes for acropolis, temple, tower of knowledge, and cult building. Analysing this predilection in 1892 in his symptomatically titled book *Architecture, Mysticism and Myth*, the English Arts and Crafts architect William Richard Lethaby concluded:

> We shall find that the intention of the temple (speaking of the temple *idea*, as we understand it) was to set up a local reduplication of the temple, not made with hands, the World Temple itself – a sort of model to scale.[38]

And there were many models to choose from: in his recent monograph on Patrick Geddes, Volker M. Welter offers a table of 'secular and quasi-religious temple projects, 1880s to 1920s', listing nearly forty projects,

I.3
J. C. van Epen,
Sketch for a
skyscraper, 1920,
NAI, Rotterdam,
007473

13

predominantly unbuilt, which range from Lethaby's own 1896 project for a 'Sacred Way dedicated to the City of London', via François Garas's 'Temple à la Pensée' of 1907, to the 'City of Light' designed by the Dutch architect Frederick van Eeden in 1921.[39]

Geddes's own Outlook Tower was constructed in Edinburgh in the 1890s. He conceived it as an aid to the comprehension of the natural and cultural histories not only of the city, but of human evolution, enlisting visuality as a mode of cognition. Turning the process inside out in the 1920s, Le Corbusier produced his mysterious scheme for a World City – the Mundaneum – drawn up in 1929 with a spiralling pyramid at the centre, the World Museum.[40] At the other, more speculative end of the spectrum, there are countless proposals by early modernists for temples or towers devoted to the investigation of spirituality through built space. In 1902 the Wagnerschule student Alois Bastl (1872–1947) submitted as his diploma project a scheme for a 'Palace for Scientific Occult Societies' to be sited on a hill on the outskirts of Paris. It was published in the *Wagnerschule* yearbook for 1902, together with a text in which Bastl attacks the materialism that has reduced man 'in the most enlightened manner' to a 'pile of chemicals', which after his death simply recombine to form other chemical combinations. But what is the source of ethics and morality? – he asks, and answers: 'This is the job of the occult sciences'. Quoting as his authority Dr Franz Hartmann, Bastl argues that, whereas the average person knows and understands only the external world of appearances, the person who has undergone an 'inner awakening and illumination' discovers a source of internal power, which is the source of the true ego ('*wahre Ich*'). This ego, in turn, creates the light that illuminates the divine truths. Bastl's 'Palace' was set on the gently rising slope at Suresnes outside Paris, directly across the River Seine from the Bois de Boulogne, 'far from the metropolitan turmoil'.[41] Although removed from the city, its gilded dome – housing a temple of immortality – and light beacons were designed to make it a constant, moral presence hovering above the city.

Speculative metaphysics were also close to H. P. Berlage's heart. In a text entitled 'Art and Society' and published in 1909, he described a religious and ethical impulse very similar to that outlined a few years earlier by Bastl. Looking to a future in which socialism and brotherhood would stimulate a revival of non-religious, contemplative faith akin, once again, to the Nietzschean model, Berlage prophesied:

> People will again go up to the religious community building, whose architectural prominence will command respect, and which can only be approached along a triumphal axis.

I.4
Alois Bastl, *Palace for Scientific Occult Sciences*, from *Wagnerschule 1902*, Leipzig, Baumgärtners Buchhandlung, 1902, p. 37

Its great internal space will inspire us again, not because of a sacredly mystic devotion that makes us long for a transcendental world, but because of a devotion characterised by a reborn Dionysian joy.

Yet it will be essentially different from the small classical temple space, which was only intended to be used by the deity. For this new space will have to contain the thousands of people who will approach the earthly god in a totally different way, and the god will be present again in this space, but only in a spiritual form.

The great acts that lead to the goal will be shown on the walls of the grand hall, and the virtues of the community will be represented in niches and on pedestals.

Orchestral music will sound from the great apse, not accompanying liturgical singing, or songs and dance, but accompanying the great choir that in glorious melodies jubilantly sings the hymn of peace.

Will this ideal remain an illusion? Even though the internationalist endeavors of Social Democracy show us a comparable ideal, will this vision of the future seem, as Kuyper thinks, to be a search for the unattainable, an attempt to realise a holy ideal in this sinful world?

No, not only may we hope for it, we can even expect it.[42]

City Crown

Berlage's dreams of brotherly love and solidarity were dealt a cruel blow only five years later with the outbreak of World War I. In response to this insanity, viewed from the neutral territory of the Netherlands, he proposed a great tower that would serve as a Pantheon of Humanity. Set on top of a hill, the octagonal Pantheon was crowned by a dome and flanked by eight towers, representing liberty, love, life, strength, peace, courage, prudence, and knowledge. The eight sectors between the towers and the Pantheon were to be dedicated to the memory of the fallen combatants of World War I, while the central domed space symbolised the unity of mankind. In Berlage's own description:

Along the galleries of reconciliation the great central hall is reached. There, rounded [sic] by the gallery of remembrance, solely lit by the light falling through the zenith of the dome, the monument of humanity stands. Further upward the galleries of

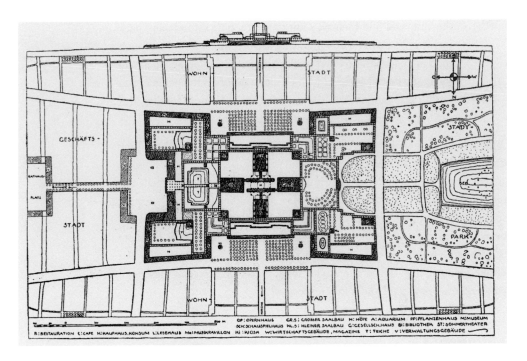

I.5
Bruno Taut, City
Crown, from *Die
Stadtkrone*, Jena,
Diederichs, 1919,
p. 73

cognition, of elevation, and of all-embracing universality are reached, while the space is vaulted by the dome of the unity of nations.[43]

The project was given no specific site, and certainly no urban context. These appeared, however, in an almost exactly contemporaneous project by Bruno Taut, who in 1915/16 drew up his vision of the city of the future under the title *Die Stadtkrone* – the city crown. In Taut's description: 'The glowing light of purity and transcendence shimmers over the carnival of unrefracted, radiant colours. The city spreads out like a sea of colour, as proof of the happiness in the new life.'[44] At its epicentre would be the *Stadtkrone*, the city crown, which would have no function beyond being beautiful and awakening in the populace a sense of communal solidarity and awe. 'Flooded by the light of the sun, the crystal house reigns over everything like a flashing diamond, sparkling in the sun as a symbol of the highest serenity, joyfulness, and spiritual delight.'[45]

This image of the Gothic cathedral as the site of social harmony and artistic cooperation was adopted by Walter Gropius in the spring of 1919 to symbolise the ambitions of the new Bauhaus in Weimar. In a gestatory text, penned just weeks before the formal opening of the Weimar Bauhaus, Walter Gropius insisted that:

the 'arts' will find their way out of their lonely solitude and back into the womb of an all-embracing architecture. For only through intimate collaboration and working together can an age generate the many-voiced orchestra which alone deserves the name of art. From time immemorial, the architect was called to conduct this orchestra. Architect, that means: Leader of the Arts.[46]

Addressing the Bauhaus students later in 1919, Gropius confirmed not only the primacy of the architect, but also the ultimate goal, which he defined as 'a universally great, enduring, spiritual-religious idea'.[47] Even though the reformed Bauhaus of the later 1920s was less inclined to such spiritual speculation, Gropius's design for the new Bauhaus Building reaffirmed the primacy of architecture over the other arts and crafts, the role of architect as Messiah. He set his own architectural office on the upper floor of the bridge element that linked the studio wing to the library and classroom wing, representing hand and mind, respectively.

Monument

But the new world order that emerged in the 1920s proved less beneficent than anticipated in the intoxicating visions of the Expressionists or of the early Bauhaus. Hyperinflation, armed uprisings, and the ruinous conditions of the Treaty of Versailles in Germany, the Stalinised Third International in the Soviet Union and the great economic slump that ended the decade bore witness to a continental Europe that was far less stable in the 1920s than in the pre-war decade. In such a condition of uncertainty and anxiety, abstraction – to invoke Worringer's dialectic of empathy and abstraction – offers itself as a refuge and as a panacea. In Worringer's definition: 'the drive for abstraction springs for a great inner anxiety of man in the face of the external world . . . I should like to call this condition an immense spiritual dread of space.'[48] Two images capture the changing condition well. In 1919 Taut in his *Alpine Architektur*, extravagantly embraces nature in a text that proclaims: 'Pillars and arches of emerald glass set upon the snow-capped summit of a high mountain project above the sea of clouds. An architecture of frames, of open space flowing into the Universe.'[49] Le Corbusier, in contrast, building a decade later, creates a timorous rectangular aperture on the roof terrace of the Villa Savoye, offering a controlled, enframed and abstracted view of the external world. This fear of space was marked by a move towards the rational and the abstract, towards the modernism of Hitchcock and Johnson's *International Style*, and the standard histories of Pevsner and Giedion. Even Taut, the arch-messiah of 1919, was moved to comment in 1929 that 'To speak of spiritualization is also impossible today. One can no longer decently and without irony utter such words as spiritualization, ennoblement and immersion in *Geist*.'[50]

The international style in the 1930s was not, of course, the *International Style* of Hitchcock and Johnson, but neoclassicism. Similarly, the international focus of architectural discussion centred less on the lightweight architecture of Neues Bauen than on monumentality. The most vocal site of this discussion was the Europe of the dictators.

In his celebrated text 'The Modern Cult of Monuments', first published in 1901, Alois Riegl notes that 'the new, in its integrity and purity, can be appreciated by anyone, regardless of education. Newness-value has always been identified with art in the eyes of the masses.'[51] At the time of writing, the public monument was dedicated to the likes of Queen Victoria, Victor Emanuel II or Otto von Bismarck. With the advent of the European dictators in the 1920s and 1930s, the monument cult became confused with the monumental urban gesture, designed to bring reassurance and, indeed, optimism to the credulous masses. The progeny of the secular temples and city crown projects of the early century were the political cult buildings of the dictators, be it the Palace of the Soviets or the Great Hall in Speer's plan for Berlin.

In *Mein Kampf*, Hitler bemoans the absence of monumental buildings in the modern metropolis: 'Our big cities of today possess no monuments dominating the city picture, which might somehow be regarded as the symbols of the whole epoch.'[52] In the great cities of the past, insisted Hitler, the great monuments – the Roman circus and basilica, the Gothic cathedral and the city hall – were public buildings that dominated the more modest architecture of dwelling and trade. Now the situation was reversed, with private and commercial interests dominating the cityscape:

> If the fate of Rome should strike Berlin, future generations would some day admire the department stores of a few Jews as the mightiest works of our era and the hotels of a few corporations as the characteristic expression of the culture of our times. Just compare the miserable discrepancy prevailing in a city like even Berlin between the structures of the Reich and those of finance and commerce.[53]

The solution, said Hitler, was a return to a monumental architecture able to capture and express the spirit of the age:

> What in antiquity found its expression in the Acropolis or the Pantheon now cloaked itself in the forms of the Gothic Cathedral. Like giants these monumental structures towered over the swarming frame, wooden, and brick buildings of the medieval city.[54]

The language used by Hitler here in the mid-1920s is disarmingly similar to that employed by the Expressionists only a few years earlier to proclaim the new architecture of social harmony, of colour and glass that would radiate out from the great temple or city crown. It seems unlikely, although by no means impossible, that Hitler would have known the text of Taut's *Die Stadtkrone*. The general argument, however, occupies similar intellectual and linguistic territory. The sentimental yearning for a pre-industrial cityscape and an even more sentimental notion of a harmonious and unfragmented society sheltering in the shadow of the temple or cathedral can be found both in *Mein Kampf*, as quoted above, and in *Die Stadtkrone*, as can the unfavourable comparison with the modern metropolis. Taut's version, published only seven years before that of Hitler, reads:

> The image of the old city is true, pure, and serene. The grandest buildings belong to the highest ideas: faith, god, religion. The house of god dominates every village, every small town, and the cathedral is enthroned mightily over the city – quite differently to how we experience it today in the cityscape of the tenement barracks, which has superseded the old city plan.[55]

The sketches for a domed hall and for a triumphal arch that Hitler drew in Landsberg prison, at the same time as he was writing *Mein Kampf*, became, on his own instructions, the anchoring elements of Albert Speer's plan for a monumental North–South axis to run through Berlin.

In his memoirs, Speer describes the Great Hall as a 'cult space' ('ein Kultraum'), designed to hold some 180,000 souls as they made their ritualistic obeisance to party and leader. The Great Hall was the focus of the movement, the heart of the cult of devotion and sacrifice, the spiritual epicentre of the Third Reich:

> The hall was essentially a place of worship. The idea was that over the centuries, by tradition and venerability, it would acquire an importance similar to that which St Peter's in Rome has for Catholic Christendom. Without some such essentially pseudo-religious background the expenditure for Hitler's central building would have been pointless and incomprehensible.[56]

I.6

Albert Speer, Model
of the Great Hall on
the projected
North/South Axis,
Berlin, 1937–40,
from *Albert Speer,
Architecture
1832–1942*,
Brussels, Archives
d'Architecture
Moderne, 1985,
p. 64

Beyond Berlin, the smaller cities echoed the same strategy of building or rebuilding around the city crown – now dedicated to the party. In one of Herbert Rimpl's proposals for the new town improbably named The City of the Hermann Göring Works ('Die Stadt der Hermann-Göring-Werke'), now Salzgitter, the party buildings formed a city crown on the Lichtenberg Hills that dominated the town below. The same strategy was adopted by the architect Peter Koller in planning the new City of the Strength through Joy Car ('Stadt des KDF-Wagens'), now Wolfsburg, where the party and cultural buildings are explicitly identified on the plan as 'Stadtkrone mit Parteibauten' – City Crown with Party Buildings.[57]

The similarity in the urban and, indeed, ideological strategies shared by both the pedigree modernists and the architects of the Third Reich should not surprise. Contradicting the Pevsnerian position, which

21

implied that all modernists were democrats, the biographies of such lumi-
naries as Walter Gropius, Mies van der Rohe, Wassili Luckhardt, and even
Bruno Taut, a convinced socialist who was to die in exile in 1938, show a
marked willingness to collaborate with the new masters in the early
months of the National Socialist regime.[58] These biographical indiscretions
support the unsettling parallels that exist between the ideological positions
adopted by the 1920s' avant-garde and those assumed by the dictators in
the 1930s. In a catalogue essay published in the late 1980s, Boris Groys
suggested that the animosity between the avant-garde and the totalitarian
regimes was not the result of radically opposing positions, but rather of
competition for the same position. For both the avant-garde architect and
the party leader shared the same goal, the total reshaping of the world
according to a single programme.[59] Developing this insight, Karsten Harries
has noted:

> I find it hard to overlook the similarity between the programme
> presented by National Socialism, which also insisted on an over-
> coming of disintegration and fragmentation, which also wanted
> to subordinate the individual to the collectivity, and the ideas
> that found expression in the manifestos of some of the leading
> modern architects. One senses the affinity that links the utopian
> wing of modern architecture to totalitarianism in texts like Bruno
> Taut's 'A Programme for Architecture' (1918) . . . The architect is
> asked to think big, to imagine large-scale housing projects in
> which theatre and music would find their place – invited to
> dream of megastructures that would collapse the distinction
> between public and private, sacred and profane.[60]

The hankering after an architecture that could carry symbolic meaning and
give expression to metaphysical precepts was not, however, limited to the
dictators. The monumental architectural gesture was also pursued throughout non-totalitarian Europe and North America. As already indicated, the
truly international style of the 1930s was monumental classicism, which
flourished not only in Moscow and Berlin, but in countless projects of
widely diverse location, function and ideological hue. All under construction in 1936–7, for example, were the Federal Triangle in Washington, the
Parliament Building in Helsinki, Walthamstow Town Hall in London and
the Brotherton Library at Leeds University.

    In the radical discourse, too, the certain belief of the late 1920s in
the ultimate triumph of a lightweight, functionalist architecture began to fade.
Writing as guest editor in a special issue of the *Architectural Review* on interior
design, published in December 1937, the British designer and Le Corbusier

I.7
Johan Sigfrid Sirén,
competition
perspective for the
Parliament House,
Helsinki, 1924,
from *J. S. Sirén:
Arkkitehti*,
exhibition
catalogue, Museum
of Finnish
Architecture,
Helsinki, 1989,
p. 86

disciple Clive Entwistle insisted that 1920s' 'functionalism' . . . 'has slowly come to be regarded by more sensitive designers as a dead end'. The architecture of the future, he hazarded, would abandon the technical and intellectual imperatives in favour of a manner of design that would appeal to 'the intellect, emotions and senses'. The new goal, said Entwistle, was 'lyricism growing from a basis of sound technics'.[61] This view, offered by a youthful enthusiast, echoed the discussions of more established voices. Many of the leading figures within the modern movement had realised by the late 1930s that 'the new aesthetic needed to be infused with a collective and symbolic content'.[62]

Spirit

At the meeting of CIAM 5 in 1937, for example, Joseph Hudnut called for 'cities which are patterned not only by those intellectual forces which seek to bend natural law to human betterment but also by those spiritual forces which throughout human history also left repeated imprints upon human environment'.[63] This position was echoed in the celebrated 'Points on Monumentality', produced in 1943 by José Luis Sert, Fernand Léger and Sigfried Giedion, which sought to reconcile architectural modernism and rhetorical monumentality. Point 1 reads:

> Monuments are human landmarks which men have created as
> symbols for their ideals, and for their actions. They are intended
> to outlive the period which originated them, and constitute a
> heritage for future generations. As such, they form a link
> between the past and the future.

Proposing an evolutionary history of modernism, Point 5 suggests that the
time for the monument has finally arrived:

> Modern architecture, like modern painting and sculpture, had to
> start the hard way. It began by tackling the simpler problems, the
> more utilitarian buildings like low-rent housing, schools, office
> buildings, hospitals and similar structures. Today modern archi-
> tects know that buildings cannot be conceived as isolated units,
> that they have to be incorporated into the vaster urban schemes.
> There are no frontiers between architecture and town planning,
> just as there are no frontiers between the city and the region. Co-
> relation between them is necessary. Monuments should consti-
> tute the most powerful accents in these vast schemes.[64]

The proposal that the architecture of the future should be able, once again,
to express metaphysical beliefs was given a vigorous impulse by the revival
of interest in spirituality that followed the end of the war. In 1948, Arnold
Toynbee predicted that Christianity might flourish in the wake of the recent
experience of secular catastrophe. He grounded his hopes for a spiritual
revival on the assumption that science and technology could not provide
answers to the great questions of metaphysics:

> Man has been a dazzling success in the field of intellect and
> 'know-how' and a dismal failure in the things of the spirit, and it
> has been the great tragedy of human life on Earth that this sensa-
> tional inequality of man's respective achievements in the non-
> human and in the spiritual sphere should, so far at any rate, have
> been this way round.[65]

The architectural discourse, too, moved away in the late 1940s from its
emphasis on scientific certainty and on the satisfaction of purely physical
necessity towards a closer enquiry into the emotional needs of man.

When CIAM 6 assembled in Bridgwater, England, in September
1947 for its first post-war meeting, it resolved 'to work for the creation of a
physical environment that will satisfy man's emotional and material needs
and stimulate his spiritual growth'.[66] Later in the same year, and in a similar
vein, Walter Gropius – in a speech to UNESCO – called for a synthesis of

'art, science and religion'. 'Only then', he said, 'will the individual be integrated with his community, carried by a new faith.'[67] And the symbolic vehicle for the aims and hopes of the community was still, as it had been in 1919, the monument, the city crown. Driven by Giedion, the status of the monument fuelled the Anglo-American architectural debate in the later 1940s, leading to the dedication of an issue of the *Architectural Review* to this topic in September 1948, with contributions by Gregor Paulsson, Henry-Russell Hitchcock, William Holford, Walter Gropius, Lúcio Costa, Alfred Roth and Sigfried Giedion. Lewis Mumford also joined the fray in 1949, with an article in the *Architectural Review* entitled 'Monumentalism, Symbolism and Style'.[68]

City core

The site of post-war communal cohesion was to be the city core. This was the intellectual focus of CIAM 8, held in Hoddesdon, England, in 1951, with its programmatic call for the creation of 'cores' or 'hearts' in cities: 'The Core is an artefact: a man-made essential element of city planning. It is expressive of the collective mind and spirit of the community, which humanises and gives meaning and form to the city itself.'[69] The Stoic historian, looking for a cyclic history of modernism, would see the city core as simply another repetition of the theme of city crown or spiritual focus. The progress-inclined reformers of the new, post-war world saw it as something essentially radical and different, as a new synthesis of art, science and religion entirely consistent with the scientific humanism that held sway in the late 1940s and early 1950s.[70] The failure of this initiative, either as Stoic trope or as harbinger of progress, heralded the social failure of heroic architectural modernism. To repeat Löwith's admonition: 'The modern mind has not made up its mind whether it should be Christian or Pagan. It sees with one eye of faith and the other of reason. Hence its vision is necessarily dim in comparison with either Greek or biblical thinking.'[71]

Epilogue

These are the themes addressed in this volume. It proposes neither a return to the cathedral nor the rediscovery of faith as the essential context for successful design. It is not concerned with the truth-claims of the spirit or of spirituality, and is neither evolutionist nor creationist. Its more modest ambition is to investigate spiritual enquiry as an architectural category in

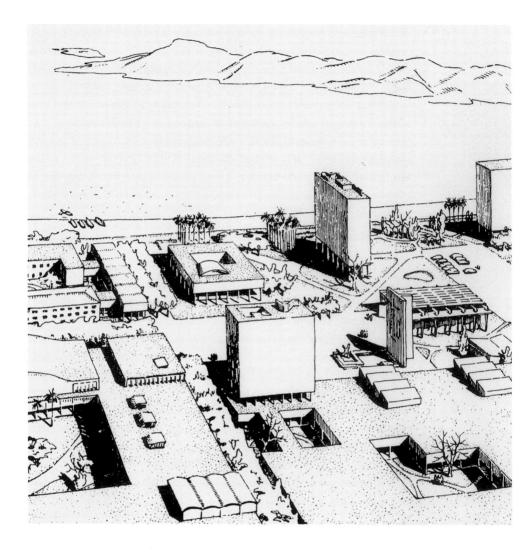

the twentieth century, and to exhume a major intellectual theme from the historiographical rubble. In the process, it offers an alternative to the pragmatics of Pevsner and Giedion, or the reactionary position of Watkin that proposes tradition, habit and repetition as an antidote to the changing demands and fashions of the *Zeitgeist*. The weakness of such a position is indicated by Anthony Giddens: 'Tradition can be justified, but only in the light of knowledge which is not itself authenticated by tradition.'[72] An understanding of the insistent metaphysical narrative of twentieth-century architecture also empowers the rejection of the postmodernist account of architecture that traduces the true complexity and diversity of modernism. In a recent essay, Sarah Williams Goldhagen notes how 'after 1930, the

I.8
P. L. Wiener and J. L. Sert, city core for Chimbote, Peru, from J. Tyrwhitt, J. L. Sert and E. N. Rogers (eds) *The Heart of the City: Towards a Humanisation of Urban Life: CIAM 8, The Heart of the City*, New York, Pellegrini and Cudahy, 1952, p. 128

fragile coalition of architects and theorists that had formed around the multivalent metaphor of the machine broke apart', and identifies a wide range of 'discursive communities' as an alternative vehicle for the study of architectural modernism.[73] In a footnote Goldhagen observes, however, that 'In this essay I will not discuss modernism's intellectual and cultural roots, which is a project distinctly different from the one undertaken here.'[74] The present volume seeks to address precisely these intellectual and cultural roots, as they found symbolic and numinous architectural expression in the first half of the twentieth century.

Notes

1 Karl Löwith, *Meaning in History*, Chicago, Chicago University Press, 1949, p. 207.
2 Karl Marx, 'Speech at the Anniversary of the People's Paper', 1856, in Robert C. Tucker (ed.) *The Marx–Engels Reader*, 2nd edn, New York, Norton, 1978, pp. 577–8.
3 Löwith, *Meaning in History*, p. 4.
4 Ibid., p. 203.
5 Le Corbusier, *Towards a New Architecture*, 2nd edn, London, Architectural Press, 1946, pp. 124–5.
6 Karsten Harries, *The Meaning of Modern Art*, Evanston, IL, Northwestern University Press, 1968, p. 18.
7 CIAM 1, 'Programme de Travail', quoted in Colin St John Wilson, *The Other Tradition of Modern Architecture*, London, Academy Editions, 1995, p. 14. The six questions were:

    1 Modern technology and its consequences
    2 Standardisation
    3 Economy
    4 Urbanism
    5 Education
    6 Realisation: Architecture and the state

    For further details of the six questions, see Martin Steinmann (ed.) *CIAM Dokumente 1928–1939*, Basel, Birkhäuser, 1979, pp. 16–21.
8 Walter Gropius, *The New Architecture and the Bauhaus*, London, Faber & Faber, 1935, p. 23.
9 Nikolaus Pevsner, 'Architecture in Our Time', *The Listener*, 29 December 1966.
10 Sigfried Giedion, *Space, Time, and Architecture*, Cambridge, MA, Harvard University Press, 1949, pp. 417–18.
11 Reyner Banham, *Theory and Design in the First Machine Age*, London, Architectural Press, 1960, p. 321.
12 David Watkin, *Architecture and Morality*, Oxford, Clarendon Press, 1977, p. 3.
13 Ibid., p. 41.
14 Ibid., p. 14.
15 Heinrich Klotz, *The History of Postmodern Architecture*, Cambridge, MA, MIT Press, 1988, p. 24.
16 Walter Benjamin, *Illuminations: Essays and Reflections*, New York, Harcourt, Brace & World, 1968, p. 256. Echoing Benjamin's insight, Hans-Georg Gadamar argues that the salvation story from the Creation to the Last Judgement

> contributes a whole dimension of hidden meaning to the self-comprehension of what has come to be and presently exists, and shows in this way that what presently exists is and means more than it knows of itself. This holds especially true for the modern age.

See Hans-Georg Gadamer, review of Hans Blumenberg, *Die Legitimät der Neuzeit* (1966), in *Philosophische Rundschau*, 1968, vol. 15, pp. 201–2.

17 Colin Rowe, *The Architecture of Good Intentions*, London, Academy Editions, 1994, p. 41.

18 The Revelation of St John the Divine, 21:10, *New English Bible*, Oxford/Cambridge, Oxford University Press/Cambridge University Press, 1970, p. 335.

19 Matthew Arnold, introduction to *Ward's English Poets* (1880), quoted in David Daiches, *Some Late Victorian Attitudes*, London, André Deutsch, 1969, p. 87.

20 Le Corbusier, *The Charter of Athens* (1941), paragraph 92, in Ulrich Conrads, *Programs and Manifestos on 20th-Century Architecture*, Cambridge, MA, MIT Press, 1971, p. 144.

21 Reinhart Koselleck, *Kritik und Krise: Ein Beitrag zur Pathogenese der bürgerlichen Welt*, Freiburg, Karl Alber, 1959, p. 8.

22 Hendrik Petrus Berlage, *Grundlagen und Entwicklung der Architektur*, Rotterdam/Berlin, Brusse/Bard, 1908, pp. 117–20. English translation from Iain Boyd Whyte, *Hendrik Petrus Berlage: Thoughts on Style*, Santa Monica, CA, Getty Center Publication programs, 1966, pp. 249–52.

23 Bruno Taut, *Die Stadtkrone*, Jena, Diederichs, 1919, p. 59.

24 Ibid., p. 59: 'ein Christentum in neuer Form', 'der soziale Gedanke'.

25 Ibid., pp. 59–60:

> Das Gefühl, irgendwie an dem Wohl der Menschheit mithelfen zu müssen, irgendwie für sich und damit auch für andere sein Seelenheil zu erringen und sich eins, solidarisch mit allen Menschen zu fühlen – es lebt, wenigstens schlummert es in allen. Der Sozialismus im unpolitischen, überpolitischen Sinne, fern von jeder Herrschaftsform als die einfache schlichte Beziehung der Menschen zueinander, schreitet über die Kluft der sich befehdenden Stände und Nationen hinweg und verbindet den Menschen mit dem Menschen.

26 Thomas Mann, 'Bilse und ich' (1906*)*, *Gesammelte Werke*, vol. 10, Frankfurt am Main/Oldenburg, Fischer/Stalling, 1960, p. 18. 'Es gibt in Europa eine Schule von Geistern – der deutsche Erkenntnis-Lyriker Friedrich Nietzsche hat sie geschaffen – in welcher man sich gewöhnt hat, den Begriff des Künstlers mit dem des Erkennenden zusammenfließen zu lassen'.

27 Paul Turner, 'The Intellectual Formation of Le Corbusier', in Russell Walden (ed.) *The Open Hand: Essays on Le Corbusier*, Cambridge, MA, MIT Press, 1982, pp. 19–20.

28 For a detailed account of Nietzsche's influence on Behrens, see Tilmann Buddensieg, 'Das Wohnhaus als Kultbau', in *Peter Behrens and Nürnberg*, exhibition catalogue, Nuremberg 1980, pp. 48–64.

29 Bruno Taut, letter to Max Taut, 8 June 1904, quoted in Iain Boyd Whyte, *Bruno Taut and the Architecture of Activism*, Cambridge, Cambridge University Press, 1982, p. 85. 'Ich habe im verlaufenen Vierteljahr Nietzsche's Zarathustra gelesen, ein Buch von ungeheurer ernster Lebenskraft –. Ich habe sehr viel davon gehabt.'

30 Friedrich Nietzsche, 'Wir Künstler', *Die fröhliche Wissenschaft*, in Werke in drei Bänden, Munich, Hauser, 1954–6, vol. 2, p. 79: 'wir steigen offnen Auges und kalt gegen alle Gefahr auf den gefährlichsten Wegen empor ... unermüdlichen Wanderer, auf Höhen, die wir nicht als Höhen sehen, sondern als unsere Ebenen, als unsere Sicherheiten'.

31 The Revelation of St John the Divine, 21: 10–11.

32 Harries, *The Meaning of Modern Art*, pp. 6–7. On the church as the City of God, see also Karsten Harries, *The Ethical Function of Architecture*, Cambridge, MA, MIT Press, 1997, pp. 102–10.

33 Rainer Maria Rilke, letter to Ellen Key, 1904, quoted in Rilke, *The Book of Hours*, translated by A. L. Peck, with an Introduction by Eudo C. Mason, London, Hogarth Press, 1961, p. 37.

34 Rainer Maria Rilke, 'Das Stunden-Buch vom Mönchischen Leben', in Rilke, *Sämtliche Werke*, vol. 1, Wiesbaden, Insel-Verlag, 1955, p. 261.

35 Wilhelm Worringer, *Formprobleme der Gotik*, 1911: English translation by Herbert Read as *Form in Gothic*, New York, Schocken, 1964, p. 106.

36 Lucretius, *The Nature of the Universe*, 2. 7–10, trans. R. E. Latham, Harmondsworth, Penguin, 1951, p. 60:

> sed nil dulcius est, bene quam munita tenere
> edita doctrina sapientum sempla serena,
> despicere unde queas alios passimque videre
> errare atque viam palantis quaerere vitae.
>
> (T. Lucreti Cari, *De rerum natura*, 2. 7–10, Stuttgart/Leipzig,
> Teubner, 1992, p. 43)

37 Antje Graevenitz, 'Hütten und Tempel: Zur Mission der Selbstbestimmung', in Harald Szeemann (ed.) *Monte Verità: Berg der Wahrheit*, Milan, Electra, 1980, p. 91; quoted in Volker M. Welter, *Biopolis: Patrick Geddes and the City of Life*, Cambridge, MA, MIT Press, 2002, p. 146.

38 W. R. Lethaby, *Architecture, Mysticism and Myth,* London, Percival, 1892, p. 5.

39 Volker M. Welter, *Biopolis*, pp. 150–1.

40 See Le Corbusier and Pierre Jeanneret, *Œuvre complète 1910–1929*, Zurich, Girsberger, 1960, p. 214; and Giuliano Gresleri, 'The Mundaneum Plan', in Carlo Palazzolo and Riccardo Vio (eds) *In the Footsteps of Le Corbusier*, New York, Rizzoli, 1991, pp. 94–117.

41 Alois Bastl, 'Palast wissenschaftlicher Vereine für Okkultismus, Paris', in *Wagnerschule 1902*, Leipzig, Baumgartners Buchhandlung, 1903, pp. 32–7.

42 Hendrik Petrus Berlage, 'Kunst en Maatschappy', in *Studies over Bouwkunst Stijl en Samenleving*, Rotterdam, 1910, pp. 3–44; translation as 'Art and Society' from Iain Boyd Whyte and Wim de Wit (eds) *Hendrik Petrus Berlage: Thoughts on Style 1886–1909*, Santa Monica, CA, Getty Center Publication Programs, 1996, p. 317.

43 H. P. Berlage, *Het Pantheon der Menschheid*, Rotterdam: W. L. & J. Brusse, 1915.

44 Taut, *Die Stadtkrone*, p. 69. 'Der Glanz, das Leuchten des Reinen, Transzendentalen schimmert über der Festlichkeit der ungebrochenen strahlenden Farben. Und als ein Farbenmeer breitet sich der Stadtbezirk rings umher aus, zum Zeichen des Glückes im neuen Leben'.

45 Ibid., p. 69.

46 Walter Gropius, 'Die freie Volkstaat und die Kunst', typescript, undated (March 1919?), Bauhaus-Archiv, Berlin, GN 2/3.

47 Walter Gropius, address to the Bauhaus students, July 1919, in Hans Maria Wingler (ed.) *The Bauhaus*, Cambridge, MA, MIT Press, 1969, p. 36.

48 Ibid.

49 Bruno Taut, *Alpine Architektur*, Hagen, Folkwang, 1919, plate 5.

50 Bruno Taut, *Die neue Baukunst in Europa und Amerika*, Stuttgart, Hoffmann, 1929, p. 40.

51 Alois Riegl, 'Der moderne Denkmalkult' (1901), English translation by Kurt W. Forster and Diane Ghirardo as 'The Modern Cult of Monuments: Its Character and Its Origin', *Oppositions*, no. 25 (Fall 1982), p. 42.

52 Adolf Hitler, *Mein Kampf,* Munich, Eher, 1933, p. 290. English translation from Hitler, *Mein Kampf*, trans. Ralph Mannheim, London, Radius Books/Hutchinson, 1972, p. 240.

53 Adolf Hitler, Ibid., p. 291: translation Ibid., p. 241.

54 Hitler, *Mein Kampf*, p. 291; trans. Mannheim, p. 241.

55 Taut, *Die Stadtkrone*, p. 53:

> Treu, rein und ungetrübt ist der Spiegel des alten Statdbildes. Die großartigsten
> Bauten gehören dem höchsten Gedanken: Glaube, Gott, Religion. Das
> Gotteshaus beherrscht jedes Dorf, jede kleine Stadt, und die Kathedrale thront
> mächtig über der großen Stadt, ganz anders, als wir es heute noch bei dem
> über den alten Plan hinausgegangenen Stadtbilde mit den Mietskaserne
> empfinden.

56 Albert Speer, *Erinnerungen*, Frankfurt/Berlin, Propylean, 1970, p. 167: translation from
Albert Speer, *Inside the Third Reich*, London, Macmillan, 1970, p. 153:

> Im Grunde handelte es sich . . . um einen Kultraum, der im Laufe der
> Jahrhunderte durch Tradition und Ehrwürdigkeit eine ähnliche Bedeutung
> gewinnen sollte, wie Sankt Peter in Rom für die katholische Christenheit. Ohne
> einen solchen kultischen Hintergrund wäre der Aufwand für Hitlers Zentralbau
> sinnlos und unverständlich gewesen.

57 See 'Die Stadt des KDF.-Wagens', plan, *Die Kunst im Dritten Reich*, 3, no. 4 (April 1939),
p. 159.

58 On Mies's relationship with National Socialism, see Elaine S. Hochman, *Architects of Fortune:
Mies van der Rohe and the Third Reich*, New York, Weidenfeld & Nicolson, 1989; on the
relationship between the architectural avant-garde and the National Socialists, see Iain Boyd
Whyte, 'Berlin, 1 May 1936', in Dawn Ades, Tim Benton et al. (eds) *Art and Power: Europe
under the Dictators*, London, Thames & Hudson, 1995, pp. 43–9.

59 See Boris Groys, 'Die totalitäre Kunst der 30er Jahre: Antiavantgardistisch in der Form und
avantgardistisch im Inhalt', in Jürgen Harten, Hans-Werner Schmidt and Marie Luise Syring
(eds) *'Die Axt hat geblüht . . .' Europäische Konflikte der 30er Jahre in Erinnerung an die frühe
Avantgarde*, exhibition catalogue, Düsseldorf, Städtische Kunsthalle, 1987.

60 Karsten Harries, *The Ethical Function of Architecture*, Cambridge, MA, MIT Press, 1997,
p. 338.

61 Clive Entwistle, 'An Approach to Interior Design', *Architectural Review*, 82, no. 12 (December
1937), pp. 225–8.

62 Joan Ockmann, *Architecture Culture 1943–1968*, New York, Columbia/Rizzoli, 1993, p. 27.

63 José Luis Sert, *Can our Cities Survive?*, Cambridge, MA, Harvard University Press, 1944, p. iv.

64 José Luís Sert, Fernand Léger and Sigfried Giedion, 'Nine Points on Monumentality' (1943),
in Ockmann, *Architecture Culture 1943–1968*, p. 29.

65 Arnold Toynbee, *Civilization on Trial*, London, Oxford University Press, 1948, p. 262.

66 CIAM 6 (1947) – Sigfried Giedion, *A Decade of New Architecture*, Zürich, Girsberg, 1951,
p. 17.

67 Walter Gropius, text of speech to UNESCO, December 1947, Getty Research Institute, CIAM
Papers, 850 856/2.

68 Lewis Mumford, 'Monumentalism, Symbolism and Style', *Architectural Review*, 105, no. 627
(April 1949), pp. 173–80.

69 CIAM 8 (1951) – Jaqueline Tyrwhitt, José Luis Sert, E. N. Rogers (eds) *The Heart of the City:
Towards the Humanisation of Urban Life*, London, Lund Humphries, 1952, p. 168.

70 On post-war scientific humanism, see Gregory Blue, 'Scientific Humanism at the Founding of
UNESCO', *Comparative Criticism*, vol. 23, Cambridge, Cambridge University Press, 2001,
pp. 173–200.

71 Karl Löwith, *Meaning in History*, Chicago, Chicago University Press, 1949, p. 207.

72 Anthony Giddens, *The Consequences of Modernity*, Stanford, CA, Stanford University Press, 1990, p. 38.

73 Sarah Williams Goldhagen, 'Coda: Reconceptualizing the Modern', in Sarah Williams Goldhagen and Réjean Legault (eds) *Anxious Modernisms*, Cambridge, MA, MIT Press, 2000, pp. 301–23.

74 Goldhagen, 'Coda', p. 321, n. 5.

Part I

Geist

The German word *Geist* defines a human quality that combines both rationality and spirituality. It embraces mind and intellect on the one hand, and metaphysical belief or spiritual faith, on the other. *Geist* points to a richness that characterised architectural modernism between the 1890s and the late 1920s, with the 'Geist der Großstadt' – the spirit of the city – defined variously as the implementation of the ultra-rationalist circulation plans at one extreme, to the construction of cultural beacons, symbols of redemption, and city crowns at the other. Diverse strategies employed to define the 'spirit' of the city are addressed in the first three chapters.

Chapter 1

From *locus genii* to heart of the city

Embracing the spirit of the city

Volker M. Welter

What is most striking in London is its vastness ... London over-powers us with its vastness. Place a Forum or an Acropolis in its centre, and the effect of the metropolitan mass, which now has neither head nor heart, instead of being stupefying, would be ennobling. Nothing more completely represents a nation than a public building ... monuments to which all should be able to look up with pride, and which should exercise an elevating influence upon the spirit of the humblest.

(Benjamin Disraeli, 1847, p. 112)[1]

Obviously, the towns which are already growing so fast will grow yet faster, or rather they will melt into the distant country ... What was once the most densely inhabited part of the city is precisely the part which is now becoming deserted, because it is becoming common property, or at least a common centre of intermittent life ... The heart of the city is the patrimony of all ... Every town should have its agora, where all who are animated by a common passion can meet together.

(Elisée Reclus, 1895, pp. 263–4)[2]

> The big city, the residential neighbourhood, small towns, and
> country villages ... each must have its own heart or nucleus or
> Core ... The Core is not the seat of civic dignity: the Core is the
> gathering place of the people ... The market place? The cathed-
> ral square? The city hall? The common? The crossroads? Some-
> where, whether planned or not planned, a place exists that
> provides a physical setting for the expression of collective
> emotion.
>
> (Jaqueline Tyrwhitt, CIAM 8, 1951, p. 103)[3]

When in 1951 the eighth Congrès Internationaux d'Architecture Moderne
(CIAM) assembled in Hoddesdon, England, its theme was the core of the
city. Following on from CIAM 6 (1947) in Bridgwater, England, and CIAM 7
(1949) in Bergamo, Italy, CIAM 8 was the third meeting since the end of
World War II dedicated to a reassessment of CIAM's principles of functional
modern architecture and urban planning. Recent scholarship has emphasised that CIAM 8 was the climax of a self-reflective interrogative process,
which had begun when CIAM reconvened, after an interval of ten years, in
1947 in order to re-establish contacts and to reaffirm its goals by surveying
which of its existing principles were still relevant.[4] The discussions about
humanism in architecture and planning during the 1951 conference
expressed an inclination among architects and planners to reconsider the
potential importance of empiricist and humanist values for modern architecture and urban planning. Pre-war CIAM conferences had investigated
housing and minimum habitations (*Existenzminimum*) or the advantageous
division of modern cities into the four functional zones of work, living,
recreation, and transportation. This rational approach to the modern urban
question had culminated in the Charter of Athens, which was based on the
CIAM 4 meeting in 1933 but only published a decade later by the French
CIAM group.[5]

   With the conference on the core of the city CIAM 8 focused its
interest on the centre of the city. One of the most obvious explanations
offered for this shift in interest was the need for the reconstruction of many
major historic European cities following their destruction during World War
II.[6] Yet this explanation falls short in two respects. First, it does not account
for the numerous designs for urban cores at the centre of new cities presented during CIAM 8. Second, it does not fully explain the interest in the
potentially symbolic function of the core of a city, in the case of CIAM 8, for
example, as the embodiment of humanist values. Indeed, the attempts made
at CIAMs 6–8 to broaden the strictly functional and rational basis of architectural and planning thought that had informed the founding tenets of

CIAM can be traced further back into the history of the discourse on the modern city than to the immediate aftermath of World War II. Since the late 1930s, urban theoreticians, historians, and architects such as Lewis Mumford, José Luis Sert, Sigfried Giedion, and Louis I. Kahn had developed an interest in notions of monumentality in urban settings.[7] Broadly speaking, they aimed at complementing, or indeed overcoming, an exclusive focus in architecture on the functional fulfilment of rationally established human needs.

A pointer to the sources of CIAM's intellectual reorientation is provided by the theme of CIAM 8, the core of the city, and the title of the subsequent published proceedings, *The Heart of the City*. Under these headings, CIAM 8 harked back to a tradition of urban thought that was relatively little concerned with a utilitarian and functional reordering and extension of the urban fabric. Instead, this particular approach to the modern city aimed first and foremost at providing a symbolic urban focus such as a prominent community building, a meeting square, or other central spaces or structures. Such a focus would bestow upon the city an ideal order by capturing and making visible the spirit of the city, the *genius loci*, in a space for the spirit, a *locus genii*. The *locus genii* as the urban core was considered to be the most important means of creating a city. It would not only transform the urban fabric into a holistic whole larger than the constituting functional zones, but would also elevate the town's inhabitants into a community of citizens.

The three quotes cited at the beginning of this chapter map out broadly the history of this concept.[8] From a literary motif to anarcho-socialist visionary essay to conference proceedings, the concept of a heart of the city gradually gained acceptance as an urban design tool, after its emergence as a reaction to the massive expansion of the city during industrialisation. Disraeli, for example, specifically demands a heart for London to counter the blandness of the modern, endlessly expanding city:

> Though London is vast, it is very monotonous. All those new districts that have sprung up within the last half-century, the creatures of our commercial and colonial wealth, it is impossible to conceive anything more tame, more insipid, more uniform. Pancras is like Mary-le-bone, Mary-le-bone is like Paddington; all the streets resemble each other ... This amount of building capital ought to have produced a great city ... It did nothing.[9]

Roughly a generation later the French geographer and anarchist Elisée Reclus argued in a comparable manner. When speculating about the origin and future of the city, Reclus stated his satisfaction that cities were expanding into the surrounding countryside, which was a sign of healthy growth of human civilisation. However, in order to incorporate fully the newly urbanised areas into the city, they had to be brought under its spell. This Reclus intended to achieve by transforming the evacuated historic urban centre into a cultural and social core of the rapidly growing city. It was this cultural core that ultimately defined the city as a city. Disraeli's prescription of a heart for London and Reclus's transformation of a historic city centre into the core of a vastly expanded modern town are early examples of the figurative and symbolically charged approach to the modern city that culminated in the discussion of the core of the city at CIAM 8.

Genius loci

The concept of a genius is of ancient Roman origin. A genius was for the Romans a tutelary spirit that existed outside the human being. Throughout their entire lives, human beings were accompanied by their genius: human life began at the very moment when a genius joined a human being and ended when the genius departed. Furthermore, the genius influenced man's character, modes of life, states of happiness, and good or bad fortunes. Yet such genii existed not only for human beings, but also for families, for professional groups such as craftsmen or artists, for societies and states, for such localities as theatres, baths, stables, streets, for whole cities as well as for rural locations. Most importantly, the genius existed outside the object of its tutelage and acted as a generator and preservator of this object, its life and characteristics. In return, the genius demanded attention from its tutee in the form, for example, of sacrifice or prayer.

In more recent times the understanding of the genius, especially of the *genius loci*, has shifted considerably. Christian Norberg-Schulz argues in his book *Genius Loci* that a location is elevated to a place when it expresses a distinct character or *genius loci*. He explains that 'this identity, or "spirit", may be described by means of the kind of concrete, "qualitative" terms Heidegger uses to characterize earth and sky'. Referring to Heidegger's idea of dwelling, which is defined as 'the way in which humans are on the earth', Norberg-Schulz states that a location that aspires to be a dwelling place has to be situated on the earth and under the sky. Even more, dwelling requires establishment of a connection between sky and earth.[10] Man does not merely live in a location, but his dwelling establishes a place which connects heaven and earth. Two quotes, from the 1890s and the 1920s may elucidate what Heidegger and Norberg-Schulz refer to. The connection between earth and heaven reminds one of the call in 1898 by the Dutch architect K.P.C. de Bazel for an architect-priest who has the power 'to present the divine order, to form a relation between earth and heaven, between the materialistic nature of man and his spiritualistic being'.[11] A comparable connection between earth and sky, to be mediated by architecture, is also made by Le Corbusier who writes in 1923 in *Vers une architecture*: 'The purpose of architecture is *to move us*.' The agency for this process is what Le Corbusier calls 'architectural emotion', which, he insists, is achieved when architecture 'rings within us in tune with a universe whose laws we obey, recognize and respect'.[12]

Another essential quality of a place which embodies a *genius loci* is to make man feel at home on earth. Norberg-Schulz quotes Heidegger's belief that 'the world is the house where the mortals dwell'.[13] This house is the dwelling place between sky and earth and 'when man is capable of dwelling, the world becomes an "inside"', an expression which, as Norberg-Schulz explains, refers to the capability of a dwelling place to condense an 'extended comprehensive totality'.[14] This idea of the world as an inside is beautifully captured by an unrealised Great Globe which the French architect Louis Bonnier designed in 1897–8 for Elisée Reclus, to be erected at the World Fair in Paris in 1900. Bonnier conceived an Art Nouveau, egg-shaped iron structure, which accommodated the globe, a library, and a series of dioramas. Around the sphere a ramp allowed visitors to climb upwards while marvelling at the earth. Reclus explains that his globe would be 'a model of the Earth ... where every man will find himself at home'. Such globes 'must be temples themselves', inspiring a feeling of awe that 'will help to strengthen within us the feeling that we are one and the same family'.[15]

Finally, to express a *genius loci* requires the creation of man-made artefacts. Again, Norberg-Schulz refers to Heidegger, who once wrote: 'The single houses, the villages, the towns are works of building which ... bring the earth as the inhabited landscape close to man, and at the same time place the closeness of neighbourly dwelling under the expanse of the sky.'[16] Thus the *genius loci* not simply joins a place or is merely a given fact. Instead, only creating a *locus genii* makes the *genius loci* appear by enclosing it. To equate symbolically the *genius loci* with the cosmological order reigning over mankind, which dwells between earth and sky, identifies the act of building a *locus genii* as a Heideggerian act of *poiesis*, 'a disclosing that lets us see what conceals itself, but ... only by guarding the concealed in its self-concealment'.[17]

A striking example of architecture as a signifier of a, in this case imperial, *genius loci* is a design by William Richard Lethaby from 1896 for a new street from Waterloo Bridge to the main portico of the British Museum in central London. On either side of the street, Lethaby proposed to erect statues of the city's worthies and at the junction with The Strand he placed an *omphalos*. During a conference on the building and decorating of the city organised by the Arts and Crafts Exhibition Society, Lethaby proposed creating this sacred way as the heart of London. He argued that in order to think of London 'as a whole – a city – there must be some sort of more or less actual, or sentimental, order and unity given to it'.[18] The sacred way would bestow upon London the much needed order and unity, it was a ceremonial street dedicated to the heart of the British Empire and to the city fathers as the guardians of this *genius loci*.

Already these few architectural examples make clear that a concern for the *genius loci* accompanied the emergence of modern architecture and planning during the late nineteenth century. From the very moment architects began to ponder solutions to the problems of the modern city, the creation of a *locus genii* was considered to be a potentially beneficial urban intervention with the power to order an entire city. Lethaby makes a strong link between building one single street and the subsequent urban reformation of London in its entirety. He suggests that the capital should be transformed by 'sweeping streets better, washing and whitewashing the houses, and taking care that such railings and lamp-posts as are required are good lamp-posts and railings, the work of the best artists attainable'.[19] The extreme modesty of this proposal underlines antithetically the hopes Lethaby placed on the sacred way as the condensation of London's *genius loci*.

From *genius loci* to *locus genii*

One of the most comprehensive accounts of a *locus genii* used as a means of urban planning was put forward around 1900 by the Scottish urbanist Patrick Geddes (1854–1932), a close friend of Reclus and an acquaintance of Lethaby.[20] According to Geddes, the *genius loci* was most suitably captured by doing not quite nothing, but nearly nothing. The best strategy was to adopt a passive position and 'wait in reverence for the genius of the place to work its miracle in its own way'. This meant an acknowledgement that events of the past 'remain an "unseen hand" in the ordering of its destiny'.[21] Furthermore, Geddes argued for a similar relation to that in Lethaby's proposal for London, between the wider urban fabric and the creation of one particular *locus genii*. He writes: 'The existing roads and lanes are the past product of practical life, its movement and experience; and observation and common sense alike show them to be in the right directions, and therefore needing only improvements.'[22] While the existing urban fabric required only improvements, the awareness of the continuous presence of the *genius loci* needed to be reawakened. Consequently, Geddes concentrated in his urban planning work on ambitious proposals to create a visible place for the spirit in order to make its beneficial presence felt again throughout the city. Geddes expected that the *genius loci* condensed in a *locus genii* would 'express, stimulate and develop its [the city's] highest possibility, and so deal all the more effectively with its material and fundamental needs'.[23]

Geddes's work in Palestine for the Zionist movement illustrates his particular approach to the city. When asked in 1919 by Chaim Weizmann to produce a master plan for the newly founded Hebrew University at Jerusalem, Geddes responded with a design for a large university complex to be located on Mount Scopus to the east of the Old Town.[24] His design incorporated not only faculty buildings and teaching facilities, but also research institutes, staff and student accommodation, workshops, artists' studios, a teacher training college, a museum for the history of Palestine, exhibition and performance spaces including an amphitheatre, and a domed graduation hall that was conceived iconographically as a quasi-religious temple of life. In short, Geddes widened significantly the intellectual setting of his commission in order to ensure that the Hebrew University would become a new cultural-spiritual centre for the city of Jerusalem and for the region of Palestine beyond.

In 1925, Geddes worked on a master plan for a large extension of the city of Tel Aviv, which had been founded in 1909. The intellectual centre of the master plan was an assembly of cultural, educational, artistic, and civic institutions set on a slightly raised site, adjacent to the border between the existing Tel Aviv and the planned extension to the north. Geddes explains:

> Every city of the past which has adequately risen to the conception of the Culture-Institutions seen and felt appropriate to the expression of its ideals, and of its developing civilisation . . . has chosen for these purposes the very noblest site within its area. Hence the sublime situation of the Temple of Jerusalem; and so too of every Acropolis throughout the Hellenic world: and so again for the Cathedrals of the Middle Ages, their Town Houses and civic Belfries as well.[25]

The extension of Tel Aviv was built according to Geddes's master plan, but private property speculation and a reluctance by the municipality to commit itself to the financial consequences of Geddes's cultural centre prevented the realisation of the heart of Tel Aviv. The idea itself, however, retained its

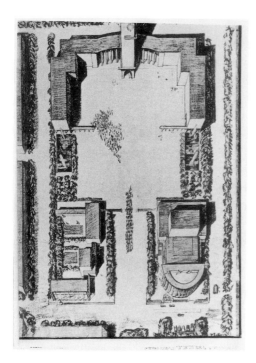

1.1
Oskar Kaufmann, bird's-eye
view of a design for a core of
the city of Tel Aviv (project),
comprising a theatre (right),
town hall with clock tower,
and further public buildings
(left), 1934.
Volker M. Welter

fascination. In 1934, the Austro-Hungarian – formerly Berlin-based, Jewish émigré architect Oscar Kaufmann (1873–1956) published a design for a civic forum for Tel Aviv, roughly on the site of Geddes's cultural centre.[26] When commissioned to plan a new theatre for the *Habimah* theatre company, Kaufmann extended his plan to create a cultural-political forum combining the theatre, a municipal town hall, and further public buildings in order to capture the spirit of Tel Aviv as a city of culture. The Hebrew caption to his design reads 'A proposal for the buildings on the site of the head [*rosh*] of Tel Aviv'.

When Geddes arrived in Jerusalem in late 1919, a close friend of his, the English architect Charles Robert Ashbee, had already been working in Palestine since mid-1918 as adviser to the British military administration of Jerusalem. The year before, Ashbee had published a major study on the modern city and its planning entitled *Where the Great City Stands: A Study in the New Civics*. In the final chapter of the book, Ashbee develops as a general palliative for the modern city the idea of an art institute.[27] Ashbee's concern was to implant groups of artists and craftsmen into the 'empty shells' of existing cities, arguing that 'unless in every city there are men inventing, dreaming, *finding the city its soul*', every attempt to reform life in cities would be in vain.[28] The accompanying plan for the art institute shows workshops, galleries and a central municipal museum, arranged in a circular form, so that the institute's influence could literally 'radiate outwards from the power centre' into the wider urban fabric.[29] With public complexes such as the Hebrew University, the cultural centre of Tel Aviv, and the art institute, Geddes and Ashbee hoped to condense the spirit of a city in a symbolic *locus genii* in order to initiate urban renewal.

These projects raise an interesting issue, which is the apparent contradiction between the claims to condense the spirit of a particular city by proposing, however, a palliative universally applicable to every city. Ashbee's art institute was not specifically intended for Jerusalem but for any city, as its inclusion in a book on town planning suggests. Likewise, wherever Geddes worked, he usually conceived an assembly of institutions similar to his designs for Jerusalem and Tel Aviv. Elsewhere in early twentieth-century thought about the modern city a comparable phenomenon is encountered. To draw in just one non-British example from the same period, the book *Die Stadtkrone* by the German architect Bruno Taut poses a similar question.

As a pacifist, Taut directed his creativity during World War I to the question of rebuilding civilisation once the war was over. Taut focused on the question of how to restore human community by engaging humankind in the task of building a symbol of cooperation. The city crown was the communal centre of an imaginative future city. It assembled cultural and educational institutions at the heart of an extended city, which Taut modelled on garden suburb housing outside Berlin that he had designed prior to the war. At the centre of the city crown precinct Taut placed a crystal house, a glass beacon containing 'nothing apart from an incredibly beautiful room, reached by steps and walkways to the right and left of the theatre and the small *Volkshaus*'.[30] Elsewhere in the book, Taut identifies the city crown as a building which embodies the *Geist* (spirit) of the community and establishes a connection between the community on earth and its godhead in heaven.[31] The city crown fulfilled another function, which the German art critic Adolf Behne exemplified in an essay included in *Die Stadtkrone*. Behne echoes Reclus's description of the historic city centre as a new cultural focus for the expanding modern city when he identifies historic Indian temples as examples of community foci with the power to unify human life – its material and immaterial manifestations – into a holistic whole: 'The Indian temple penetrates deep into the surrounding countryside. The simple huts belong to it, for they derive from the same sensibility.'[32] In the language of Heidegger and Norberg-Schulz, projects such as those discussed above are attempts to offer man a home on earth. Yet their diagrammatic, rather than place-specific, presentations imply, however, that the *genius loci* of one city does not differ much from that of another. A possible way out of this impasse is shown by Immanuel Kant's notion of a genius, a third type of genius beside the ancient tutelary spirit and the spirit of a place.

The architect as genius

In *The Critique of Judgment* Kant discusses human beings of outstanding capacities as having genius. Two points of Kant's discussion are particularly important in the context of this chapter. First, Kant's genius is a talent to generate works of originality thanks to an 'innate mental aptitude (*ingenium*)', a disposition other human beings do not have. This unique disposition allows a genius to produce with the works of originality 'that for which no definite rule can be given', meaning that which cannot be comprehended according to known rules and to which only the genius has access.[33] However, and this is the second point, in order to be works of originality, the genius's creations must, according to Kant, 'at the same time be models, i.e. be *exemplary*' for others 'as a standard or rule of estimating'.[34] Rather than potentially representing what Kant calls 'original nonsense', these works should constitute what one may call original sense, which can be understood as 'extending the realm of rules'.[35] The genius as a talent to offer through works of originality new and original sense to others provides a useful analogue to understand the intentions of, for example, Geddes's, Ashbee's, and Taut's designs for urban cores.

One of the problems of the early modern city was that it did not appear to make sense. The British positivist and historian Frederic Harrison (1831–1923) had already described this difficulty in 1862 with outstanding lucidity: 'The Modern City is ever changing, loose in its organisation, casual in its form. It grows up, or extends suddenly, no man knows how … a Modern City is … wholly without defined limits, form, permanence, organisation, or beauty.'[36] A typical nineteenth-century attempt to make sense of the modern city was to approach specific urban problems with a strictly rational methodology; for example, by mapping the location of cholera deaths in their spatial relation to sources of water supply, when London was hit by an outbreak of the disease in 1854.[37] Such a scientific approach made functional sense of the city, and from such insights gained into the workings of a city, rules of town planning gradually emerged, and were subsequently disseminated in handbooks of city planning to be applied to cities everywhere. However, this materialist understanding of the city no longer required the architect as an artist for it perceived the city as a mechanism, if not a machine, but not as an original work of architecture and art.

In opposition to this scientific approach, schemes such as Taut's, Geddes's, and Ashbee's are attempts to make sense of the modern city in a way which is only open to the architect considered to be an ingenious Kantian artist. As discussed above, the genius creates works of originality which make original sense. That said, Kant's argument turns subsequently to the difference between art and science, making out as one dividing line the character of the respective rules governing both.[38] Despite the works of originality capturing new rules, ultimately, the ingenious artist cannot indicate these rules scientifically. For the same reason, science and mechanical art can never constitute original works of (fine) art 'for they follow determinate rules which can be set down in a formula and can be both taught and learnt'.[39]

Transferred into the urban realm, a distinction between art and science comparable to Kant's governs the divide between the endeavours of Taut, Geddes, and Ashbee on the one hand, and, for example, those of municipal engineers and hygiene experts on the other. The latter concentrate primarily on the scientific rules which make a city work as a mechanism; the former focus on the spirit of the city as the primal generator of a city's life and character, similar to an ancient tutelary genius granting both to human beings or man-made artefacts. Even if the ordering principles a *genius loci* bestows upon a city remain ultimately inexplicable and concealed, according to Kant and Heidegger respectively, the ingenious architect can nevertheless bring them to the ordinary city dwellers by designing a *locus genii*, a work of originality in the Kantian meaning and thus inviting the *genius loci* to join the city. In the face of the competing claims about how to order the modern city by the emerging professions of municipal engineers, sociologists, or hygiene experts, some architects refused to be drawn into primarily functional arguments about such mundane things as the width and length of roads or the merits of straight or crooked streets. Instead, they claimed that architects have a unique insight into the spirit of the city, and that only they, as ingenious artists, can condense that spirit in an appropriate *locus genii*, be this a city crown or, after World War II, a new city core – the heart of the city.

Monumentality and the city

In 1937, Lewis Mumford proclaimed in an essay the death of the monument, a hypothesis he returned to a year later in *The Culture of Cities*.[40] Mumford rejected nineteenth-century monuments for springing from death and for displaying a fixation with the past rather than contributing to 'one of the most important attributes of a vital urban environment . . . the capacity for renewal'.[41] Yet with the rejection of the monument did not come a rejection of monumentality. On the contrary, Mumford wished to clear existing cities of dead monuments in order to create space for a new monumentality. His new monumentality was rooted in Geddes's vitalism with its emphasis upon life as a perpetual process of renewal which, accordingly, would continuously re-create its urban environment. As Mumford argued: 'the fact is exterior form can only confirm an inner life: it is not a substitute'.[42] The inner life that required concrete materialistic confirmation in exterior form was man's perpetual communal existence: 'What men cannot imagine as a vague formless society, they can live through and experience as citizens in a city.'[43] As the appropriate means to achieve exterior urban order as a reflection of human society, Mumford identified, in the tradition of Lethaby, Geddes, and Taut, the creation of a symbolic urban core, to be taken care of before attention was given to the satisfaction of practical human needs. The previous century, Mumford explains, focused on expanding the urban fabric and treated symbolic urban spaces and structures 'as mere afterthoughts, today we must treat the social nucleus as the essential elements in every valid city plan'.[44] To cast into built form the 'inter-relationship of schools, libraries, theatres, community centres, is the first task in . . . laying down the outlines of an integrated city'.[45] This process would give rise to a new, religiously inspired monumentality, as Mumford describes in a language full of pathos on the final pages of *The Culture of Cities*: 'the care of those whose labors and plans create the solid structure of the community's life must be to unite culture in all its forms', but in particular 'as the transformation of power into polity, . . . of life into the unity and significance of art: of the whole into that tissue of values that men are willing to die for rather than forswear – religion'.[46]

Symbolic monumentality in the urban context also informed a manifesto entitled 'Nine Points on Monumentality', which was drafted in 1943 by the architect José Luis Sert, the artist Fernand Léger, and the architectural polemicist and historian Sigfried Giedion. Following in part Mumford's argument, the manifesto describes monuments as a link between past and future, identifies as the most vital monuments those which 'represent the spirit or the collective feeling of modern times',[47] and, finally, names the creation of monuments as the climax of the project of modern architecture. This had begun initially with 'utilitarian buildings', which became embedded into 'vaster urban schemes' until architecture and town planning had merged. The next tasks were to overcome the division between city and region, and to unite the diverse elements of the modern city and region into a coherent whole; the genuine responsibility of the monument: 'Co-relation

... is necessary. Monuments should constitute the most powerful accents in these vast schemes.'[48] To make physically tangible this new monumentality, the manifesto recommended, somewhat vaguely, a process of collaboration between planner, architect, painter, sculptor, and landscape architect, which made use of light, modern materials, incorporated mobile elements, and took into account the siting of the monuments when viewed from the air.

Louis I. Kahn was more specific in elucidating how a monumental urban environment might look. In 1944, he presented a paper entitled 'Monumentality' to a symposium on architecture and city planning in New York, an event to which Sert and Giedion likewise contributed.[49] Kahn defines monumentality as 'a spiritual quality inherent in a structure which conveys the feeling of eternity'. He detects such qualities in medieval cathedrals, but asks if an equivalent 'full architectural expression' for 'social monuments' such as schools, community or culture centres can be achieved.[50] From an analysis of modern materials, especially the structural possibilities of tubular steel, he develops his proposal for a Gothicising structure which defines space in an 'emotionally stirring way' by carrying a roof of glass domes. This 'spiritually emotional environment' not only opens up a connection with the sky, but also establishes a new relation with the earth for 'delicate ground sculpture' underneath and next to the glass roof 'stretches beyond the rolling contours and vegetation to the surrounding land and continues farther out to the distant hill'.[51] Interspersed in the space, Kahn envisions small shelters for 'specific use', an amphitheatre, and a 'community museum of sculpture, painting, and crafts'.[52] To create such a monumental urban setting was the obligation of an architect of genius: the

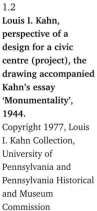

1.2
Louis I. Kahn, perspective of a design for a civic centre (project), the drawing accompanied Kahn's essay 'Monumentality', 1944.
Copyright 1977, Louis I. Kahn Collection, University of Pennsylvania and Pennsylvania Historical and Museum Commission

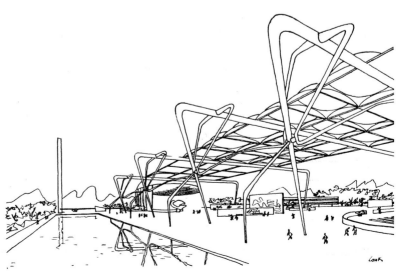

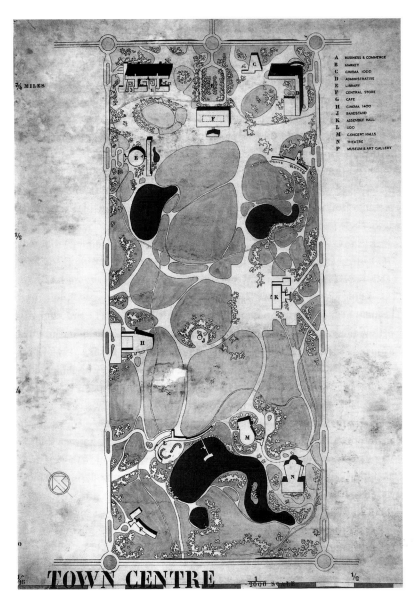

1.4
Students of Unit 12,
Architectural
Association,
London, site plan
for town centre of
Tomorrow Town
(project), *c*.1937.
Special Collections,
University Library,
University of
Edinburgh

urban core which assembled public and communal buildings such as library, central store, café, theatre, museum and galleries in a park setting. While the buildings show the influence of Le Corbusier, their respectful placing along the edges of a large park indicates a belated reference to the central park of Ebenezer Howard's garden city.

Three years later, the English architect Ralph Tubbs included in the *Living Cities* exhibition (1940) a speculative design for a core to be

implanted into bombed cities. When he re-created the exhibition in book
form in 1942, Tubbs juxtaposed under the heading 'The Heart of the City' a
sketch of this core with a photograph of the Piazza San Marco in Venice, an
obvious inspiration for his design.[60] Tubbs published a much revised version
of this sketch in 1945 in his book *The Englishman Builds*, in which he proposed a new urban core on an elevated platform with parking underneath.[61]
At the centre of that scheme, a public square is surrounded by shallow rectangular buildings, which are connected on the raised ground level by a
continuous colonnade. Tucked away near a corner, a trapezoidal theatre or
assembly hall is located behind one of the shallow buildings and can be
accessed through the colonnade. Opposite this public venue, the square
opens to its surroundings and the elevated platform extends across a road
to the banks of a river. A few years later, Sert and Wiener's scheme for a
square at the core of the Cidade dos Motores employed comparable architectural elements, most notably a trapezoidal structure incorporated within
lower, continuous buildings following the edges of the square.

In the light of the above, the importance of CIAM 8 can now be
reassessed. To hold a congress under the rubric of the core of the city was a

revolutionary step for CIAM because it meant the final farewell to the rigid urban functionalism that had characterised its earlier position. Yet, in retrospect, the congress was not the hoped-for beginning to a new phase in urbanism, rather, it was the climax of a historical development stretching at least as far back as the mid-nineteenth century. The suggestion for the congress theme seems to have come from the British MARS group, which defined the core in its invitation for CIAM 8 as 'the element which makes the community a community'. MARS also provided the framework for the presentation of designs at the meeting by defining five hierarchical levels for the provision of cores, namely village, neighbourhood, town, city, and 'metropolis or multiple city'.[62] Reading through the lavishly published proceedings one is struck by the repeated references to the recent history of the core of the city as set out in this chapter. The core as an element that 'made the city a city' as opposed to 'an aggregate of individuals' (Sigfried Giedion), as 'a meeting place of the arts' (Le Corbusier), as 'the repository of the community's collective memory' (J. M. Richards), as 'natural expression of contemplation, . . . quiet enjoyment of body and spirit' (Ernesto N. Rogers), as 'background for spontaneity' and 'feeling of processional development' (Philip Johnson), and as 'expression of the collective mind and spirit of the community' (Jaqueline Tyrwhitt), are all statements that are anticipated, for example, in Reclus's communal city centre, Geddes's cultural acropolis, Taut's city crown, and Mumford's social core.[63] The participants at CIAM 8, however, did not make obvious their references to these recent predecessors of their conference theme. This does not indicate ignorance on their side, but rather how deeply the idea was embedded in early to mid-twentieth-century thought about the modern city. Le Corbusier's seminal master plan from 1945 for a new core for the French city of St Dié, Vosges, is a prime example of the continuity of this urban design theme. For all its modern architectural idiom and urban environment, the design evolves around a prominent reference to the history of the core. The proposed spiral-shaped museum for St Dié is a successor to Le Corbusier's controversial project from 1929 for the *Mundaneum*. This was intended to house universal 'Culture-Resources' (Geddes) at the core of a world city as the epitome of human civilisation. The initiator of the *Mundaneum* project was the Belgian Paul Otlet, who had developed the initial idea for a world city in collaboration with Patrick Geddes after the two had met in 1900 at the Paris World Fair.

Between the 1890s and the 1950s not only the architectural form of a *genius loci* and core of the city changed radically, but also the symbolic meaning that these interventions were to bestow upon a city. Reclus's and Geddes's generation still appealed to some higher authority such as a monistic understanding of nature. In the aftermath of National Socialism and Fascism, however, appeals to narratives and higher authorities fell from favour. As a consequence, the proposals for urban cores made in the 1940s and 1950s proposed human interaction as the cores' authority for social meaning and urban order. The longed-for community was to emerge out of the interaction between equal beings, rather than be forced upon city and citizens through the nexus of mankind and a higher authority. To search for legitimacy, however, at the heart of the city by charging chance human encounters with a particular meaning does not necessarily create an order, or even contribute to the understanding of the functioning of the modern city. Instead, it illustrates how little modern architects had moved away from, or how much they had returned to, the romantic notion of their profession as an artistic calling, with the architect as a vessel for the transmission of redemptive ideals.

Nevertheless, in focusing on the spiritual and social potential of the city core, CIAM 8 did, indeed, address a fundamental concern of postwar reality, the reduction of man to an atomised and fragmented existence in both city and society. By searching with the help of architecture, art, and culture in their widest possible definitions for meaning where there is little or no meaning, CIAM 8, inadvertently one suspects, endorsed belatedly what Horkheimer and Adorno had already argued in the *Dialectic of Enlightenment*. In the chapter entitled 'Cultural Industry: Enlightenment as Deception', when reflecting upon the relation of the inhabitants of functionalist mass housing to the centre of their city, they write:

> Yet the city housing projects designed to perpetuate the individual as a supposedly independent unit in a small hygienic dwelling make him all the more subservient to his adversary, the absolute power of capitalism. Because the inhabitants, as producers and as consumers, are drawn into the center in search of work and pleasure, all the living units crystallize into well-organized complexes. The striking unity of microcosm and macrocosm presents men with a model of their culture: the false identity of the general and the particular.[64]

Notes

1 Benjamin Disraeli, *Tancred or the New Crusade* (1847), London, Longmans, Green and Co., 1881.

2 Elisée Reclus, 'The Evolution of Cities', *Contemporary Review*, 1895, vol. 67, pp. 246–64.

3 Jaqueline Tyrwhitt, 'Cores within the Urban Constellation', in Congrès Internationaux d'Architecture Moderne, *The Heart of the City: Towards the Humanisation of Urban Life*, ed. by J. Tyrwhitt, J. L. Sert, and E. N. Rogers, London, Lund Humphries, 1951, pp. 103–7.

4   For CIAM's post-war history see Congrès Internationaux d'Architecture Moderne, *Ten Years of Modern Architecture*, ed. Sigfried Giedion, Zürich, Girsberger, 1954. 'The Last CIAMs', *Rassegna*, 1992, vol. 14, no. 4 (December). Joan Ockman (ed.) *Architecture Culture 1943–1968: A Documentary Anthology*, New York, Rizzoli, 1993. Joan Ockman, 'Los años de la Guerra: Nueva York, Nueva Monumentalidad', in Xavier Costa and Guido Hartray (eds) *Sert Arquitecto en Nueva York*, Barcelona, Museu d'Art Contemporani de Barcelona, 1997, pp. 22–47. Barry Curtis, 'The Heart of the City', in Jonathan Hughes and Simon Sadler (eds) *Non-Plan; Essays on Freedom, Participation and Change in Modern Architecture and Urbanism*, Oxford, Architectural Press, 2000, pp. 52–64. Eric Mumford, *The CIAM Discourse on Urbanism 1928–1960*, Cambridge, MA, MIT Press, 2000.

5   Le Groupe CIAM-France, *Urbanisme de C.I.A.M. La charte d'Athènes*, Paris, Plon, 1943.

6   Most recently, for example, Claire Zimmermann in her review of Eric Mumford, *The CIAM Discourse on Urbanism 1928–1960*, in *Journal of the Society of Architectural Historians*, 2001, vol. 60, pp. 98–100.

7   For example, Lewis Mumford, *The Culture of Cities* (1938), London, Secker and Warburg, 1940, Chapter VII, 'Social Basis of the New Urban Order', section 6, 'The Death of the Monument', a version of which was originally published in J. L. Martin, Ben Nicholson, and Naum Gabo (eds) *Circle: International Survey of Constructive Art*, London, Faber and Faber, 1937. José Luis Sert, Fernand Léger, and Sigfried Giedion, 'Nine Points on Monumentality' (1943) in Ockman, *Architecture Culture*, pp. 29–30. For the history of this text, consult Ockman, 'Los años de la Guerra', in Costa and Hartray (eds) *Sert Arquitecto*, pp. 22–47. Louis I. Kahn, 'Monumentality' (1944), in Ockman, *Architecture Culture*, pp. 48–54. Kahn's text was originally published in Paul Zucker (ed.) *New Architecture and City Planning*, New York, Philosophical Library, 1944. Zucker's volume also includes 'The Need for a New Monumentality', by Giedion, and 'The Human Scale in Planning', an essay by Sert.

8   To begin this chapter with a quote on an urban core by Disraeli does not imply that the emergence of this approach to the city was restricted to the UK. For example, nearly at the same time as Disraeli, the German art historian Friedrich Theodor Vischer demanded in his *Ästhetik oder Wissenschaft des Schönen* (3 vols, 1848–51) that architects should create central spaces within cities suitable to accommodate a renewed public life in order to reaffirm a sense of community across all classes. At the centre of theses spaces, Vischer envisioned a temple which together with public buildings would dominate the surrounding masses of private dwellings. See Gerhard Fehl, *Kleindach, Steildach, Volksgemeinschaft: Zum 'reaktionären Modernismus' in Bau- und Stadtbaukunst*, Braunschweig, Vieweg, 1995, pp. 40–1.

9   Disraeli, *Tancred*, p. 113.

10 Christian Norberg-Schulz, *Genius Loci: Towards a Phenomenology of Architecture* (1979), New York, Rizzoli, 1980, p. 10.

11 K. P. C. de Bazel, 'Bouwkunst', in *Bouw- en Sierkunst*, 1898, vol. 1, p. 32.

12 Quoted from Norberg-Schulz, *Genius Loci*, p. 6, emphasis in original.

13 Norberg-Schulz, *Genius Loci*, p. 10.

14 Ibid.

15 Elisée Reclus, 'A Great Globe', in *Geographical Journal*, 1898, vol. 12, pp. 401–9 (p. 406).

16 Quoted from Norberg-Schulz, *Genius loci*, p. 10.

17 Martin Heidegger, 'Poetically Man Dwells' (1971, trans. Albert Hofstadter), quoted from Neil Leach (ed.) *Rethinking Architecture: A Reader in Cultural Theory*, London, Routledge, 1997, pp. 109–19 (p. 115).

18 William Richard Lethaby, 'Of Beautiful Cities', in *Art and Life, and the Building and Decoration of Cities*, London, Percival, 1897, pp. 45–110 (p. 104).

19 Lethaby, 'Of Beautiful Cities', pp. 103–4.

20 For Geddes's theory of the city, see Volker M. Welter, *Biopolis: Patrick Geddes and the City of Life*, Cambridge, MA, MIT Press, 2002.

21 Victor Branford and Patrick Geddes, *Our Social Inheritance*, London, Williams & Norgate, 1919, pp. 280, 183.

22 Patrick Geddes, *Town Planning in Lahore: A Report to the Municipal Council*, Lahore, Commercial Printing Works, 1917, p. 7.

23 Patrick Geddes, *Cities in Evolution: An Introduction to the Town Planning Movement and the Studies of Civics*, London, Williams & Norgate, 1915, pp. vii, vi.

24 For Geddes's work in Palestine, see Volker M. Welter, 'The Geddes Vision of the Region as City: Palestine as a Polis', in Jeannine Fiedler (ed.) *Social Utopias of the Twenties: Bauhaus, Kibbutz, and the Dream of the New Man*, Wuppertal, Müller + Busmann Press, 1995, pp. 72–9.

25 Patrick Geddes, 'Town Planning Report Jaffa and Tel-Aviv', unpublished typescript, 1925, p. 56.

26 *Yedioth Iriat Tel Aviv* (Hebrew), 1934, no. 6–7, p. 283, and *Bamah* (Hebrew), 1934, no. 3, pp. 9–11. For Kaufmann, see Antje Hansen, *Oskar Kaufmann: Ein Theaterarchitekt zwischen Tradition und Moderne*, Berlin, Gebr. Mann Verlag, 2001.

27 Charles Robert Ashbee, *Where the Great City Stands: A Study in the New Civics*, London, Essex House Press, 1917, pp. 113–22.

28 Ashbee, *Great City*, p. 113, my emphasis.

29 Ibid, pp. 119–20.

30 Bruno Taut, *Die Stadtkrone*, Jena, Diederichs, 1919, p. 52, quoted from Iain Boyd Whyte, *Bruno Taut and the Architecture of Activism*, Cambridge, Cambridge University Press, 1982, p. 78.

31 Whyte, *Taut*, pp. 55–60.

32 Adolf Behne, 'Wiedergeburt der Baukunst', in Taut, *Stadtkrone*, pp. 130–1, quoted from Whyte, *Taut*, p. 56.

33 Immanuel Kant, *The Critique of Judgment*, trans. James Creed Meredith, Oxford, Clarendon Press, 1961, § 46, p. 168.

34 Kant, *Critique of Judgment*, § 46, p. 168, p. 169.

35 Timothy Gould, 'The Audience of Originality: Kant and Wordsworth on the Reception of Genius', in Ted Cohen and Paul Guyer (eds) *Essays in Kant's Aesthetic*, Chicago, Chicago University Press, 1982, pp. 179–93 (p. 185).

36 Frederic Harrison, *The Meaning of History and other Historical Pieces* (1862), London, Macmillan & Co., 1894, p. 251.

37 See, for example, Leonardo Benevolo, *Storia della Città*, Roma-Bari, Editori Laterza, 1975, p. 799.

38 Kant, *Critique of Judgment*, § 46 [(3)–(4)], § 47, pp. 169–72.

39 H. W. Cassirer, *A Commentary on Kant's Critique of Judgment*, London, Methuen, 1938, p. 274.

40 Mumford, *Culture of Cities*, pp. 433–40. For the essay, see note 7.

41 Ibid., p. 433.

42 Ibid., p. 435.

43 Ibid., p. 481.

44 Ibid., p. 482.

45 Ibid.

46 Ibid., p. 492.

47 Sert, Léger, and Giedion, *Nine Points*, quoted from Ockman, *Architecture Culture*, p. 29.

48 Ibid.

49 See note 7.

50 Kahn, 'Monumentality', quoted from Ockman, *Architecture Culture*, p. 48.

51 Kahn, 'Monumentality', quoted from Ockman, *Architecture Culture*, pp. 51, 49, 53.

52 Kahn, 'Monumentality', quoted from Ockman, *Architecture Culture*, p. 53.

53 Kahn, 'Monumentality', quoted from Ockman, *Architecture Culture*, p. 54.

54 E. Mumford, *CIAM Discourse*, p. 144.

55 José Luis Sert and CIAM, *Can Our Cities Survive? An ABC of Urban Problems, their Analysis, their Solutions*, Cambridge, MA, Harvard University Press, 1944.

56 E. Mumford, *CIAM Discourse*, p. 133, emphasis in original.

57 Walter Gropius, *Rebuilding our Communities*, Chicago, Paul Theobald, 1945, p. 54, emphasis in original.

58 Jos Bosma, 'CIAM after the War: A Balance of the Modern Movement', *Rassegna*, 1992, vol. 14, no. 4 (December), pp. 6–21 (p. 8).

59 Mary O. Ashton, '"Tomorrow Town": Patrick Geddes, Walter Gropius, and Le Corbusier', in Volker M. Welter and James Lawson (eds) *The City after Patrick Geddes*, Bern, Peter Lang, 2000, pp. 191–209.

60 Ralph Tubbs, *Living in Cities*, Harmondsworth, Penguin, 1942, p. 35.

61 Ralph Tubbs, *The Englishman Builds*, Harmondsworth, Penguin, 1945, p. 57.

62 E. Mumford, *CIAM Discourse*, p. 203. The sequence from village to metropolis follows Patrick Geddes's well-known diagram of the valley section.

63 CIAM, *Heart of the City*, pp. 6, 41, 61, 73, 77, 78, 168.

64 Theodor W. Adorno and Max Horkheimer, *Dialectic of Enlightenment* (1944), trans. John Cumming, London, Verso, 1997, pp. 120–1.

Chapter 2

Straight or crooked streets?

The contested rational spirit of the modern metropolis

David Frisby

The street . . . the only valid field of experience.

(André Breton)

TO CIRCULATE

It is an important modern word. In architecture and city planning, circulation is everything.

(Le Corbusier)

Circulation proceeds in time and space.

(Marx)[1]

I

In the course of his provocative *The Practice of Everyday Life*, Michel de
Certeau draws a distinction between the activities of urban planning, the
everyday practices of urban dwellers, and the corresponding results of their
divergent practices.[2] On the one hand, we have the 'aloof' activity of 'the

space planner urbanist, city planner or cartographer' concerned with 'the "geometrical" or "geographical" space of visual, panoptic or theoretical constructions'. The product of their constructions is 'the panorama-city ... a "theoretical" (that is, visual) simulacrum, in short a picture, whose condition of possibility is an oblivion and a misunderstanding of practices'. On the other hand, we have 'the ordinary practitioners of the city' who live '"down below", below the thresholds at which visibility begins', and who 'walk' the city, 'make use of spaces that cannot be seen', and whose bodies 'follow the thicks and thins of an urban "text" they write without being able to read'. These practices create 'a manifold story that has neither author nor spectator, shaped out of fragments of trajectories and alterations of spaces: in relation to representations, it remains daily and infinitely other'. Whereas the activities of the city planner are preoccupied with 'surmounting and articulating the contradictions arising from urban agglomeration', the 'ordinary practitioners' engage in

> a specific form of *operations* ('ways of operating'), ... 'another spatiality' (an 'anthropological', poetic and mythic experience of space), and ... an *opaque* and *blind* mobility characteristic of the bustling city. A *migrational*, or metaphorical, city thus slips into the clear text of the planned and readable city.[3]

This distinction between the practices of city planning and everyday urban practices is not confined to de Certeau's writings but is found also in other theoretical traditions, such as the more Marxist-inspired work of Henri Lefebvre.[4] But what such distinctions have in common is an assumption that the practices of city planning are unconnected to ordinary, everyday urban practices in de Certeau's sense. Now it may be that city planners seek to represent their productions as 'extraordinary'. But such productions are also rooted in everyday practices and problems and in the 'ordinary'. This implies, however, that the planners' reading of the city and the practices necessary for the production of that reading rest ultimately upon everyday readings and practices. At the very least, the grounds for privileging the first reading (that of the planner) require to be demonstrated. Second, the notion of 'the clear text of the planned and readable city' already concedes the 'clarity' of geometrical or geographical space. Yet should we not at least question whether city planning commenced from or created the clarity which de Certeau ascribes to it?

The 'clear text' produced by the city planner glosses over the contested nature of such productions. If we return to the early history of city planning and the claims to establishing and constructing a 'privileged' body of 'systematic' knowledge in the late nineteenth century, then we may be able to explore more fully these and other issues. In other words, the uniform interpretation of city planning may be challenged by investigating debates *within* discourses on city planning in the late nineteenth century.[5] Such debates may reveal a more richly textured constellation of issues surrounding the nature of the modern city that directly impacted upon the everyday practices of which de Certeau speaks. In fact, far from the new spaces of modern cities going unquestioned within planning discourses, there is evidence that they were heavily contested. And in this respect, to highlight but one significant dimension, such spaces were associated – as Esther da Costa Meyer,[6] Anthony Vidler,[7] Christine Boyer[8] and others have demonstrated – with the generation of urban pathologies. A case can be made for the identification of not merely the more obvious spatial pathologies such as agoraphobia or claustrophobia in planning discourses in the late nineteenth century but also, within wider debates on urban culture, pathologies such as amnesia, neurasthenia, hyperaesthesia, monomania, and so on. The 'formally rational' spaces could be regarded as the breeding ground for 'irrational' pathological responses.

II

The 'exemplary instance' which we will explore is the seemingly obscure debate that commenced around 1890 in German-speaking architectural and city planning discourse on 'straight or crooked streets' ('*Gerade oder krumme Straßen*'), echoes of which, in a different context, continued to surface decades later in the notion of 'the really straight street' – the German *Autobahn* – and to reveal a more obvious connection between street construction and power relations. Yet the original debate in the 1890s displayed many other dimensions associated with the power of capital, the circulation of commodities and individuals, traffic configurations, the aesthetics of the street, historical memory, modernity and anti-modernity, street infrastructure and the pathologies of urban life. The initial protagonists in the debate were the German city planners Karl Henrici and Joseph Stübben and its textual venue was the *Deutsche Bauzeitung*, published in Berlin.[9] Yet active behind this debate and sometimes intimately connected with it were the Austrian architects Camillo Sitte and Otto Wagner.[10] This debate, therefore, was not confined to textual exchanges in a Berlin journal but was incorporated (and this was especially true of Sitte) in practical confrontations in Vienna, where the creation of a Greater Vienna (*Groß Wien*) as a new administrative entity in 1890 demanded new plans for restructuring the city. What this implies is that, far from the debate on straight or crooked streets being merely *theoretical*, it had a significant impact upon the *practices* of city planning and, for post-1890 Vienna, upon a much wider confrontation between a contested 'Old' and 'New' Vienna.[11]

The general question of straight or crooked streets had already been raised by Joseph Stübben as early as 1877.[12] The wider controversy, however, was sparked by the responses to two major works on city planning: Sitte's *City Planning According to Aesthetic Principles* (1889) and Stübben's *City Planning* (1890), which was reviewed by Karl Henrici, a supporter of Sitte.[13] The ensuing debate between Henrici and Stübben on the principles of city planning extended into the 1890s,[14] and found echoes both in Henrici's review of Otto Wagner's monograph *Moderne Architektur*, first published in 1896,[15] and in the controversy surrounding the planning of Greater Vienna. The administrative creation of Greater Vienna was accompanied by a competition for the planning of the city (won initially by Stübben and Wagner but eventually in 1894 solely by Wagner), and by a heated debate that included Sitte's critical newspaper articles in the *Neues Wiener Tagblatt*.[16]

III

Sitte begins his monograph by acknowledging the technical achievements in urban planning 'with respect to traffic, the advantageous use of building sites, and especially, hygienic improvements', but insisting that, 'artistically we have achieved almost nothing, modern majestic and monumental buildings being usually seen against the most awkward of public squares and the most badly divided lots'. His recommendation for modern city planning is 'to go to school with Nature and the old masters also in matters of town planning'.[17] In fact, after Vienna, Florence and Rome are most often cited as exemplars in his text. Sitte maintains that our contemporary urban arrangements can be improved by recalling distant, aesthetic memories:

> Enchanting recollections of travel form part of our most pleasant reveries. Magnificent town views, monuments and public squares, beautiful vistas all parade before our musing eye, and we savour again the delights of those sublime and graceful things in whose presence we were once so happy.[18]

This pastoral opening passage suggests the need for us to recall the past as a guide to constructing our present – one in which 'the process of enlarging and laying out cities has become an almost purely *technical* concern'.[19] It is a present accustomed to 'the already proverbial tedium of modern city plans', but one in which 'something of value and beauty' can be constructed, if we find

> an escape from the modern apartment house block system, in order to save, wherever practical, the beautiful old parts of towns from falling prey to continuing demolition, and in the end to bring forth something in the spirit of the old masterpieces.[20]

Of particular importance for Sitte are open spaces and squares in cities (Renaissance and Baroque instances dominate his text) that facilitated active public life within them rather than, as today, serving to provide 'more air and light' or 'a certain interruption in the sea of houses'.

In contrast to the often irregular and nonetheless effective old squares (that run counter to the modern 'rage' for 'striving for symmetry'), Sitte maintains that a blank space in the modern city is not yet a city square since, 'just as there are furnished and empty rooms, so one might also speak of furnished and unfurnished squares, since the main requirement for a square, as for a room, is the enclosed character of its space'.[21] Sitte's analogy of the space of the square with interior spaces prompts different reflections compared with Stübben's earlier similar analogy. A decidedly enclosed quality of 'space' is therefore required for a square to be aesthetically effective. But there is another more modern reason, relating to modern metropolitan existence, for the enclosed square. Sitte notes that:

> Recently a unique nervous disorder has been diagnosed – 'agoraphobia'. Numerous people are said to suffer from it, always experiencing a certain anxiety or discomfort whenever they have to walk across of vast empty space . . . Agoraphobia is a very new and modern ailment. One naturally feels very cozy in small, old plazas, and only in our memory do they loom gigantic, because in our imagination the magnitude of the artistic effect takes the place of actual size. On our modern gigantic plazas, with their yawning emptiness and oppressive ennui, the inhabitants of snug old towns suffer attacks of this fashionable agoraphobia.[22]

Here Sitte assumes that those afflicted with this new disorder are those who migrate to or visit the new metropolitan centres from small old towns. He approves Richard Baumeister's objections to excessively large open squares as 'bringing no benefit to health, but only causing heat, dust and occasional traffic jams'.[23]

In general, Sitte's treatment of the pathology of modern urban spatial interactions is predicated upon an often implicit distinction between the *natural* development of older urban configurations and the *abstract*,

artificial development of modern ones. Irregular old squares are aesthetically attractive, for instance, since they were not 'conceived on the draught board, but instead developed gradually *in natura*, allowing for all that the eye notices *in natura* and treating with indifference that which would be apparent only on paper'. In contrast, the set shape of modern squares, 'laid out with a ruler ... is only ever-so-many square yards of empty surface'.[24] Modern planning and architectural practice create empty surfaces, set shapes and mechanical reproductions. This arises out of the architect's abstract relationship to that which is commissioned since

> often we have never in our lives seen the square for which a competition project may be intended. Should one be satisfied then to place this *mechanically produced project*, conceived to fit any situation, into the middle of an empty place *without organic*

2.1
Camillo Sitte, Building plan for Marienberg, from *Der Städtebau*, 1, no. 10 (November 1904), plate 73/74

KIRCHENPLATZ.   MARIENBERG.

2.2
Camillo Sitte,
Kirchenplatz,
Marienberg, from
Der Städtebau, 1,
no. 10 (November
1904), plate 75

relation to its surroundings or to the dimensions of any particular building? *'Manufactured product' is here as everywhere the trademark of modernity*; everything is punched out by the same die; also in this field it is the trend of our time.[25]

What the modern planner offers 'to compete with the wealth of the past' is merely 'the precisely straight house-line and the cubic building-block' and the result is that, of the good artistic features of the past, 'nothing is left of them, not even a memory'.

Sitte's task therefore is to reverse this situation in which city planning is 'only . . . a technical problem' by recalling good exemplars of past planning that create a positive artistic effect in the cityscape. The particular modern features to be countered – besides the cubic building block – are the specific problems created by the straight line and rectilinearity. Modern streets, continually breached by wide cross-streets, 'so that on both sides nothing is left out a row of separated blocks of buildings', fail to create a unified impression. Continuity is lacking in a modern street 'made up primarily of corner buildings. A row of isolated blocks of buildings is going to look bad, under any circumstances, even if placed in a curved line'.[26]

In contrast to the felicitous irregular creations of the past, 'the artistic disadvantage of the modern' is also revealed in the preference for the straight street, 'the universal horizontal termination' of buildings 'all to the maximum allowable height, emphasising the harshness of that line with a real roster of ostentatious cornices', 'the endless rows of windows of identical size and shape, the overabundance of small pilasters and continuously repeated curlicues . . . and the absence of large, quiet wall surfaces'.[27] The harshness and monotony of the building line must be viewed in the context of the modern technical approach to urban street layout dominated by traffic and transportation concerns. Most brutal of the three major systems – the gridiron, the radial and the triangular system – is the gridiron system, whose checkerboard system has major traffic disadvantages at street crossings. The disadvantages of crossing streets, which Sitte highlights for carriage traffic, consists in traffic dramatically slowing down in modern city sections whereas 'in the narrow alleys of the old part of town, crowded with traffic as they are, . . . [the driver] can proceed quite nicely at a trot . . . [since] a street seldom crosses there, and even simple street openings are relatively infrequent'. For pedestrians negotiating the gridiron system, 'every hundred steps they have to leave the sidewalk in order to cross another street' and 'miss the natural protection of uninterrupted house fronts' (as in medieval streets and where promenades exist).[28]

The radial system creates even more traffic problems, necessitating police traffic control and the construction of 'refuges' for pedestrians,

> a small safety island on which a beautiful slender gas light rises like a lighthouse amidst the stormy waves of the ocean of vehicles. This safety island with its gas lamp is perhaps the most magnificent and original invention of modern city planning![29]

Such reflections confirm his view that earlier times were more conducive to artistic concerns than 'our mathematically precise modern life' in which 'man himself has become almost a machine'. Modern living conditions have transformed the range of possibilities for achieving an aesthetic effect by the diminution of the public sphere in which, for instance, market and consumption activity has been increasingly withdrawn into 'inartistic commercial structures' and artistic works 'are straying increasingly from streets and squares into the "art cages" of the museums'.[30]

More spectacularly, the sheer size of urban expansion has been accompanied by the parcelling of building lots, with their high price leading to their maximum utilisation. In turn, this has meant the disappearance of many external features – such as 'projections, porches, ornamental staircases', which have 'retreated from street and square into the interior of buildings, yielding to the universal trend of the time, the fear of open spaces (*Platzscheu*)'.[31] What was originally exterior – stairways and galleries that constituted the charm of medieval structures – has given way to modern design with stairs as an exclusively interior feature. Indeed,

> we have become so sensitive ... and so unaccustomed to the hub-bub of streets and squares that we cannot work when someone is watching us, we don't like to dine by an open window because somebody could look in, and the balconies of our houses usually remain empty.[32]

Again Sitte is indicating a retreat from the public sphere implicitly into the bourgeois *interieur*, though his analysis of city planning makes no reference to the stratification of the capitalist city. Similarly, his extensive examination of traffic problems makes no reference to the possibility of other forms of transport than the horse carriage and the street car. The railway, in its city or underground variants, receives no mention.

Thus, while recognising technical developments in engineering and sanitation, Sitte's preoccupation is with artistic effect and, despite his disclaimers to the contrary, his negative assessment of modernity leads him to propose improvements in the modern system of city planning that rest upon the 'imperative to study the works of the past'.[33] He does recognise that any modern city planning must take account of population, traffic circulation and social structure projects to facilitate city zoning. At the same time, this is accompanied by a call to resist the tenement block which has 'actually taken over modern cities almost completely'. Sitte further recognises that, on the basis of the above projections, the 'number, size and approximate form of ... public buildings' should also be assessed. The absence of attention to artistic effect in this and other spheres of the modern city leads to a lack of public attachment or identification with the city 'as one can in fact see among the dwellers of the artless, tedious, new sections of cities'.[34] Indeed, we modern city dwellers are forced to pass our lives in formless mass housing with the depressing sight of externally similar apartment house blocks and unbroken frontage lines. It is probably the gentle force of habit that hardens us to them. We ought to consider, however, the impression we receive upon returning home from Venice or Florence – *how painfully our banal modernity affects us*. This may be ... why the fortunate inhabitants of those marvellously artistic cities have no need to leave them, while we every year for a few weeks must get away into nature in order to be able to *endure our city for another year*.[35]

The 'banal modernity' of Vienna is here contrasted with a nostalgic perception of Venice and Florence, thereby reinforcing a reliance upon historical exemplars when exploring the aesthetics of the modern city.

IV

Stübben's *Der Städtebau* (1890) does not possess the same polemical content as Sitte's volume. Running to over 550 pages, it has the appearance more of a compendium or encyclopedia of city planning that covers in detail city plans, streets, dwellings, parks, transport, traffic, lighting, water and drainage, telegraph networks, monuments, all the street 'furniture' of the late nineteenth century from public conveniences to street signs, and much more. With some justification, Gerhard Fehl has suggested that, together with Baumeister's earlier work, its content is located within an interpretation of 'Städtebau' as city planning (*Stadtplannung*), in contrast to the art of city planning (*Städtebaukunst*) exemplified in the work of Sitte, Henrici and Theodor Fischer.[36]

Although theoretically informed, the guiding threads do not present themselves as a sustained theoretical argument. If Sitte's programme focuses upon the monumental buildings and squares of the centre of the city – as if the rest of the city did not exist, except as monotonous suburbs – Stübben's work encompasses the whole of the modern city, with one significant exception: the industrial areas of the city. Yet whereas Sitte refers only to machine-like construction of buildings and human beings reduced to machines and completely ignores the development of an urban industrial society, Stübben is more aware of the importance of new technology in the city. Yet he too is uninterested in the actual industrial sectors of the city. Nonetheless, Stübben's conception of city building is wider in scope than Sitte's. Its object is

all these building constructions ... whose purpose it is, on the one hand, to make possible the provision of appropriate dwellings and workplaces for city dwellers, their interaction with one another and movement out of the city, on the other, to make possible for the communality the provision of built structures for administration, religious service, education, art and science, traffic and other public purposes.[37]

City planning not merely creates the spatial preconditions for citizens' dwelling, city transport and communal public activities:

> Nor is it merely the totality of those constructions that make possible dwellings for the city population, and transport as well as for the communality the provision of public buildings; *Städtebau* creates not merely the ground and the framework for the development of individual building activity: rather, at the same time, it is a comprehensive social activity for the physical and mental welfare of the citizenry; it is the fundamental, practical, public hygiene; it is the cradle, the clothing, the adornment of the city.[38]

What Stübben emphasises here is the social goal of city planning, whose 'creations are as much for the poor as they are for the rich'. City planning participates in 'equalising justice, a co-operation in the removal of social grievances and thereby an influential co-operation in social appeasement and welfare'.[39]

This ethical and technical project distinguishes Stübben's position on city planning from Sitte's aesthetic concerns, and is further distinguished by its focus upon modern, internationally varied city examples (if not in fact a surfeit of them). The technical orientation to the city and its necessary infrastructure are further accompanied often by socio-economic reflections. Thus, the opening section on housing distinguishes individual family houses and multi-occupancy apartment blocks. The rental apartment block offers 'all too often a barrack-like uniformity', at best 'an enormous illusory monumentality'. Yet unlike Sitte, whose interest in such structures lies in their aesthetic effect, Stübben emphasises their socio-economic foundation:

> The rented apartment block, above all else, fulfils the purpose of financial investments, resting upon the housing needs of others; its task is to extract the highest possible rent as is made obvious by the name 'interest-generating house' (*Zinshaus*) ... The rented apartment block changes its inhabitants and its owners just like the commodity its owners; it has no intimate or one could say inner relationship to its inhabitants. It must suit everyone, deny all uniqueness. The inhabitants do not love their house; they only take care of the part used by themselves. The entrance hall, the

stairway are really an appendage of the public street and, as a rule, open to anyone.[40]

Stübben views the widespread nature of this mode of dense urban living to be 'a sad shadowside of our civilisation'. Unlike many of his contemporaries, he is concerned with all modes of accommodation for all social strata.

In the Stübben–Henrici debate, it was Stübben's alleged emphasis upon city traffic which was contested – summarised in the statement that 'like country roads, city streets are in the first instance traffic routes; only in the second instance do they serve the extension of buildings.'[41] Traffic density serves to condition where the best commercial opportunities are located and increases the likelihood of substitution of commercial premises for dwellings. This 'density of traffic on a city street is not fortuitous or arbitrary but rather a direct consequence of its position in the city plan' and is less affected by the structures along it than those such as bridges, gates, and so on, that influence the flow of traffic. Traffic is a dynamic factor in the city, as is its focal point 'which is not something spatially fixed and unmoving'.[42] Although the focal point of traffic at the centre of many cities is the 'city' itself, in some (such as Paris, Cologne, Budapest and Vienna), radial traffic on its ring roads is also dense.

Stübben is also concerned with the interaction between public buildings and monuments and the circulation of traffic, beyond the 'fully jammed narrow main streets and dead adjacent streets' found in many cities. The location of public buildings and monuments should be governed by two considerations – 'considerations of functional appropriateness and considerations of beauty':

> Functional appropriateness (*Zweckmässigkeit*) requires easy access, ready locatability, much light and air. Beauty requires a distinctive location in comparison to the neighbouring structures and an artistically effective position in the whole section of the city. It is almost always the case that considerations of functional appropriateness and beauty mutually support one another; they seldom stand in contradiction to one another.[43]

This issue is disputed by Sitte, Henrici and others and raised in a somewhat different manner subsequently by Wagner.

What cannot be disputed is Stübben's concern with both utility and beauty, a concern which extends to all the metropolitan infrastructure down to its drainage, lighting, signposting systems as well as public toilets, advertising hoardings, trees and plants, telegraph wire systems, and so on. Unlike Henrici, his comparative approach to these dimensions does not lead him to favour his own nation's solutions to any or all of the issues. Rather, Stübben sought to extend the new discipline beyond 'street pavements and the building alignment line' to the form 'which the city offers to our gaze and which is represented for friends of humanity alike as one of the noblest works for the welfare of fellow human beings'.

With respect to our present concerns, Stübben's volume elaborates upon the significance of traffic (*Verkehr*) which, in its broadest sense, involves the circulation of goods, mobile vehicles and individuals increasing in both density and speed. In addition, facilitation of urban traffic requires a massive investment in and creation of a material culture for such transportation. It is not merely a matter of streets and squares and their configuration but the whole range of material artefacts that accompany traffic flows which Stübben's volume explores in meticulous detail: street signs, bridges, viaducts, vegetation planted along streets, advertising boards and columns, street lighting system, needs of those circulating such as public lavatories, street car stands, railway stations, and so on. All were proliferating in the second half of the nineteenth century. And many were new and required classification for use. In part, this is Stübben's concern. It is a project which has crucially influenced our modes of metropolitan experience and the space of the city with its urban furniture.

More specifically, and as merely one section of his larger compendium, Stübben addresses the issue of the straight street versus the street rendered irregular in the context of an extensive, comparative discussion of the length and breadth of streets. His proposals encapsulate some of the issues in the subsequent debate. Stübben recommends that:

> From the standpoint of traffic a street should be extended as long as possible in a straight line. From the standpoint of health a careful restriction of the length already recommends itself due to dust accumulation and to the sharp wind that in long straight streets, especially when they correspond to the dominant wind direction, can be quite unpleasant. Beauty dictates this restriction most of all. If a street is to correspond to a sense of beauty and if the traffic on the street is not to tire the eye but rather guarantee a satisfying prospect, then its length must to a certain extent be a function of its breadth. Just as in the case of dwelling spaces and ceremonial salons one accepts at the outer margins the relationship of length to breadth of 2:1, so there are specific artistic parameters too for city streets that should not be exceeded.[44]

Stübben recommends 'a relationship of 1:25 as the artistic boundary for straight streets', and goes on to compare the profiles of European streets in terms of their length and cross-section. This narrower focus upon streets, squares and intersections, which constitutes part of both Sitte's and Stübben's volumes, becomes the focus of contestation.

V

The debate's starting point is Henrici's 1891 review of Stübben's *Der Städtebau* which he views as a work that does not represent 'something totally new' but rather what has been observed as new in the last decade.[45] In particular, Henrici juxtaposes Stübben's *technical* standpoint with Sitte's *artistic* standpoint, exemplified in Henrici's assertion that 'our present-day architecture strives towards the picturesque (*dem Malerischen*)'.[46] Specifically, Henrici laments the modern urban planning system's preference for the '*unGerman*':

> is it really necessary that this striving, derived from the primal German essence and directed towards the picturesque square, must make way for the *unGerman, Italian or French* type, because the latter adapts better to the equally unGerman *modern* system of 'city planning'?

The attempt to preserve the original beautiful squares and streets should, of course, not merely copy them in new constructs for it is impossible to copy such old originals. Rather, this striving for copying the old is precisely what is recommended by modern city planning 'with its classifications and with its squares and street figuration by means of circles and lines'.[47] But Henrici sees the major defect of the modern system in the identification of streets with traffic flows. The linear grid crossing systems proposed by the modern system create significant loss of time at major intersections, thus contradicting the view that the straight line is the shortest way between two points, since such crossings are 'conceptual (*reflektiert*) and unnatural, arbitrary'.[48] Henrici therefore favours other solutions including curved streets and indirect linear street crossing.

Indeed, Henrici sees the straight street as associated in the modern system with 'individual public buildings in a parade' and parallel housing rows. Instead, the location of public buildings should be interspersed with dwellings since it is from there that one should be able to appreciate and achieve the beautiful perspective. However:

> The average public is in fact alienated from the artistic vision and at present finds in the richly bedecked shop display windows,

above whose huge reflecting glass the monumental façades swirl in the air and in the attire which on foot, in the coach or on horseback rush by and are reflected in the glass windows, complete satisfaction for the enjoyment of a cityscape. But should one concede that this is a justified and justifiable taste?[49]

Henrici's intention is to educate the public in its artistic taste but not by the adoption of a foreign model such as Stübben's praise for Parisian *points de vue* but rather 'by taking up again genuine, old, primal German (*Urdeutsch*)' examples.

Responding to this proposal, Stübben rejects this exclusive identification of straight streets and street crossings with modern city planning systems, and rejects the identification of curved streets and the abscence of street crossings as the model for a 'genuine old primal German type'.[50] Stübben deconstructs the 'modern city planning system' which Henrici seems to abhor by pointing out, first, that his own *Städtebau* volume drew on many historical and contemporary instances of good practice from many countries and, second, that 'in my view, city planning in the last thirty years has still not been incorporated into a completed "system" '.[51] The juxtaposition of this 'unGerman' system with the crooked street as 'primal German' is illusory insofar as there are countless instances of 'unregulated irregular and crossing' systems in French and Italian cities. Stübben further notes that he himself discussed the distinction between straight and curved streets almost two decades earlier and, certainly, more recently took account of valuable elements in Sitte's study of city planning. Thus, contrary to Henrici's opposition between (old) artistic and (new) modern systems, Stübben insists that city planning be concerned with the reconciliation of the demands of traffic, and 'the naked acquisitive interest' with aesthetic interests.

With respect to this aesthetic interest, Stübben argues that the fact that many medieval churches, town halls and the like were built on irregular plans cannot be adduced as a reason to follow the principle of irregularity in modern constructions in order to produce an artistic effect. Indeed, both modern life and modern technology no longer allow a true imitation of old city layouts, and on public health grounds such crooked and irregular arrangements should not be favoured. Thus, although artistic considerations should be increasingly taken into account, 'aesthetic "reflection", and artistic temper unfortunately have no right of precedence over consideration of technical traffic factors, economic and health considerations'.[52] We must recognise that: 'A city building plan is not just an ideal work of art but rather is something which decides upon important economic questions, upon mine and yours, upon the future welfare of many inhabitants.'[53] It has to comply with many building regulations, rules for loss compensation and many other factors.

Henrici's reply to Stübben, 'Individualism in City Planning' (1891)[54] returns to the modern city planning system's one-sided privileging of traffic interests, which in turn create traffic problems by favouring direct or unmediated street crossings. This arises out of 'the modern mode of building cities [which], as I believe, does not really connect with historical traditions. It commences, under the new establishment of normal street widths, with the primitive rectangular or chessboard scheme'.[55] In contrast to this system, Henrici detects the emergence of a new current based upon 'a healthy individualism', not in the sense of the planner's or architect's personal qualities being displayed in a city plan, but rather 'the individualisation must be appropriate to the distinctive features of the place that is to be built upon'.[56] It therefore follows that there can be no single universally valid system or scheme for this approach, but merely to take account of traffic, building or dwelling and beauty. Of these three it is the building dimension that 'represents the *bodily element* of the whole city sector, the flesh which with the healthy content and in a beautiful form is to produce the street. In contrast, streets – without building – in themselves form merely surfaces without content'.[57] The variations in street formation should include irregularities and deviations from the rigid chessboard system.

Henrici addresses the effect of ring-roads in this context. Although without specific reference to the Vienna Ringstraße, his reflections are revealing. For him:

> Ring-roads are also mostly to be seen as auxiliary lines (*Nebenlinien*), and will probably only exceptionally and for only part of their length bear continuous commercial traffic. In most instances they are especially appropriate as promenade installations, because they bring with them, as one goes round them, rapidly changing images and impressions. Such promenade ring-roads are largely walked upon or travelled upon by persons who have a great deal of time.[58]

The early images of the Vienna Ringstraße and guidebook accounts suggest that significant sections of the street at least were viewed as for the purposes of the promenade, for refined *flânerie*. Henrici's concern here, however, is to argue for greater differentiation of streets, for the dispersal of public buildings instead of their concentrations, for greater individualism in city planning. To much of this Stübben concurs, since

It is indeed better to take into account some individual weaknesses and errors than to give over the formation of the city to schematism. Since the much repeated critique of the boring and barren nature of modern city areas is often only too true, so it is urgently to be desired that artistically trained colleagues concern themselves more than previously with the questions of city planning.[59]

But, once more, Stübben defends his claim that his own *Städtebau* volume reflected diverse demands upon city planning and did not put forward a single modern system.

The debate took a somewhat different turn two years later in Henrici's 'Boring and Pleasant Streets' ('Langweilige und kurzweilige Straßen') in which he terms a street *'boring* if the wanderer along it gets the impression that the route is longer than it actually is; I term it *pleasant* if the reverse is the case'.[60] Henrici's objection here is to the perspective of the straight street, his argument being that the more one sees of the continuous ground surface and walls of the street, the more boring will a street be. The more a street is denied the endless perspective, by giving it curves for example, the more changes of perspective are available and the more interesting it will be. In terms of landscape the difference is between two hours walking along a flat poplar avenue and two hours in the hills. Between the boring and the pleasant street is the 'normal' street which has breaks in its building line and does not deceive as to its time length. Even the long straight street may be broken up by artificial means such as planting of bushes and trees in the middle, lanterns or introducing curves into the street. The deliberate intervention of city planners gives the opportunity to reduce the amount of fortuitousness which Henrici views as having had a more deleterious than beneficial effect with regard to the beauty of cities.

Stübben's reply, 'On the Beautiful Formation of Urban Streets', again points out that, though coming from a different standpoint and based upon other foundations, he had already indicated the beneficial effect of concave lines in streets and squares as preventing boredom on the part of the wanderer and encouraging a changing perspective.[61] But rather than be preoccupied with introducing details to produce distractions, Stübben insists that the problem goes much deeper if we recognise that:

Major traffic arteries are unavoidable in our times. It is our modern task to construct them in an artistically beautiful manner, a task that is perhaps more difficult than but nonetheless equally important to the designing of an artistic detail according to models from previous centuries.[62]

The latter procedure hardly addresses the real problems faced by metropolitan traffic and the attempt to cater for it in an aesthetically appealing manner.

Although this exchange between Henrici and Stübben concludes in 1894, the challenge to contemporary conceptions of urban modernity was also taking place in Sitte's newspaper articles.[63] It is also evident in Henrici's review of Otto Wagner's *Moderne Architektur* which

> suffers from a certain one-sidedness insofar as it focuses almost exclusively upon the technical achievements of the modern period, on the anticipated ever increasing perfection of *modern means of transport* and upon *metropolitan life*. But . . . this part of the spirit of the times with its *tendency towards uniformity*, penetrating through all the pores of the life of the people in such a manner that hardly any place for other things remains, which lies outside that of *world transport* and the *life of acquisition*, and which I wish to indicate with the term *soul of the people* (*Volksgemüth*).[64]

For Henrici, Wagner's problems of modern life and his tasks for modern architecture 'are already solved in a practical sense in America'. Rather than give expression to modern metropolitan life, 'artists of all countries' should take as their most important task 'the *cultivation of a distinctive national art*', one that moves beyond Wagner's 'horizontals' and the straight line, one that – outside Berlin at least – seeks out 'active progressive works delivering us from the yoke of traffic lines'. More pointedly, in one of his newspaper articles on planning a new Vienna, Sitte decried Wagner's relationship to Stübben:

> whose book he has apparently taken to be authoritative . . . with [its] precise knowledge of the metropolitan building office . . . [Its] reference book on everything possible is very useful . . . but not at all appropriate for extracting principles from it since Stübben himself does not have any at all.[65]

Such judgements by Henrici and Sitte confirm the extent to which this ostensibly narrow debate was part of a wider attack upon architectural programmes such as Wagner's that sought to focus upon an architecture and city planning appropriate to their conceptions of the modern metropolis.

VI

If we step back from the specific details of this debate, we can begin to reveal some of its general features. First, the volumes by Sitte and Stübben on city planning form the foundation for the controversy in the 1890s, even though some of its features were already intimated by Stübben well over a decade earlier. Second, although this is a German debate, the fact that Henrici is a supporter of Sitte's position and that Henrici's critique of Wagner's *Moderne Architektur* accords with his critique of Stübben's position suggests a Viennese debate between Sitte and Wagner. This is confirmed by Sitte in his contemporary newspaper attacks upon Wagner's plans, as well as in some of Wagner's own critical comments in his *Moderne Architektur*. Third, this debate had a wider impact in Vienna upon the much broader controversy, stemming from the 1890 extension of Vienna's boundaries, between the supporters of 'Old' Vienna and 'New' Vienna. But rather than take up this extensive Viennese debate, which extends up to the First World War, we will highlight the general features of the straight or crooked streets debate while drawing upon some of the issues that arise in Sitte's critique of Wagner. In order to do so, it may be useful to set out somewhat schematically the specific areas of controversy.

The notion that the modern metropolis reflects or should mirror the spirit of the times in this period most commonly identifies this spirit (*Geist*) with a rational structuring of the city. In contrast, the aesthetic focus upon the city is often identified with preserving the historical soul (*Seele*) of its inner core. Such a contrast is drawn by Sitte when questioning whether the modern city should be a 'human storehouse' or a 'work of art'.[66] The 'mechanical' outline of the modern city's street network and building blocks is contrasted with a conception of a more harmonious cityscape that preserves existing irregular structures worthy of protection. In turn, the 'mechanical' outline of modern urban expansion facilitates an infinitely expandable and open city in contrast to an enclosed historical core. The formal, rational expansion of the city into a universal world city (*Weltstadt*) is contrasted with the historically grounded city as work of art. In some contemporary discourse, at least, these two conceptions of the modern city are embodied in the contrast between Berlin and Vienna.[67]

Similarly, the virtues of the straight or crooked (irregular) street that ostensibly constitute the focus of the 1890s' controversy are not confined to 'linearity' versus 'fantasy'. Rather, the discourses on streets are obviously embedded not merely in different conceptions of the metropolis but also in the nature of its dynamic (of which circulation is a significant dimension), the nature of the practical orientations to its construction and

THE STRAIGHT OR CROOKED STREETS DEBATE

Otto Wagner	Camillo Sitte
Joseph Stübben	Carl Henrici

CITY

Spirit (*Geist*)	Soul (*Seele*)
City as 'human warehouse'	City as 'work of art'
'Mechanical' cityscape	Harmonious cityscape
Open (expandable) city	Closed (enclosed) city

STREETS

Straight streets ('linearity')	Crooked or irregular streets ('fantasy')
Symmetry	Asymmetry
Wide streets	Enclosed squares
'Boring' streets	'Pleasant' streets

CIRCULATION

Circulation	Regulation
Traffic	*Flânerie*
Interchangeability	Uniqueness
Anonymity	Intimacy
Indifference	Cosiness (*Gemütlichkeit*)
Uniformity	Diversity
Surface (superficiality)	Embeddedness (depth)
Abstract mass	Concrete individuals
'Geometric man'	Natural inhabitants

TECHNICAL/AESTHETIC PROBLEMATICS

Technical problematic	Aesthetic problematic
(Street infrastructure)	(Street aesthetics)
Contemporary comparative	Historical exemplary
('Gallic', 'unGerman')	(Renaissance, Baroque)
'Use' style (*Nutzstil*)	Artistic style
Fashion	Taste

PATHOLOGIES

Agoraphobia	Claustrophobia
Amnesia	Pillars of memory
Momentary presentness	Nostalgia

perceived positive or negative consequences of modern urban built patterns. The width of the modern street in relation to the height of buildings along it, and the possibility of a *point de vue* may contrast with the broken façade and building line and, especially, with the enclosed square. 'Boring' streets may be juxtaposed to 'pleasant' streets. But other dimensions of this controversy are not necessarily highlighted by its participants. The broad, straight avenue might also have a political significance as potential barrier to insurrection as Walter Benjamin and others argued for Haussmann's *grands boulevards*.[68] The contrast between the symmetry of straight street layout with the asymmetry of crooked or irregular streets may also have a political dimension as Georg Simmel, a major explorer of the mental life (*Geistesleben*) of the modern metropolis, intimated when he argued (in 1896) that this 'tendency towards symmetry, to identically formed arrangement of elements according to universal principles is . . . shared by all despotic social formations . . . The symmetrical arrangement renders easier the domination of many from a single point.'[69] This political dimension of an aesthetic form contrasts, for Simmel, with the 'rhapsodic fortuitousness' of liberal state formations and other groupings whose 'inner structure and boundaries of the parts are irregular and fluctuating'. And without any evidence of his acquaintance with our debate, we find Simmel formulating in his essay on Rome (1898) one aesthetic dimension of the controversy on straight or crooked streets. The virtue of Rome's urban form lies in the 'fortuitousness, contradictoriness and absence of principle' in its building history, and creating the effect of a 'work of art of the highest order':

> This is emphasised by its streetscape just as it is determined by the hilly nature of its terrain. Almost everywhere its buildings stand in the contradictory relationship of above and below. Thereby, they relate to one another with a totally different significance than if they lay on a flat surface, merely alongside one another . . . Where the elements of a landscape lie on a single level they are more indifferent to one another, each has as it were its position for itself, compared with the former where they are defined in terms of each other.[70]

In the 1890s' debate, 'fortuitousness, contradictoriness and absence of principle' contrast with rational calculation, lack of contradiction and regulation by principles.

Yet at issue is not merely the structure of street and square patterns in the city. Rather, it is the relationship of such structures to their different functions. Above all, the frequency of references to street intersections, their diverse constructions and consequences highlights the problem of *circulation*. The accelerated movement of individuals, commodities and transport vehicles in expanding metropolitan centres raised issues around the prioritisation of vehicular traffic, the optimum street formation and width for intended traffic and the maximisation of traffic flows at street intersections. What did not feature in the 1890s' debate at least was the possibility of multi-level intersections (although there were some examples in Stübben's compendium) or the construction of city and underground railways and their relationship to street traffic systems (already functioning in Berlin and, with respect to a city railway, under construction in Vienna from 1894). Although not always openly stated, the issue of the separation of traffic and pedestrians concealed another division between the removal or restriction of traffic in the old inner core of the city and its location in the new, modern sectors of the city. In more than one respect, the dialectic of inside and outside was never far away.

The issue of circulation itself went far beyond straight or irregular streets and intersections. The sphere of circulation of commodities, which Marx viewed as the sphere of total alienation and indifference in which commodities mysteriously exchanged one for another through their equivalent exchange values and not by virtue of their use values, was associated with a free market for all that could be commodified.[71] This implied *open* spaces of circulation in which commodities could *freely* move. In turn, this 'daily traffic of bourgeois life' (Marx) proceeds on the *surface* of a capitalist economy. The sphere of commodity circulation can generate a series of attributes of its own process of mobilising commodities and commodity signs that include interchangeability, anonymity, indifference, uniformity (all intimately connected with the equivalence of exchange values of commodities). This process of circulation taking place on the surface of a capitalist economy could also be readily associated with superficiality. The countervailing symbolic universe resisting capitalist modernity would emphasise uniqueness, intimacy, cosiness, diversity and embeddedness. Capitalist circulation generates an abstract mass of commodities and individuals. The latter, circulating and driven by the principles of 'time is money' (highlighted by Max Weber as a feature of the spirit of modern capitalism and by Otto Wagner as a feature of the spirit of the modern metropolis), as an abstract mass of individuals with what Weber termed a purposive rational orientation to social and economic interaction, required an appropriate urban means within which to circulate.[72] Sitte viewed this modern urban network as one conceived by 'geometric man' – an epithet he ascribed to Wagner.

The valorisation of the circulation process in capitalist modernity to some degree extends into architectural modernism too, insofar as the focus upon sites of *production* appears relatively late. For example, in the avant-garde Viennese journal *Der Architekt*, the first modern design of a factory building appears only in 1909. The negative valorisation of circulation is located in the concept of *regulation*. Both sides of the 1890s' debate are concerned with the regulation of traffic flows. The problem of the street crossing and the acceleration or retardation of traffic circulation is a concrete issue which becomes an increasingly formal problem susceptible to mathematical calculation (as in a 1913 article in the journal *Der Städtebau*).[73] Traffic is also crucial to urban land values, commercial property values and ground rents. Circulation is essential for the infrastructure beneath the urban streets, whether it be sewage, gas, water supply, pneumatic postal systems, and so on (which feature in Stübben's compendium). On the street surface, the street intersection implies an interruption of circulation and a conflict of interests with respect to modes of traffic. The intersection of systems of purposive rational action requires separation and regulation. Viewed abstractly, the indifference of the sphere of circulation in which anything can circulate is threatening to pre-capitalist hierarchies. The social regulation of classes of individuals as masses might therefore require spatial regulation. To give but one example, the lines of the Vienna city railway (constructed 1894–1901) were constructed around the centre of the city and not to its political and administrative centre. Access to centres of power became increasingly regulated in the nineteenth century, driven in part by fear of insurrections. In the context of the 1890s' debate, the political parameters remained hidden.

What were the aesthetic parameters within which the 1890s' debate operated? At first sight, the opposition between a technical problematic focusing upon street infrastructure and an aesthetic problematic oriented towards an aesthetics of the street seems self-evident. Yet it becomes clear that both sides had an aesthetic interest, but with a different focus. Stübben (and Wagner with his emphasis upon the *modern* metropolis) favoured a contemporary and comparative orientation to aesthetic models that were denounced by Henrici as 'Gallic' and 'unGerman', whereas Sitte (and Henrici) largely, though not exclusively, favoured historical exemplary models (drawn from the Italian Renaissance and Baroque). If we extend the debate to include the reception of Wagner's city planning proposals and opposition to them, then there is an opposition between his conception of a use-style (*Nutzstil*) and an (historicist) artistic style. This heretical connection drawn between fashion and contemporary architecture provoked a defence of a historically rooted and hierarchically confirmed conception of taste.

Finally, what are the consequences of the different conceptions of urban space for what Simmel termed the 'mental life' (*Geistesleben*) of its inhabitants? As indicated earlier, several authors have identified discourses on urban pathologies in the late nineteenth century. Simmel, for instance, names neurasthenia, hyperaesthesia, amnesia and claustrophobia with reference to modern metropolitan life and existence in a mature capitalist money economy.[74] Sitte highlights agoraphobia with reference to large open squares surrounded by buildings from which the individual can be observed. He also suggests that people in their own homes do not wish to be observed from outside, a state indicative of the precarious bourgeois interior and retreat and, in extreme cases, paranoia. The uniformity of the straight street and anonymous apartment block might be a source of amnesia, or at least spatial disorientation. Entrapment in the ever momentary presentness of modernity might also generate a kind of forgetting. The converse of these pathologies are claustrophobia (the negative interpretation of Sitte's cosy squares), the historically preserved memory and nostalgia for a pastoral image of a past that is *elsewhere*, and certainly far away from 'our banal modernity'.

The juxtaposition of straight and crooked streets in the 1890s could have a practical resolution in their spatial differentiation. The crooked, irregular streets of the historical core of the city often contrasted with the regular straight layout of modern suburbs, especially if they were home to the working classes. Perhaps Wittgenstein was thinking of Vienna when he drew the analogy between language and the city in the following terms:

> Our language can be seen as an ancient city: a maze of little streets and squares, of old and new houses, and of houses with additions from various periods; and this surrounded by a multitude of new districts with straight regular streets and uniform houses.[75]

The dialectic of inside and outside, of old and new, of crooked and straight streets could be resolved in their spatial separation.

But Sitte and Stübben draw another analogy between inside and outside in their albeit different treatments of the outside spaces of squares as insides, as spatial interiors. Yet in both instances this outside as inside is that of a readily assembled bourgeois interior. It is a space that is not conceived for those who live in the street, who as 'ordinary practitioners', in de Certeau's sense, live '"down below", below the thresholds at which visibility begins'. For them, as Benjamin suggested, the street exterior is actively transformed into an interior. This 'other' group of users

> is an eternally alert, eternally moving being that witnesses, experiences, perceives and devises as much between the house

walls outside as do individuals within the protection of their own four walls. To the collective, the shining enamel signs of a store or company are just as good as, or better than, the decorative oil paintings on the walls of the bourgeois salon. Walls with the sign *Défense d'Afficher* are the collective's writing desk, newspaper stands its libraries, mail boxes, its bronze sculptures, benches, its bedroom furnishings, and the café terraces are the alcoves from which it looks down at its home. Where the asphalt worker lets his coat hang on the rail, that is the vestibule. And the gateway, leading out into the open from multiple courtyards is the long corridor which frightens the bourgeoisie but is to them the entrance into the chambers of the city.[76]

This 'other' conception of the street or square is not merely *perceived* differently but also *experienced* and *used* differently.

Viewed from above in de Certeau's sense, and with respect to attempts to construct monumental straight streets such as Haussmann intended for Paris with his north–south and east–west axes, such projects were unsuccessful in both Berlin and Vienna from the 1890s and through to the end of the Second World War. In Berlin, neither the ambitious projects entered for the 1910 Greater Berlin competition, nor the various plans for a north–south boulevard after the First World War drawn up by Martin Mächler and others came to fruition. Still less were Albert Speer's plans for a *via triumphalis* in Berlin realised. In Vienna, the projects for a grand avenue from the Karlsplatz to Schönbrunn (supported by Wagner) and a straight boulevard from the inner core of the city at the Stephansdom to the Praterstern advanced by Riehl and Lotz before 1914 came to nothing. The same fate befell a Nazi *via triumphalis* that would have erased large sections of the Leopoldstadt district – which originally had a substantial Jewish population. The monumental straight streets within these metropoles remained on paper.[77]

Notes

1 Breton cited in P. Jukes, *A Shout in the Street*, Berkeley, CA, University of California Press, 1991, p. xi; Le Corbusier, *Precisions*, Cambridge, MA, MIT Press, p. 128; K. Marx, *Grundrisse*, Harmondsworth, Penguin, 1973, p. 533.

2 M. de Certeau, *The Practice of Everyday Life*, Berkeley, CA, University of California Press, 1984, p. 93.

3 Ibid.

4 H. Lefebvre, *The Production of Space*, Oxford, Blackwell, 1991.

5 On German city planning, see B. Ladd, *Urban Planning and Civil Order in Germany*, Cambridge, MA, Harvard University Press, 1990.

6 E. da Costa Meyer, 'La Donna è Mobile', in L. Durning and R. Wrigley (eds) *Gender and Architecture*, Chichester, John Wiley, 2000, pp. 155–70.

7 Anthony Vidler, *Warped Space: Art, Architecture and Anxiety in Modern Culture*, Cambridge, MA, MIT Press, 2000.

8 C. M. Boyer, *The City of Collective Memory*, Cambridge, MA, MIT Press, 1996.

9 See Section V on p. 70.

10 On Sitte, see M. Mönninger, *Vom Ornament zum Nationalkunstwerk: Zur Kunst- und Architekturtheorie Camillo Sittes*, Braunschweig/Wiesbaden, Vieweg, 1998. On Wagner, see D. Frisby, *Metropolitan Architecture and Modernity: Otto Wagner's Vienna*, Minneapolis, University of Minnesota Press (forthcoming).

11 See D. Frisby, *Cityscapes of Modernity: Critical Explorations*, Cambridge, Polity Press, 2001, Chapter 5.

12 See J. Stübben, 'Gerade oder krumme Strassen?', *Deutsche Bauzeitung*, vol. 11, 1877, pp. 132–4. See also in the same volume his 'Ueber die Anlage öffentliche Plätze', *Deutsche Bauzeitung*, vol. 11, 1877, pp. 393–5, 403–6. On Stübben's early contributions see my *Metropolitan Architecture and Modernity*. In the second article, he makes an interesting comparison between the forms of squares with rooms in a house:

> Just as the different kinds of construction of squares with respect to their determination and location allow themselves to be compared in an appropriate manner with the room of a house, the traffic square with the vestibule, the market square with the office, the architectonic square with the ballroom or the drawing room, the English square, finally, with the bedroom or the secluded family chamber, so this comparison equates almost completely with respect to the dimensions of size. The claim to the largest dimensions, accordingly, go to the architectonic and traffic squares, whereas English and market squares require less space. In the case of the latter, this should not be forgotten since on too large a market square the buyers feel themselves isolated and the public's desire to buy is not realised; it is indeed a *specific* confinement that is a necessary attribute of busy market transactions. Just as the salon must stand in a correct relationship to its decor, so the size of the architectonic square must stand in relation to the buildings upon it or around it.
>
> (Ibid., p. 404)

13 C. Sitte, *Der Städtebau nach seiner künstlerischen Grundsätzen*, Vienna, C. Graezer, 1889. English translation G. R. and C. C. Collins, *Camillo Sitte: The Birth of Modern City Planning*, New York, Rizzoli, 1986. Joseph Stübben, *Der Städtebau*, Darmstadt, A. Bergstrasse, 1890; reprinted Braunschweig/Wiesbaden, Vieweg, 1980.

14 The last intervention is by Stübben in 1894.

15 See Otto Wagner, *Moderne Architektur*, Vienna, Scholl, 1896. In English see *Modern Architecture*, trans. H. Malgrave, Santa Monica, CA, Getty, 1988. For the review see C. Henrici, 'Moderne Architektur', *Deutsche Bauzeitung*, vol. 31, 1897, pp. 14–20.

16 Most of these pieces remain unpublished in volume form. For a recent discussion of Sitte, see K. Wilhelm, '"Städtebautheorie" als Kulturtheorie – Camillo Sittes "Der Städtebau nach seinen künstlerischen Grundsätzen"', in L. Musner, G. Wunberg and C. Lutter (eds) *Cultural Turn: Zur Geschichte der Kulturwissenschaften*, Vienna, Turia + Kant, 2001, pp. 89–109.

17 Sitte, *City Planning*, p. 138.

18 Ibid., p. 141.

19 Ibid., p. 142 (my emphasis).

20 Ibid., p. 170.

21 Ibid., p. 183.

22 Ibid., p. 183.

23 Ibid., p. 184.

24 Ibid., p. 197.

25 Ibid., pp. 213–14 (my emphasis).

26 Ibid., p. 225.

27 Ibid., p. 228. For a recent discussion of the plain (white) wall, see M. Wrigley, *White Walls, Designer Dresses: The Fashioning of Modern Architecture*, Cambridge, MA, MIT Press, 1995.

28 Sitte, *City Planning*, p. 233.

29 Ibid., p. 234.

30 Ibid., p. 243.

31 Ibid., p. 245.

32 Ibid., p. 246.

33 Ibid., p. 263.

34 Ibid., p. 270.

35 Ibid., p. 271.

36 See G. Fehl, 'Camillo Sitte als Volkserzieher', in G. Fehl (ed.) *Städtebau um die Jahrhundertwende*, Hamburg, W. Kohlhammer, 1980, pp. 173–221.

37 Stübben, *Der Städtebau*, p. 514.

38 Ibid.

39 Ibid., p. 515.

40 Ibid., p. 16.

41 Ibid., p. 32.

42 Ibid., p. 33.

43 Ibid., p. 40.

44 Ibid.

45 K. Henrici, 'Gedanken über das moderne Städte-Bausystem', *Deutsche Bauzeitung*, vol. 25, 1891, pp. 81–3, 86–91.

46 Ibid., p. 83.

47 Ibid.

48 Ibid., p. 88.

49 Ibid., p. 90.

50 J. Stübben, 'Über Fragen der Städtebaukunst', *Deutsche Bauzeitung*, vol. 25, 1891, pp. 122–8, 150–5, 122.

51 Ibid., p. 123.

52 Ibid., p. 154.

53 Ibid.

54 K. Henrici, 'Der Individualismus im Städtebau', *Deutsche Bauzeitung*, vol. 25, 1891, pp. 295–8, 301–2, 320–2.

55 Ibid., p. 296.

56 Ibid., p. 297.

57 Ibid.

58 Ibid., p. 301.

59 J. Stübben, 'Der Individualismus im Städtebau', *Deutsche Bauzeitung*, vol. 25, 1891, p. 362.

60 K. Henrici, 'Langweilige und kurzweilige Strassen', *Deutsche Bauzeitung*, vol. 27, 1893, pp. 271–4, especially p. 271.

61 J. Stübben, 'Zur schönheitlichen Gestaltung städtische Strassen', *Deutsche Bauzeitung*, vol. 27, 1893, pp. 294–6.

62 Ibid., p. 296.

63 Several newspaper articles, though not those attacking Wagner, are included in Mönninger, op. cit.

Beginning without end

It seems that every art form, every aesthetic, has one goal, namely order. Either the intention is to support an established order – witness the Greek temple, the reliquary, the Baroque garden design – or to create a new order. This was the goal that Classical Modernism had in its sights, although artists or groups of artists all took different directions depending on their own particular persuasion. Artistic and cultural trends followed hot on each other's heels, stumbling through the early twentieth century.

Writing in 1892, it was the heavily moustached philosopher Friedrich Nietzsche who identified for future generations the reasons for these developments. In his *Fröhliche Wissenschaft*, Nietzsche's Madman declares God dead. And the death of God also heralded the death of a historic language of forms and semantics that was to celebrate its own existence just one last time in the eclecticism of the late nineteenth century. Wilhelm II's Siegesallese, laid out in 1901, was no more than retrospective defiance. The more forward-looking artists of the early twentieth century set out on a search for a living culture. Lacking in any common tradition, the Modernists were united in their recognition of the need to construct their own language and customs. Classical Modernism was searching for a model of order worthy of the name: an exemplary yardstick. While the functional and material constraints imposed on the applied arts and architecture led to a degree of consensus, by and large discord was the order of the day. A spiral of mutually exclusive '-isms' ensued, each setting itself the goal of renewing art, and each one living by its own dogma. The 'functionalism' since associated with that period in fact never existed in the homogenous form that the term implies. One exception to that supposed functionalism was August Endell (1871–1925): a champion of Modernism but too unpragmatic and unorthodox to adopt any external schema of the kind normally associated with functionalism.

An example: August Endell and the beauty of the city

The cities of Munich, Berlin and Wroclaw were the geographical poles of Endell's life and artistic output. He carried out his first architectural commission in 1898: the Photoatelier Elvira in Munich, which was perfectly located for him to make a provocative statement promoting a new style of architecture.

His task was primarily to produce a design for the façade and the interior. And it was his design for the façade that went against the grain of bourgeois notions of decency. Instead of ordering successive storeys in a

3.2
August Endell,
Atelier Elvira,
189/1900, façade,
from *Hof-Atelier
Elvira 1887–1928:
Ästheten, Emanzen,
Aristokraten,*
exhibition
catalogue,
Fotomuseum im
Münchener
Stadtmuseum,
1986, p. 37

clear hierarchy, he created a design that related to the internal structure of
the building but which neither legibly reflected that structure nor laid bare
the actual construction. The façade – as Endell himself reported in 1900 in
his article 'Architektonische Erstlinge' – in fact corresponded to the arrangement and sizes of the internal spaces: large window/large room, small
window/small room. On the upper floor there was a photo studio which
was not to have any windows in the façade. This provided the opportunity
for the truly provocative feature of his design: an ornament larger than anything anyone had ever seen, unconstrained and beholden only to itself,
dominating the façade. It was not recognisably anything in particular.
Indeed, this ornament dared to enter the domain of the liberal arts although
it was part of an architectural design. Not to mention the colours –
cyclamen-red detail on a sea-green ground.

    This first architectural statement by Endell sets the agenda for his
subsequent works. These perhaps strike a rather quieter note, but they
always take the same basic approach. August Endell makes art from forms:
art to be lived in and lived with, or simply art to be wondered at.

    From 1901 onwards Endell lived, wrote and worked in Berlin. As
a city Berlin was a moloch, its architecture riddled with inner courtyards; as

a place to live there was scarcely a more exciting city in Europe. Here Endell built his apartment blocks, Salamander shoe shops, the Wolzogen Theatre, the Hackesche Höfe, the Mariendorf trotting course. Endell took an active interest in urban planning and demanded that 'plans should be drawn up for extending the city in keeping with certain hygienic and artistic principles'.[1] His goal was an artistic culture for everyone. He set about achieving this goal in various different ways. He designed urban spaces, he passed on his knowledge to the next generation in his 'Schule für Formkunst'; in articles and lectures addressed to a wider public he discussed the beauty in everyday life. In his view, art and culture do not belong in museums: they should be lived and experienced each day.

In 1908 Endell published a slim volume with the title *Die Schönheit der großen Stadt*. This publication, on 'the beauty of the city', is Endell's widest-ranging and freest text; in it he elucidates his aesthetic in the context of the city of Berlin – a credo for a form of beauty that is not always immediately apparent: 'I want only to discuss the design of the modern city, which is, with ever fewer exceptions, loathsome.'[2] For all its loathsome qualities Endell still paid tribute to the 'miraculous sights' that Berlin had to offer. And this is not necessarily a contradiction. For Endell's aesthetic is as much an aesthetic of production as of reception. And where ugliness is the norm, proper perception is the first step to a more beautiful, better world.

On seeing and the visible world

On arrival in Berlin, the first task for the unpractised visitor was, in Endell's view, to abandon all customary modes of functional perception geared solely towards the everyday. Only what Endell calls 'pure seeing' will free the form from its context:

> But those who have learnt to yield themselves up to their visual impressions completely without making other associations, without any kind of extraneous thoughts, those who have even just once had their emotions affected by forms and colours will find in these impressions an inexhaustible source of extraordinary and undreamt of pleasure. It is indeed a new world that opens up in such circumstances.[3]

Endell treats perception as a psychological matter. Other than in the case of learnt perception, pure seeing also involves a response to the form itself. Everything a person perceives through pure seeing induces an immediate emotional reaction. Every line, every shape has a particular emotional effect. And this applies to all human beings alike. The coordinates that determine the form's effect – namely tension and tempo – together generate a response somewhere on our scale of pleasure and displeasure.

Endell's psychological model of perception takes up one of the best-known topoi of Modernity: the lost unity of the 'I', existence and nature. With his 'pure seeing', Endell sought to create unmediated moments that know nothing of this separation. However, it was not romantic longing that brought him to this point but scientific reality. Influenced by his study of psychology he arrived at his 'aesthetic geometry' in which he described the harmonic structures and function of form.[4] This aesthetic geometry was based on widely accepted findings concerning the effect of forms on the human psyche. His own researches then led him to the conclusion that art 'affects us by virtue of freely invented forms, as does music with free sounds'.[5] The direct impact of form without any intellectual input on the part of the recipient also forms the basis of the theory of 'aesthetic empathy' developed by Theodor Lipps.

In 1894 Theodor Lipps (1851–1914), having previously held posts in Bonn and Wroclaw, was appointed Professor and Dean of the Department of Psychology at the Ludwig Maximilian University in Munich. Endell, who had been studying there since 1892, attended his lectures and seminars on psychology and aesthetics. In Lipps he at last found a scientific authority who confirmed his own thinking. Endell started work on a doctorate on 'Emotional Contrasts' with Lipps as his supervisor, but he never submitted his research.

Lipps' theory of aesthetic empathy reduces the meaning of the object to no more than a focus of perception; it thus loses its autonomous meaning in its aesthetic reception. 'Complete empathy means the complete absorption of myself into the object perceived optically and into that which I experience within it. – Such complete empathy may be called aesthetic empathy.'[6] This supposed secure scientific foundation is a cornerstone of Endell's own aesthetic. With this as his starting point he can liberate functional seeing so that it may become pure seeing. In an act of empathetic seeing the separation of object and subject is annulled. The 'I' is not defined by its activity: 'How do I behave towards the object?' – perception and emotional response are as one.

The spirit in the visible

He misses the spiritual, the ideal, that he can only think of in intellectual terms, never guessing that the visible – when it is experienced by the soul – is of course just as spiritual, ideal, valuable as every other great emotional agitation of the soul. Here, too, what is crucial is not the object, but the feeling, the emotion it induces.[7]

The platonic separation of pure ideal from the materialisation of the idea is abandoned here by Endell. In his terms an abstract idea is only of any value when it is experienced by a human being. But with that the idea is no longer abstract, it becomes concrete. The world as a phenomenon is defined by human perception. Every object that is created must be created with a beholder in mind. It is Nietzsche's 'reversed Platonism' that declares 'existence in appearance' as its goal.[8] Only then can the visible be one with the ideal.

At the turn of the century Nietzsche's philosophy occupied many hearts and minds. Endell, too, encountered Nietzsche and his work in many different forms. There were Nietzscheans amongst his friends, he himself was in touch with the circle around Elisabeth Förster-Nietzsche, Nietzsche's sister, who reputedly had her own will to power. In 1898 and 1899 two volumes of Nietzsche were brought out by the publishers C. G. Naumann, with covers designed by Endell.[9] Furthermore, since 1896 Endell had been acquainted with Nietzsche's friend and biographer Lou Andreas-Salomé. 'And it was already part of Nietzsche's notion of the highest ideal that appearance has the right to present itself as existence and being – indeed, that the highest truth is to be found in the impact of the appearance, in its effect on others.'[10] The effect of the appearance on others is also a core issue in Endell's aesthetic. Here the spiritual finds expression in the visible, in the appearance, in the form. Here ethics and aesthetics become one.

As Endell wrote to his cousin Kurt Breysig in early 1896, he learnt about creating appearances – using 'form and sound' – from Stefan George.[11] Endell's contact with the circle around Stefan George, above all with the 'Schwabing Jupiter' Karl Wolfskehl, goes back to the time before 1894. Wolfskehl's salon was a meeting place for artists and intellectuals living in and around the Munich district of Schwabing; these included August Endell, Ludwig Klages and Franziska von Reventlow. Stefan George himself was well enough acquainted with August Endell to avoid him as far as possible. For Endell, very much an individual, had found his own voice, had his own thoughts and was certainly not prepared to submit to some other authority. But he had taken to heart at least one principle of George's poetry. In *Blätter für die Kunst*, the journal published by one section of the George circle, this principle is formulated as follows:

> And those who constantly exhort us to change, whose feelings have become rigidified through sheer force of habit and whose gaze is dulled would be well advised before they turn to art again to spend seven years thinking solely about why a poem is more beautiful than a speech saying the same, a painting more beauti-

ful than the more exact coloured photograph, a sculpture more beautiful than the more faithful wax model.[12]

It is not functional form, nor more precise representation, nor greater accuracy and objectivity that determine the value of art. It is that infinitesimal 'more' that we are aware of in the work of art: the non-factual aspect of the facticity of the work of art which Adorno calls its 'spirit'.[13]

Stefan George's notion of the spiritual as an earthly resonance of the ideal takes root in Endell's aesthetic theory as the realisation of the ideal in experienced form. Plato's enduringly 'remembrable' idea becomes the enduringly 'experienceable' for Endell. Thus he stays within the realms of the earthly-human, but liberates himself from the constraints of the functional and the material. His work in the field of the applied arts and architecture is not determined by technical necessity but primarily from the inner need to create something beautiful, something spiritual. Thus in Endell's work, form is the spiritual made visible.

Endell uses psychology to detach this form and one's experience of it from arbitrary subjectivity, and this in turn leads to his aesthetic geometry. Beauty, this great 'agitation of the soul' is here governed by concrete laws. And in this context, Endell firmly believed, psychology is to perception as physics is to the natural sciences. Psychology defines the laws that apply. Psychology provides our sensual experience of the form with a rational corset. The spirituality of the visible needs the aestheticisation of the world around us either through forming or perception. Other than in the elite circles around Stefan George, it was Endell's firm conviction that every individual could heighten his/her own existence by means of pure seeing and experience his/her surroundings anew.

For Endell, the spiritual is bound up with human existence. A thing must be experienced by a human being for it to exist on an emotional level. While functional perception helps human beings to react to the world around them, the aesthetic process requires the active involvement of the individual. For only pure, unmediated seeing 'is one with the deed'.[14] And it is at this point that Endell's project of an artistic culture overcomes the divided oneness of being and connects the ideal with the deed. The indispensable precondition for this is an unconditional acceptance of the present. For only the actively experienced present will find its fulfilment in the Here and Now.

The city

The city, the most visible and perhaps strangest fruit of our lives today, the most striking, most self-contained manifestation of our doing and wanting.[15]

The city embodies the modern present. Here we hear the 'melody of life'. Here Modernity thrives. But what disturbed Endell about Berlin, and he made no bones about it, was the lack of considered design. Industrial society, with its technical demands, now took up too much space. Endell complained that 'the wonderful melody of our working lives' did not resonate in the ways people took their leisure or in the ways they shaped their surroundings.[16] There was an urgent need to re-establish this lost unity. But since the WHAT – the city of Berlin – was not in itself beautiful, Endell concentrated on the mechanism described in his aesthetic, the HOW, that is to say pure, artistic seeing. As in an Impressionist picture, everything becomes form and colour. Everything can be and is viewed as form: 'squat horseless carriages' became 'gigantic bumble-bees',[17] need and poverty acquired an aesthetic appeal. Disinterested looking, purely morphological observation, underwent a paradigmatic change from knowing to seeing. And only when the beauty of the city is accepted as readily as the beauty of the mountains, can – in Endell's view – 'the power of all-embracing forming flourish on this sure foundation of "seeing" enjoyment'.[18]

Observing and forming are acts that both create and preserve culture. Seemingly superfluous – in Endell's case often excessive – ornament has a high potential for the spiritual in art. Without functional obligations the form is freer. The form and its counterpart in the third dimension, namely space, are there to be experienced. Their utilisation is only ever secondary.

The ontological reduction to the reality of the world of experiencing may mean leaving behind traditional metaphysical concepts, yet in Endell's aesthetic it retains a spiritual dimension. His 'immoralism' of pure seeing generates moments of poetry. The unmediated experience of the city by the human subject, the unconditional acceptance of the city – these all acquire what Nietzsche has elsewhere called 'human meaning'.[19] Endell's name for it is beauty.

Notes

1 August Endell, 'Kultur und Bauordnung', in *Die Werkkunst: Zeitschrift des Vereins für deutsches Kunstgewerbe in Berlin*, vol. 1, part 4, 16 November 1905, p. 65: 'Planung der Stadterweiterung nach hygienischen und künstlerischen Grundsätzen'.

2 August Endell, *Die Schönheit der großen Stadt*, Stuttgart: Strecker and Schröder, 1908, p. 47: 'Ich will nur von der modernen Stadt reden, die als Gestaltung mit verschwindenden Ausnahmen abscheulich ist.'

3 August Endell, *Um die Schönheit*, Munich, 1896, p. 11:

      Wer es aber gelernt hat, sich seinen visuelle Eindrücken völlig ohne
      Associationen, ohne irgend welche Nebengedanken hinzugeben, wer nur

einmal die Gefühlswirkung der Formen and Farben verspürt hat, der wird darin einen nie versiegende Quelle ausserordentlichen und ungeahnten Genusses finden. Es ist in der That eine neue Welt, die sich da auftut.

4 August Endell, 'Kunstgewerbliche Erziehung', in *Der Zeitgeist*, no. 33, supplement to the *Berliner Tagblatt*, 13 August 1904, unpaginated.

5 August Endell, 'Formkunst', in *Dekorative Kunst 1*, 1897/98, part 6, March 1898, p. 280: 'durch frei gefundene Formen wirkt, wie Musik durch freie Töne'.

6 Theodor Lipps, *Ästhetik*, vol. 1, Hamburg & Leipzig, L. Voss, 1903, p. 125: 'Die vollkommene Einfühlung ist eben ein vollkommenes Aufgehen meiner in dem optisch Wahrgenommenen und dem, was ich darin erlebe. – Solch vollkommene Einfühlung ist die ästhetische Einfühlung.'

7 Endell, *Die Schönheit der großen Stadt*, 1908, p. 42:

> Er vermißt das Geistige, das Ideale, das er sich nur begrifflich denken kann, und ahnt nicht, daß das Sichtbare als seelisches Erlebnis natürlich genau so geistig, genau so ideal, genau so wertvoll ist, als jede andere große Erregung der Seele. Auch hier ist das Wesentliche überall nicht das Objekt, sondern das Gefühl, die Erregung, die es hervorruft.

8 See Helge Hultberg, *Die Kunstauffassung Nietzsches*, Bergen, Norwegian Universities Press, 1964, p. 8.

9 See Tilmann Buddensieg, 'Der erste moderne Bucheinband? August Endell and Friedrich Nietzsche', in *Ars naturam adiuvans. Festschrift für Matthias Winner zum 11. März 1996*, ed. by Victoria v. Flemming and Sebastian Schütze, Mainz, P. von Zabern, 1996, pp. 662–9.

10 Lou Andreas-Salomé, *Friedrich Nietzsche in seinen Werken*, Berlin, Mann, undated [1924 (1984)], p. 203: 'Doch es liegt ja schon in Nietzsches Auffassung des höchsten Ideals, daß der Schein das Recht hat, sich als Sein und Wesen zu geben, – ja, daß alle höchste Wahrheit in der Scheinwirkung, im Effekt auf andere besteht.'

11 Tilmann Buddensieg, 'Zur Frühzeit von August Endell. Seine Münchener Briefe an Kurt Breysig', in *Festschrift für Eduart Trier zum 60. Geburtstag*, ed. by Justus Müller Hofstede and Werner Spies, Berlin, Mann, 1981, pp. 223–50.

12 *Blätter für die Kunst*, 4th series, vols 1–2, Nov. 1897, p. 2 (orthography as in original):

> Auch denen die jetzt zur allgemeinen umkehr mahnen ist durch die lange gewohnheit so das gefühl erstarrt und der Blick getrübt dass ehe sie sich wieder mit Kunst beschäftigen man ihnen raten muss sieben jahre hindurch über nichts nachzudenken als über das: warum ein gedicht schöner sei als eine gleiches sagende rede, ein gemälde schöner als das genauere farbige lichtbild, ein bildwerk schöner als die treuere wachsform.

13 Theodor Wiesengrund Adorno, *Ästhetische Theorie*, Frankfurt am Main, Suhrkamp, 1970, p. 134.

14 Endell, *Die Schönheit der großen Stadt,* 1908, p. 19: 'eins mit der Tat'.

15 Ibid., p. 21: 'Die große Stadt, die sichtbarste und vielleicht eigentümlichste Frucht unseres heutigen Lebens, die augenfälligste, geschlossenste Gestaltung unseres Wirkens und Wollens'.

16 Ibid., p. 9: 'die wunderbare Melodie unseres Arbeitslebens'.

17 Ibid., p. 84: 'kurzgebaute Automobildroschken' . . . 'riesenhafte Hummeln'.

18 Ibid., pp. 87–8: 'auf diesem sicheren Fundament des sehendes Genießens die Kraft umfassenden Gestaltens erwachsen'.

19 Friedrich Nietzsche, *Thus Spoke Zarathustra*, Part I, 1883, 'Of the Bestowing Virtue', 2, translated by R. H. Hollingdale, Harmondsworth, Penguin, 1961, p. 102.

Part II

Place

Once defined, the 'spirit' of the place demands tangible, physical expression. The three essays that follow explore this impulse in the context of political, commercial, urban and domestic imperatives.

Chapter 4

Embodying the spirit of the metropolis

The Warenhaus Wertheim, Berlin, 1896–1904

Helen Shiner

Many apologists of modernist architecture have dismissed the entrance façade of the Wertheim department store, on the Leipziger Platz, Berlin, 1904, as 'historicist', and hence 'not modern'.[1] Such writing does not acknowledge the seminal importance, as a model solution for a new building type, which the design was accorded by its contemporary critics. An examination of its reception demonstrates that the store was taken to express the spirit of the modern metropolis in which it stood. Moreover, the force of its architectural design would seem to have been compounded, for some of its chroniclers, by the vitalist utopian ideals with which it was felt to resonate.

Evidently eclectic in stylistic terms, the Wertheim department store was considered, nonetheless, by admirers and detractors alike, as an apposite translation into architectural form of the prevailing *Zeitgeist*.[2] The influential progressive architect and designer Peter Behrens deemed it the first instance of the expression of a modern monumental art; modern, he claimed, because it boldly acknowledged the true requirements of the age and employed them as a creative tool.[3] Commissioned by a family of Jewish

businessmen, the entrance façade on the Leipziger Platz was felt, perhaps surprisingly, to point the way forward for a national architecture, then struggling to find a suitable mode in which to articulate the ideals of the recently founded German Reich. That it achieved this on the Leipziger Platz, a square with Francophobic historical resonance, only served to intensify its approbation. Its understated design disavowed the supposed perils of consumption. Instead the façade asserted the store owners' assimilationist allegiance to the key liberal middle-class values of humanistic education and social respectability.[4]

The sculptural programme on the Leipziger Platz façade presented its viewers with an array of characters drawn from the Old Testament and from ancient myth. The simple appeal of the series of figures surmounting the pilasters of the entrance arcade was heightened by the architectonic surround, reminiscent for many of a medieval cathedral or guildhall, despite its evident *Jugendstil* and orientalising references. Reformist both in stylistic terms and in its iconography, this sculpture can be seen to have been employed as the most direct means of communicating the building's utopian aims to its passing public.

4.1
Alfred Messel, Wertheim Store, Berlin, 1896–1904, view of Leipziger **Platz façades (1903–4) into** Leipziger Strasse, Landesarchiv, Berlin

4.2
Alfred Messel,
Wertheim Store,
Berlin, 1896–1904,
detail of portal on
Leipziger Platz
(1903–4), with
sculptural
decoration by Josef
Rauch, from *Blätter
für Architektur und
Kunsthandwerk*,
XVIII, no. 6 (June
1905), plate 50

The commission in 1896, from the four Wertheim brothers, of a design for a large-scale, purpose-built, flagship store on the prestigious Leipziger Straße was to prove the culmination of a continuing and fruitful relationship between the Jewish patrons and their chosen architect. The family had come from a lowly background, starting business selling goods to a working-class public from a retail outlet described by one critic at the time as something akin to a penny bazaar.[5] In 1876 their father had opened his first shop in the northern town of Stralsund. Less than twenty years later the brothers had a chain of six stores to their name. Alfred Messel had been employed twice previously as architect by the Wertheim family for outlets on the Rosenthaler Straße and the Oranienstraße in Berlin, both in areas

4.3
Alfred Messel,
Wertheim Store,
Berlin, 1896–7,
central court, with
sculpture *Work* by
Ludwig Manzel.
Bildarchiv Foto
Marburg

an almost uninterrupted view of all floors within. For Messel, the essential elements of contemporary architecture were simplicity and functionality, wielded jointly to create an aesthetic whole.[19] It was this fusion which was registered by the young Bruno Taut on first viewing the Leipziger Straße store in 1902. He declared himself:

> captivated by its clarity and dignity. I had never seen a building before which exposed itself, so to speak, so nakedly to the observer, which said so directly, simply and without pathos: 'I am the way I am and nothing else.'[20]

4.4
Alfred Messel,
Wertheim Store,
Berlin, 1903–4,
great court.
Bildarchiv Foto
Marburg

4.5
Alfred Messel,
Wertheim Store,
Berlin, 1896–7,
Leipzigerstrasse
façade, from *Alfred
Messel, 5. Sonderheft
des Berliner
Architecturwelt*,
1905, p. 80

Nonetheless, the exterior of Messel's Leipziger Platz façade, at least, belied the opulence inside. Messel had been criticised in some quarters for constructional severity in the first phases of this building; now his entrance façade was hailed as a return to *Baukunst*.[21] The coeval reception of the near-contemporary store for the Tietz concern, erected on the other side of society as destructive of the pre-existing community.[36] Society, for him, was typified by contractual exchange, urbanisation, and an attendant mutual alienation of people. Community, on the other hand, drew its strength from the co-operative endeavour and 'spiritual friendship' of supportive human relationships.

At the turn of the twentieth century, it became common practice to associate the Jew with all the negative aspects of modernity.[37] Excluded from most trades, Europe's Jews had developed skills in the retail and banking sectors. Most of the department stores of this period in Berlin were in Jewish ownership. In his influential book *Modern Capitalism* of 1902, Werner Sombart portrayed capitalism as an alien force stemming from European Jewish endeavours. Contemporaries found it easy to blame the new pace of life on the supposed Jewish tendencies of rootlessness and rest-lessness. In the process of assimilation, Jews frequently faced political and social obstacles of varying kinds. Most tellingly, perhaps, they had to seek to adjust themselves to the differing notions of nationhood and citizenship, which were being played out among several constituencies at the time.[38] Jews had traditionally espoused a liberal political viewpoint, an allegiance most likely to engender their safety as citizens. The period in which they had been emancipated into German society had been one of a liberal and relatively tolerant nationalism. For Jews, as for other groupings within the contemporary society, the image of the nation resonated with a desire for community, during a period when the fractures of modernity were becoming ever more evident and traditional links were dissolving. Alfred Messel had been born a Jew, but had been baptised by the time he was working on the design of the Wertheim store. It is recorded that, although Georg Wertheim was still a member of the Jewish community, largely in deference to his father, he longed to follow Messel's precedent.[39]

Georg Wertheim was all too aware of the audacity of his latest commercial venture. It is apparent from his diaries that he was painfully prescient of the barrage of anti-Semitic criticism that he was likely to have to face.[40] The moves he made to pre-empt such abuse are indicative also of his social concerns, and his apparent liberal political stance. The resistance, noted by critics, from 'interested official and disinterested private circles' to the presence of such a vast, modern retail outlet in a primarily residential area, must have been clear to him and to his architect, Messel.[41] In order for the design to be socially acceptable, it would have been necessary above all to give the appearance of exercising 'good taste'. The influential American social analyst Theodor Veblen had spoken for many of his generation when he wrote bitingly in criticism of 'conspicuous consumption', as he termed it.[42] The discontinuity between the use value of merchandise and evident attempts to create hitherto unfelt desire created great unease at the turn of the century. Shopping had become intimately linked in many countries with fears about a nation's degeneration. In Germany, particularly, it was seen as something inherently Parisian, and, hence, artificial and decadent. Burgeoning consumption had altered in a very significant way the known boundaries between public and private arenas. Fears of moral confusion and decline in the face of increased female autonomy had led to a yearning for more simplified civic ideals in many European countries.[43]

Responding to this perception, the entrance façade of the Wertheim store on the Leipziger Platz was seen by contemporaries as understated and dignified in its design. It was particularly praised for its lack of a forthright declaration of its true commercial identity:

> Silently in the loud noise, proud and self-possessed like the giant trees before it, the corner building reaches up gracefully, almost solemnly to the heights ... But no sign, no banner, nothing colourful by day, no lighting effect by night, declares its purpose.[44]

It was in this disavowing of its intention that the critic saw its strength:

> The building looms from across the other side of the square, to be truthful, not in the manner of commercial premises, but rather like part of an old Gothic cathedral, on which everything fanciful has been spared, or like one of the most noble, earnestly charming chapels of an Oxford college. If you stand of an evening at a distance from it and watch the window masses sparkle with scattered and yet restrained lights – you feel you have to wait there until the first organ tones sound across to you from those high halls.[45]

Georg Wertheim sought, above all, to give the appearance of trading in an irreproachable manner. He was at pains to avert any criticism of his newspaper publicity, which was acclaimed for its lack of visual imagery, thought by some at the time to be much too strong in its seductive appeal. He contented himself with subtle use of lettering and other graphic elements. The fleet of delivery vans operated by the Wertheim firm, despite its presumably highly visible presence on the street, also maintained a dignified appearance by the use of similar graphics and of uniformed drivers. Wertheim offered relatively good employment terms for the period.[46] Women, especially, could expect better treatment from him than from other employers and might advance to the position of a supervisory role, given suitable aptitude. He provided unprecedented leisure facilities for his staff, such as the roof-garden where they could relax during the exceptionally long lunch-break.[47] He was also keen to ensure that his employees received correct and ample nourishment throughout the day from the staff restaurant. Wertheim's projection of a paternalistic persona might be seen as an attempt to control the threatening aspects of consumption by veiling it as an extension of the domestic realm.[48] The firm equally made great efforts to improve and educate its clientele with services of didactic intent: housed within the store's confines, for instance, were an art gallery, a lending library and a theatre ticket agency.

Messel unfailingly asserted the sophistication of his architectural work by recourse to fine and applied art. In Wertheim he found an ideal col-laborator. Contemporaries saw in this exceptional businessman a cultured patron of the arts, someone who deemed the inclusion of art in his depart-ment stores as the most effective advertising for his concern.[49] Wrapping a prime site of consumption in the vestiges of high art was also intended to deflect the claims of seduction and immorality connoted for many by such a space. One commentator enthused that Wertheim's sophisticated display of goods would train consumer taste to the benefit of the national economy.[50] Ultimately, however, it is apparent that Wertheim was not averse to employing spectacular, populist means to attract his customers. A standard device of the department store had always been the use of light. Wertheim's publicity underlined the number of lightbulbs used within the complex, focusing attention additionally on the natural lighting permitted by the three glass-covered courts: 'The whole building, including the courtyards and shop windows, is illuminated by means of electricity, in fact by 486 arc lamps and about 4,600 lightbulbs.'[51]

Of particular importance to the reception of the Wertheim store were the ways in which sculpture was mobilised for diverse purposes beyond those of mere decoration. The democratisation of sites of entertain-ment and leisure was something which had become familiar to the residents of many large European cities in the guise of International Expositions; zoo-logical gardens; and the smaller-scale touring exhibitions of 'exotic' peoples and animals, which fell somewhere between the two.[52] August Gaul's *Bear Fountain*, sited at the furthest end of the entrance arcade, for instance, had resonances of such sites of popular entertainment, alongside its obvious iconographical assertion of Berlin's identity in its employment of the city's symbol, the bear. That Messel and Wertheim were keen to address a popular audience is further evidenced by a series of reliefs belonging to an earlier phase of the building, which depicted scenes from the well-loved Grimm's *Fairy Tales*.[53] Ludwig Manzel's large-scale sculpture of a female industrial worker, *Work*, which was placed very prominently in one of the main courts, might also be read as having similar intentions.[54] Certainly, a contemporary critic saw it as an attempt by the Wertheim brothers to demonstrate their indebtedness to the firm's earliest customers in Stralsund and in the working districts of Berlin.[55] Its naturalistic simplicity of finish contrasted markedly with the opulence and intricacy of its surroundings.[56]

As Messel was working on the construction of earlier phases of the Leipziger Straße store, it is recorded that he became dissatisfied with the work produced by some of the sculptors employed by him.[57] Architectural sculpture in Berlin at that time was barely seen as fitting work for an independent practitioner. Very few sculptors based in the city seemed capable to Messel of carrying out such commissions.[58] Having undertaken an extensive national search, Messel recruited additional assistance from independent sculptors from the Munich school.[59] He was drawn in particular to artists whose conception of the architectonic, informed by Adolf von Hildebrand's theories, largely corresponded with his ideas.[60] Hildebrand had espoused a return to classical relief principles and had called for direct-carving techniques to be employed. Adopting a generalised vision of the human form, his own production privileged understated and static figures of a simple classical nature. Munich had witnessed a recuperation of its medieval architectural tradition, which had favoured a rich decoration of buildings. The city had become known for the craft skills displayed by its sculptors, particularly in their response to the possibilities of an architectonic siting. As here, the use of a coarsely textured shell-limestone allowed for an immediacy in the sculpture, which was often produced directly on site. Key amongst such practitioners were Josef Rauch, Ignatius Taschner and Josef Floßmann, all of whom were employed by Messel on the Leipziger Platz façade.[61] It is illuminating for the present argument that some of the sculptors in question had adopted artistic identities strongly influenced by the practices and concerns of their medieval counterparts. Georg Wrba, who had produced work for the interior of the store, and Ignatius Taschner were both members of the Albrecht-Dürer-Verein, a grouping of Academy students keen to emulate the art of the late Middle Ages and Renaissance.[62] Taschner was also an active member of the associated German Society for Christian Art.[63] The art critic Fritz Stahl stressed Messel's innovation in according his chosen sculptors autonomy of design, as opposed to relying on the mass-produced repetitions of the firms of decorative sculptors more normally employed on projects of this scope.[64] Scheffler contrasted the conventionality of the sculptural decoration of the earlier Leipziger Straße façade with the naturalism of that belonging to the later phase. He felt that the latter had developed as a response to the demands of the construction itself, achieving a far greater monumentality for

4.6
Alfred Messel,
Wertheim Store,
Berlin, Leipziger
Platz façade,
1903–4, figures of
David and Hercules
(?) by Josef Rauch.
Bildarchiv Foto
Marburg

architecture and sculpture. For him, naturalism in sculpture equated with functionality in architecture to the benefit of the architectonic whole.[65] Scheffler described the ensuing sculptural work, with its comparative crudeness of manufacture, primitivising style, and lack of a more prevalent Neo-classical pomp and writhing eroticism, as exhibiting 'a synthetic archaising modernity'.[66]

4.7
Alfred Messel,
Wertheim Store,
Berlin, Leipziger
Platz façade,
1903–4, figure of
Mercury by Josef
Rauch, from
*Wertheim Berlin,
Leipziger Strasse,*
Berlin, Adolf
Eckstein, 1909/10

Stahl claimed that the Leipziger Platz façade was the first building of the time to restore sculpture to its true architectonic relationship.[67]
Messel's reticence in the use of decoration, he argued, was reminiscent of
Schinkel's designs. This was not *Klebeplastik*, sculpture stuck on in an irrelevant and inappropriate manner; it responded, he claimed, to the spirit of
the time. Thematically, as well as in the fusion of styles, the sculptural work
closely echoes the project's aims. The Gothicising, and at turns *Jugendstil*-
influenced, upper reliefs may well have been intended to make light-
hearted reference to the operation of trade in their depiction of the realms
of the goddesses Fortune and Industry. The lower free-standing figures

111

depict mythological and biblical characters and demonstrate, in the simplicity of their form and understated iconography, the sculptors' concern with the theme of the *Neuer Mensch*, that staple of reform movements of the period, so favoured by Hildebrand's followers.[68]

In seeking to attain acceptability as an assimilated member of the German upper middle classes, it had been necessary since emancipation for a Jew to demonstrate the acquisition of *Bildung*. A peculiarly German concept entailing self-improvement achieved through a classical education, *Bildung* had lost its currency to some degree by the turn of the century within non-Jewish circles. It has been noted that Jews, however, clung to its ideals.[69] The attainment of such an education was seen in part as a means of countering the disquiet about racial and social degeneration, which informed the medical and socio-political discourses of the period. Many contemporary polemicists, writing on the subject of Jewish assimilation, saw the task as having physical ramifications.[70] Perhaps most prominent among them, the doctor and dilettante art critic, Max Nordau, author of the controversial *Degeneration* of 1892, made an unfavourable distinction between the 'Muscle Jew' and the 'Coffee-House Jew'.[71] He called for the creation of a 'New Jew' to counter the physical weakness and nervousness then supposed to be prevalent among his co-religionists. Many European nationalist movements had emphasised the need for physical rejuvenation and had founded gymnastic clubs to mould the new manly body (women figured little in Nordau's polemic, although he did suggest that they learn to dance).[72] Nordau's work was particularly influential in an upsurge of interest in such activity. He called upon Jews to re-establish links with their ancient and heroic past and cited biblical heroes as appropriate role models.[73] It has been pointed out that the archetype of the New Jew was very close to the ideal of masculinity then pertaining amongst the *Bildungsbürgertum*, which had been inspired largely by Winckelmann's recuperation of male physical beauty from Greek sculpture.[74] Messel, himself a keen gymnast in his younger days, and his patron, Wertheim, would surely have been aware that this depiction of the reformed body in dignified, chaste repose would form the most intimate link with the passing public. It would have spoken, not only of the regenerated biblical heroes of Nordau's rhetoric, available to Christian and Jew alike, but also of the classical figures known to possessors of the requisite *Bildung*. That it did so within a framework redolent of civic ideals, yearned for by many modern city dwellers, would only have underlined its inclusive, reformative force. Messel spoke, in fact, of his employment of sculpture, among other architectonic elements, as a means of introducing a human-scale focal point to assist comprehension of his architectural design.[75]

Presaging developments in architecture and sculpture that would preoccupy artists and commentators working in the first two decades of the twentieth century, Messel's building complex for the Wertheim family came to be seen as a model for future practice. In its referencing and unifying of past architectural styles, it spoke insistently to a generation seeking a national style for all forms of the arts in Germany. The spectacular architectural and sculptural appeal of its main entrance façade on the Leipziger Platz was rooted in reforming ideals of the turn of the century. Envisioning a vitalist utopia based on an idealised, specifically anti-French, national past, the entrance façade belied the primarily commercial function and interior opulence of the store behind. The adoption of an apparently spiritual and regenerative mode of address was ultimately a reconciling move on behalf of its Jewish clients keen to demonstrate their assimilation within an increasingly nationalistic culture, ill at ease with many of the manifestations of a burgeoning and irresistible modernity. Long fêted as a sociological and cultural 'Stadtkrone' of profoundly influential nature far beyond its mercantile intent, one might claim finally that the Wertheim department store resonated positively for those like Karl Scheffler in search of a *heimatlich* focus for the modern metropolis.

Acknowledgements

The author wishes to convey her gratitude to the following institutions for generous grants that have permitted research to be undertaken towards this chapter: the Henry Moore Foundation; the Central Research Fund, University of London; and the Courtauld Institute of Art. She would also like to thank Dr Shulamith Behr, Professor Iain Boyd Whyte, Dr Matthew Craske, Dr Josephine Gabler, Arie Hartog and Dr Simone Ladwig-Winters for their fruitful criticism and kind assistance in the preparation of this chapter. The material here presented forms part of a forthcoming Ph.D. registered at the Courtauld Institute of Art on the subject of the patronage of sculpture in Germany, 1890–1933.

Notes

1   This chapter deals with the Wertheim store until the completion of its third phase. Extensions to the complex continued until 1914. Julius Posener claimed that the store's design stood somewhere between the poles of historicism and modernity. His analysis concentrates on the

second phase and interior of the building, barely discussing the Leipziger Platz façade. Julius Posener, *Berlin auf dem Wege zu einer neuen Architektur: Das Zeitalter Wilhelms II*, Munich, Prestel-Verlag, 1979, p. 377. On the contemporary legal definition of a department store, engendered in relation to the recent department store tax, see Simone Ladwig-Winters, *Wertheim: Geschichte eines Warenhauses*, Berlin, be.bra verlag, 1997, p. 32.

2   See, for example, M. Rapsilber, 'Das Werk Alfred Messels', *5. Sonderheft der Berliner Architekturwelt*, vol. 1, Berlin, Ernst Wasmuth, 1911, 2nd edn, p. 4 and Otto Grautoff, 'Zwei neue Münchener Warenhäuser', *Dekorative Kunst*, VIII, 8 May 1905, p. 297.

3   Peter Behrens, 'Alfred Messel: Ein Nachruf', *Frankfurter Zeitung*, 6 April 1909, Morgenblatt, reproduced in Fritz Hoeber, *Peter Behrens*, Munich, Georg Miller und Eugen Rentsch, 1913, p. 225.

4   On the terms *Bildung* and *Sittlichkeit* and their relevance to the contemporary Jewish population of Germany, see George L. Mosse, *Confronting the Nation: Jewish and Western Nationalism*, Hanover/London, Brandeis University Press/University Press of New England, 1993, p. 143f.

5   Paul Göhre, *Das Warenhaus*, Frankfurt am Main, Rütten & Loening, 1907, p. 17. For very detailed, contextualised accounts of the history of the Wertheim firm and family, see Simone Ladwig-Winters, *Wertheim: Geschichte* and *Wertheim – ein Warenhausunternehmen und seine Eigentümer: Ein Beispiel der Entwicklung der Berliner Warenhäuser bis zur 'Arisierung'*. Münster, Lit Verlag, 1997.

6   Ladwig-Winters, *Wertheim: Geschichte*, pp. 17–23.

7   Ludwig Hoffmann, *Lebenserinnerungen eines Architekten. Die Bau- und Kunstdenkmäler von Berlin*, Beiheft 10, Berlin, Gebrüder Mann, 1983, p. 165.

8   Hoffmann, *Lebenserinnerungen.*, pp. 189–90, also p. 192. Messel received the commission for the Pergamon Museum in 1906. He did not live to carry out the project, which was completed by his colleague, Ludwig Hoffmann. See, for instance, Thomas W. Gaeghtgens, *Die Berliner Museumsinsel im Deutschen Kaiserreich: Zur Kulturpolitik der Museen in der wilhelminischen Epoche*, Munich, Dt. Kunstverlag, 1992.

9   The cultural theorist Guy Debord famously asserted that capitalism, in all its publicly visible manifestations, operates on the terrain of the spectacle towards the end of social control. In this Marxist account, the purpose of such a strategy is to inculcate a distracting false consciousness in the working class. The term 'spectacle' is here used, however, in the manner employed by John MacAloon, who has argued for a rejection of Debord's analysis, positing spectacle as a genre of cultural performance. He claims that 'spectacle produces and consists of images, and that the triangular relationship between the spectacle, its contents, and its contextual cultures is "about" the relationship between image and reality, appearing and being.' See Guy Debord, *The Society of the Spectacle*, New York, Zone Books, 1994 (1st publ. in French, Buchet-Chastel, 1967); and J. J. MacAloon, 'Olympic Games and the Theory of Spectacle in Modern Societies', in J. J. MacAloon (ed.) *Rite, Drama, Festival, Spectacle: Rehearsals Toward a Theory of Cultural Performance*, Philadelphia, PA, Institute for the Study of Human Issues, 1984, p. 270.

10   *Berlin für Kenner: Ein Bärenführer bei Tag und Nacht durch die deutsche Reichshauptstadt*, Berlin, Boll und Pickardt, 1912 (*Großstadtführer für Kenner*, vol. 1), excerpts published in Jürgen Schutte and Peter Sprengel (eds) *Die Berliner Moderne 1885–1914*, Stuttgart, Reclam, 1997 (1st publ. 1987), p. 96f.

11   Ibid.

12   Vor uns flutet die Masse der Menschen und Wagen dahin, rastlos, ununterbrochen, dem Engpaß der Leipziger Straße zu. . . . als der runde Rahmen des schönen, lebenstrotzenden Bildes, die hohen Häuser des Platzes, von denen doch nur eins dem Schauenden in die Augen fällt, in den Augen

bleibt, auf das der Strom der hastenden Menschen und rasselnden Wagen ewig
zustürzt . . .: das Warenhaus Wertheim.

(Göhre, *Das Warenhaus*, p. 7)

Translations are the author's unless otherwise indicated.

13 See Alan Balfour, *Berlin: The Politics of Order, 1737–1989,* New York, Rizzoli, 1990 for an
account of the history of the Leipziger Platz and adjacent Potsdamer Platz.

14 See Alste Oncken, *Friedrich Gilly 1772–1800: Die Bauwerke und Kunstdenkmäler von Berlin,*
Beiheft 7, Berlin, Gebrüder Mann, 1981, p. 43.

15 Cited in Erik Forssman, 'Karl Friedrich Schinkel', in Wolfgang Ribbe and Wolfgang Schäche
(eds) *Baumeister, Architekten, Stadtplaner: Biographien zur baulichen Entwicklung Berlins,*
Berlin, Stapp Verlag, 1987, p. 153.

16 The recuperation of the Gothic as a nationalistic tool had been made problematic in the early
1840s by the discovery of the immense debt, in the design of Cologne Cathedral, to that of
Amiens. No longer with any credibility able to claim Germany as progenitor of this style, the
debate had had to shift. Some continued to argue that, at the time of the construction of the
great cathedrals, France had been ruled by the Franks, a Germanic tribe. Others, however,
satisfied themselves with the employment of the Gothic as a potent regenerative and
reformative symbol of a cherished and lost way of life. On the Gothic and cultural
nationalism, see, for instance, Robin Reisenfeld, 'Cultural Nationalism, Brücke and the
German Woodcut: the formation of a collective identity', *Art History,* vol. 20, no. 2, June
1997, pp. 289–312.

17 Göhre, *Das Warenhaus*, pp. 12–13.

18 See Kathleen James, 'From Messel to Mendelsohn: German Department Store Architecture in
Defence of Urban and Economic Change', in Geoffrey Crossick and Serge Jaumain (eds)
Cathedrals of Consumption: The European Department Store, 1850–1939, Aldershot, Ashgate,
1999, p. 257.

19 Messel called specifically for simplicity, functionality and beauty. See letter from Messel to
Herwarth Walden, Berlin, 12 October 1905, Staatsbibliothek zu Berlin, Sturm Archiv: Alfred
Messel.

20 Translation by Iain Boyd Whyte. As cited in Whyte, *Bruno Taut and the Architecture of
Activism,* Cambridge, Cambridge University Press, 1982, p. 17.

21 Fritz Stahl, 'Alfred Messel', *9. Sonderheft der Berliner Architekturwelt,* vol. 2, Berlin: Ernst
Wasmuth, 1911, p. XIII.

22 Ibid.

23 Behrens, 'Alfred Messel', p. 225. On the term *Gesamtkunstwerk,* see Peter Vergo, 'The Origins
of Expressionism and the Notion of the *Gesamtkunstwerk*', in Shulamith Behr, David Fanning
and Douglas Jarman (eds) *Expressionism Reassessed,* Manchester and New York, Manchester
University Press, 1993, pp. 11–19.

24 'Vor diesem Werke empfindet man unwillkürlich Stimmungen, wie sie einem vor alten
Kaufmannshäusern der Renaissance oder Zopfzeit kommen, man denkt an den sozialen
Stilgedanken in alten Zunftwesen und alles Monumentale, das der Kaufmannsberuf in seinem
höchsten Aufschwung haben kann.' (Karl Scheffler, 'Wertheims Baumeister', *Kunst und
Künstler*, 3, no. 4, 1905, p. 163).

25 Anon., 'Die Neue Nationalbank', *Kunst und Künstler,* 6, 1908, p. 165.

26 Seidl's designs included the Bayerisches Nationalmuseum (1894–9), the Künstlerhaus
(1896–1900) and the neo-Romanesque church of St Anna (1887–92), all in Munich. The
buildings are notable for their integral sculptural works.

27 See, for instance, Scheffler, 'Die Bedeutung Messels', in Walter Curt Behrendt, *Alfred Messel,*
Berlin, Bruno Cassirer, 1911, p.16f.

28 Karl Scheffler, *Die Architektur der Großstadt,* Berlin, Bruno Cassirer, 1913.

29   Ibid., pp. 8–10. Here Scheffler develops ideas already intimated at in earlier articles on the Wertheim store.

30   Ibid., p. 10.

31   Theodor Fritsch, *Die Stadt der Zukunft*, Leipzig, 1896. The first translation into German of Howard's *Garden Cities of Tomorrow* was published as *Gartenstädte in Sicht*, Jena, Diederichs, 1907. I am grateful to Prof. Iain Boyd Whyte for this information.

32   Scheffler, *Die Architektur der Großstadt*, p. 14 and p. 44.

33   Even as late as 1905 Messel's early designs were still being acknowledged as seminal in planning circles. See Anon., 'Berliner Wohnbaublöcke', *Der Städtebau*, 11, 1905, p. 143. For more on Messel's housing designs, see Siegfried Jaik, 'Arbeiterwohnungen – ein beispielhaftes Projekt von Valentin Weisbach und Alfred Messel, Berlin 1893', in Karl Schwarz (ed.) *Die Zukunft der Metropolen: Paris. London. New York. Berlin. Ein Beitrag der Technischen Universität Berlin zur Internationalen Bauausstellung Berlin. Berichtsjahr 1984. Band I: Aufsätze*, Technische Universität Berlin, exhibition catalogue, 20 Oct.–16 Dec. 1984, pp. 295–302 and Jan Fenstel, *Wilhelminisches Lächeln: Bauten von Hoffmann und Messel im Bezirk Friedrichshain*, Berlin, Heimatmuseum Friedrichshain, 1994.

34   Georg Simmel, 'The Metropolis and Mental Life', reproduced in David Frisby and Mike Featherstone (eds) *Simmel on Culture: Selected Writings*, London, Sage Publications, 1997, pp. 174–85.

35   See Tim Coles, 'Department Stores as Retail Innovations in Germany: A Historical-Geographical Perspective on the Period 1870 to 1914', in Crossick and Jaumain, *Cathedrals of Consumption*, especially p. 78f.

36   See David Frisby, 'Social Theory, the Metropolis, and Expressionism', in Timothy O Benson, *Expressionist Utopias: Paradise, Metropolis, Architectural Fantasy*, exhibition catalogue, Los Angeles County Museum of Art, 1993, pp. 88–111, recently republished in David Frisby, *Cityscapes of Modernity*, Cambridge, Polity, 2001, pp. 236–63.

37   Brian Ladd, *The Ghosts of Berlin: Confronting German History in the Urban Landscape*, Chicago, University of Chicago Press, 1998.

38   Mosse, *Confronting the Nation*, pp. 121–30.

39   It was not until his marriage to a Christian woman in 1909 that Wertheim finally took this step. He did not see himself as bound by religion, although the nature of his family life was, nonetheless, distinctly orthodox, Jewish culture being valued highly. Ladwig-Winters, *Wertheim: Geschichte*, pp. 24–6.

40   Ladwig-Winters, *Wertheim – ein Warenhausunternehmen*, p. 341f.

41   Scheffler, 'Wertheims Baumeister', p. 156.

42   Thorstein Veblen, *The Theory of the Leisure Class*, New York, Dover, 1994 (1st publ. New York, Macmillan, 1899). Aimed at an American audience and as a commentary on American culture, Veblen's book was read widely and felt to be incisive in unveiling the forces behind capitalism.

43   See, for instance, Lisa Tiersten, 'Marianne in the Department Store: Gender and the Politics of Consumption in Turn-of-the-Century Paris', Crossick and Jaumain, *Cathedrals of Consumption*, pp. 117–18.

44   'Stumm in dem lauten Lärm, stolz und selbstbewußt wie die Riesenbäume vor ihm, hoheitsvoll, fast feierlich hebt sich sein Eckbau in die Höhe. . . . Aber kein Schild, keine Fahne, nichts Buntes kündet am Tage, keine Lichteffekte am Abend seinen Zweck.' Göhre, *Das Warenhaus*, p. 7f.

45   So winkt von ferner dieser Bau über den Platz herüber, wahrlich nicht wie ein Geschäftshaus, eher ein Stück eines alten, gotischen Doms, an dem man alles Spielzeug gespart, oder wie eine der edelsten, lieblich ernsten Kapellen eines Oxforder Kollegs. Wenn du des Abends so von weitem stehst, und die Fenstermassen von zerstreutem und zugleich verhaltenem Lichte blinken – du

glaubst warten zu müssen, bis der erste Orgelton aus diesen hohen Hallen dir
entgegensingt.

(Ibid., p. 8)

Emile Zola had equated the experience of visiting a department store with that of a site of
religious observance in his *Au Bonheur des Dames*: 'it was the cathedral of modern commerce,
solid and light, made for a people of customers.' As cited in Crossick and Jaumain, *Cathedrals
of Consumption*, p. 36f.

46 Göhre, *Das Warenhaus*, pp. 73–8. Parallels with the treatment of staff by larger industrial
firms, such as Krupp and Borsig, would be illuminating.

47 Ibid., p. 33. Such moves had long been associated with department store culture throughout
Europe. See, for instance, Michael B. Miller, *The Bon Marché: Bourgeois Culture and the
Department Store, 1869–1920*, London, Allen & Unwin, 1981.

48 For more on Wertheim's measures to avert criticism, see Ladwig-Winters, *Wertheim:
Geschichte*, p. 27.

49 For a contemporary assessment of Georg Wertheim's achievements, see Hans Schliepmann,
Geschäfts- und Warenhäuser, II, Die weitere Entwicklung der Kaufhäuser, Berlin/Leipzig,
G. J. Göschen'sche Verlagshandlung, 1913, p. 15f.

50 Göhre, *Das Warenhaus*, p. 136f.

51 'Das ganze Gebäude einschl. Lichthof und Schaufenster wird mittels Elektrizität und zwar
durch 486 Bogen- und etwa 4600 Glühlampen beleuchtet'. Albert Hoffmann, 'Das Warenhaus
A Wertheim in der Leipziger', *Deutsche Bauzeitung*, 32, no. 35 (30 April 1898), p. 230.

52 For detailed discussions of the growth in popularity of these cultural manifestations see
Annie E. Coombes, *Reinventing Africa: Museums, Material Culture and Popular Imagination*,
New Haven, CT, Yale University Press, 1997; and Martin Wörner, *Vergnügung und Belehrung:
Volkskultur auf den Weltausstellungen 1851–1900*, Münster, Waxmann, 1999.

53 Illustrated in Ladwig-Winters, *Wertheim: Geschichte*, p. 43.

54 Depictions of workers in realistic vein proliferated at this time in many European countries,
of course. Meanings depended greatly on context and commission. It cannot be clear without
supporting documentation what the purpose was behind such a key siting of this work.

55 While the Leipziger Straße store sought to appeal to a 'better class' of customer, it is claimed
that the working population also frequented this branch of the concern. See Göhre, *Das
Warenhaus*, p. 110. Other commentators countered this argument: see, for instance, Leo
Colze, *Berliner Warenhäuser*, Berliner Texte, vol. 4, ed. Detlef Bluhm, Berlin, Fannei & Walz,
1989 (1st publ. 1908), p. 12.

56 This sculpture quickly became known as *Frau Wertheim* amongst the staff. Ladwig-Winters,
Wertheim: Geschichte, p. 43.

57 Hoffmann, *Lebenserinnerungen*, p. 189. Employed on the Leipziger Platz façade were Josef
Rauch, Josef Floßmann, Ernst Westphal and August Vogel. Each sculptor was responsible for
one of the main arches and surrounds, although Rauch also produced work for the arcading
on the Leipziger Straße side of the entrance. The sculpture adorning the interior of the
entrance arcade was by August Gaul and Ignatius Taschner among others.

58 Messel must have considered Ernst Westphal (1851–1926) and August Vogel (1859–1932) to
be exceptions. Westphal was also employed by the architect on the Wertheim store on the
Rosenthaler Straße. He had made his name for work on the Theater am Schiffbauerdamm
and the Schloß, both in Berlin. Vogel was known for his sculpture for the Reichstag building
and the *Feuerwehrdenkmal*.

59 Hoffmann, *Lebenserinnerungen*, p. 164.

60 A. Heilmeyer, *Die moderne Plastik in Deutschland*, Bielefeld und Leipzig, Verlag von Velhagen
& Klasing, 1903, pp. 77–8 and 'Von Münchner Plastik', *Freie Kunst (Die Kunst)*, XXIX, 1914,
pp. 131–44.

61 Josef Rauch had come to Messel's attention through his work on the Künstlerhaus and on Seidl's Bayerisches Nationalmuseum. Deemed by Heilmeyer to be strongly influenced by Hildebrand, Floßmann had worked with Theodor Fischer on the Bismarck Tower on the Starnberger See. A. Heilmeyer, *Plastik des 19. Jahrhunderts in München*, Munich, Knorr & Hirth, 1931, p. 114.

62 On Taschner's career, see Norbert Götz and Ursel Berger (eds) *Ignatius Taschner: ein Künstlerleben zwischen Jugendstil und Neoklassizismus*, Munich, Klinkhardt & Biermann, 1992. On Georg Wrba, see G. Kloss, *Georg Wrba, 1872–1939: Ein Bildhauer zwischen Historismus und Moderne*, Petersburg, M. Imhof, 1998.

63 For more on the Munich art scene, see Peter-Klaus Schuster (ed) *'München leuchtete': Karl Caspar und die Erneuerung christlicher Kunst in München um 1900*, Haus der Kunst Munich, Prestel, 1984.

64 Fritz Stahl, 'Alfred Messel', p. XIII.

65 Scheffler, 'Die Bedeutung Messels', pp. 14–15.

66 'eine künstlich altertümliche Modernität'; Scheffler, 'Wertheims Baumeister', p. 166.

67 Fritz Stahl, 'Alfred Messel', p. XIII.

68 The nude as subject-matter is key to an understanding of reformist tendencies in sculptural circles at this time, following Hildebrand's repositioning of this genre as the most worthy for sculpture. Alexander Heilmeyer, *Adolf Hildebrand*, Bielefeld/Leipzig, Knackfuß, 1902, p. 39. On the *Neuer Mensch*, see Nicola Lepp, Martin Roth and Klaus Vogel (eds) *Der Neue Mensch: Obsessionen des 20. Jahrhunderts*, exhibition catalogue, Deutschen Hygiene-Museum Dresden, 22 April–8 August 1999. This overview of the subject does not, however, deal with artists' responses to the theme.

69 Mosse, *Confronting the Nation*, pp. 132–5.

70 See Walter Rathenau, 'Höre, Israel', *Die Zukunft*, vol. 5, no. 23, 1897, pp. 454–62, reproduced in Schütte and Sprengel, *Die Berliner Moderne*, pp. 172–7.

71 Nordau also wrote unfavourably about consumption, detecting degeneracy in purchasers of ephemeral, fashionable articles. Max Nordau, *Entartung,* vol. 1, Berlin, Carl Dunder, 2nd edn., 1893, pp. 50–1.

72 Some of the female figures depicted in the relief panels exhibit sinuous lines common to 'exotic' Eastern renderings of the dance. For a discussion of the signification of the nude figure in relation to reform ideals and the dance in Expressionist sculpture, see Helen Shiner, *Artistic Radicalism and Radical Conservatism: Moïssy Kogan and his German Patrons, 1903–1928*, MA diss., Birmingham Institute of Art and Design, University of Central England, 1997, pp. 89–101.

73 On Nordau's influence, see Mosse, *Confronting the Nation*, pp. 161–75.

74 Ibid., p. 166.

75 Posener, *Berlin auf dem Wege*, p. 47.

Chapter 5

The Hamburg Bismarck as city crown and national monument

Karen Lang

> What one wanted was a more simple art than the ever-growing complexity of life would naturally admit. One wanted something new. The fact that this something new was precisely the most primitive weighed heavily in its favour.
>
> (J. Meier-Graefe, 1905)[1]

Modern man, writes the historian Ernst Gellner, 'is not loyal to a monarch or a land or a faith, whatever he may say, but to a culture'.[2] Just as a sense of culture implies cultural unity, so the effectiveness of nationalism requires political unity. When definitions of culture and nationalism are sublated into national culture, then allegiance to a cultural ideal becomes congruent with membership in a political nation–state.[3] The effectiveness of national culture arises from a coherent image of 'nation' – a seamless intertwining of the national, the political, and the cultural into an ideology at once structural and invisible. The national monument might be considered an image of national culture *par excellence*. Karl Scheffler implied as much when, writing on modern architecture in 1907, he labelled the monuments of this period *Reichsplakate*, or advertisements in stone for the new German Reich.[4]

Like the advertisements or photographs in illustrated magazines, the monuments of this period were intended for a mass audience. By effectively targeting the populace of the newly formed state, both illustrated magazines and monuments helped foster an 'imagined community' of nation.[5]

For Richard Muther, 'the nineteenth century knew only the monument and the monument was everywhere' in Germany.[6] This was especially true at the end of the century, when the unification of the nation by Bismarck in 1871 and the death of the former Chancellor in 1898 stimulated an output of monument production in keeping with the pace of industrialisation itself. As the countryside became overrun with Bismarck Towers, monuments to local and national figures were erected in urban centres and city parks. The new genre of the German national monument was accorded special significance after 1871. Rising above the cacophony of local and individual histories, the national monument proved a useful focus and stimulus for feelings of patriotism and national identity. In order to achieve this emotional effect, political, regional, and religious differences had to be subsumed into a 'national' German style.

Thomas Nipperdey defines the national monument as 'an attempt to make manifest national identity in a visible, lasting and tangible symbol'.[7] The national monument is comprised of both manifest symbols of nation, and less well-defined notions of national identity (*Nationalbewußtsein*). In the national monument the constellation of abstract ideas comprising *Nationalbewußtsein* must be translated, first of all, into concrete symbols of nation. Second, and even more importantly if the monument is to fulfil its function, these ideas of nation must be grasped by the beholder. The aesthetic problem of the national monument is, then, how to channel an abstract notion of national identity so that it will be received in the intended fashion by every beholder.[8]

In order to evoke an emotional response from the viewer, the national monument sought access to 'irrational elements'. Eric Hobsbawm suggests that after the 1870s, 'and almost certainly in connection with the emergence of mass politics, rulers and middle-class observers rediscovered the importance of "irrational" elements in the maintenance of the social fabric and the social order'.[9] The 'irrational elements' of German myths, legends, and symbols were therefore deployed in this period as an appeal to the German citizen, who, it was hoped, would emotionally vacate the actual reality of *Gesellschaft*, the contemporary industrial society, and join the community or *Gemeinschaft* of common sentiment for a shared Teutonic past. A common past was further underscored at this time through the celebration both of previously established rituals and of 'invented traditions'.[10]

Not surprisingly, Bismarck, founder of the Reich, became the most popular subject for the German national monument.[11] Unlike monuments to the Kaisers Wilhelm, the Bismarck monument addressed the citizens of the newly unified German nation, the *Volksnation*; a uniquely German form was therefore sought for these monuments, one which would convey a new and particular sense of Germanness (*Deutschtum*) to the collectivity of the nation. As the strands of genealogy, national identity, and civic pride become interwoven in the Bismarck monument, the challenges of modernism and urbanism present themselves in several competitions. German myths and legends, which formed stylistic and narrative bridges between past and present, often collide with notions of modern style, subject-matter, and location.

This chapter will consider the Hamburg Bismarck monument as city crown and national monument.[12] The stakes were high for the Hamburg Bismarck monument, as were the efforts to transform this commemoration into a worthy image of national culture. The task of the Hamburg Bismarck was made all the more difficult by the tenor of the times. We know from history, of course, that the 1890s was a decade of cultural crises and social conflicts on the domestic front in Germany, and, on a larger scale, that the death of Bismarck coincided with the beginnings of competitive empire building among the major powers. At this moment in history, as conflict and dissatisfaction reached ever-higher levels in Germany, the idea of nation had to be shored up and intensified. In their capacity to make manifest and concrete a latent and still somewhat abstract idea of nation, monuments became even more crucial in this period.

An ostensible commemoration of the port city and the national unity achieved by Bismarck, the Hamburg monument nevertheless registers an unease in local and national culture. For Alfred Lichtwark, director of the Hamburg Kunsthalle and ardent supporter of modern art, turn-of-the-century Hamburg was not so much the 'free and Hansa city-state' as the 'freely demolished city of Hamburg'. In order to support the current economic boom, the mayor and senate were all too willing to raze buildings and intact city quarters, and to transfer unlucky tenants into new-style apartment blocks that hindered easy communication, thus effectively destroying the traditional relationships in which many Hamburgers took pride and comfort. At the same time, these developments did not facilitate social and intellectual integration for the many newcomers to the city.[13] These new social conditions, which were growing more precarious as the century unfolded, were certainly not commemorated in the Hamburg monument. Just as differences are papered over in a move to national culture, so they were negated in Hamburg's official commemoration to Bismarck.

Considering Bismarck monuments produced after 1898 as

5.1
Hugo Lederer and
Emil Schaudt,
Hamburg Bismarck
monument, 1906,
from *Deutsche
Bauzeitung*, 40, no.
47 (14 June 1906),
p. 329

markers of unease diverges sharply from those who view these works as
concrete manifestations of a new self-confidence brought about by the
expansion of Germany abroad and by the rapid industrialisation of the
nation at home.[14] While it is undoubtedly true that Germany sought a
reflection of the prominence it had obtained through successful battle,
colonisation, and industrialisation, a 'new self-confidence' was not the only
impetus behind the surge of Bismarck monument production.[15] Germany's
tortuous path to unification and the attendant, tenuous sense of national
identity for the recently unified country speak of a strong need for legitimi-
sation. The 'invention of tradition', or of what might be termed the national
self-fashioning witnessed in the creation and deployment of national monuments, served to engender and to cement emotion *pro patria*.

The figure of Bismarck was particularly useful in this process. As the man considered responsible for German unification, the appeal of Bismarck crossed regional, class, and – to a lesser degree – political lines, and was consequently more effective symbolically than the figure of the Kaiser, who, as a symbol, stood more for Prussia than for Germany *per se*. Whereas Bismarck had eased Germany's unification 'from above', the figure of Bismarck, when used symbolically, could finesse a unification of the country from below. As an image of national culture, Bismarck served a useful political and symbolic function as the object to which Germans could respond with thankfulness and longing.

The Hamburg Bismarck was the most expensive German monument to date. This, and the fact that the money for the commemoration was raised exclusively from public subscription, made the Hamburg monument competition noteworthy from the outset. If we consider the Hamburg Bismarck monument in the contemporary force field of debate over the monument itself, and the intended effects of the monument on the part of the viewer, then the monument operates as a hinge, or mediation, of national culture. In this sense disputes over location, design, and monumentality register an attempt to achieve political, cultural, and artistic consensus as well as the symbolic coherence necessary for the monument to become an image of national culture. Part of this attempt involved aligning the Hamburg particular and the German national, or, in short, to make of the commemoration both a city crown and a national monument. While artistic achievement might have qualified the monument as a jewel in the city crown, the strength of the Hamburg mercantile industry could be conveyed through a symbol of the powerful nation, or *Machtstaat*. As we shall see, mediated through a notion of 'monumental decorum', these seemingly competing interests could be coordinated into a coherent image of national culture.

> It will also be seen from the river, so that the gaze of the seafarers returning to their homeland will fall first on the man who created the empire, taking trade and shipping under his wing.
>
> (Executive Committee, Hamburg Bismarck Monument, January 1899)[16]

One of three port cities in the Hanseatic league, Hamburg was the home of the Hamburg–Amerika line, the largest steamship company in the world at the turn of the century. Not surprisingly, the wealthiest industrialists in the city were part of the merchant community, and it was they who set the tone in local politics through their membership on the Senate. Free trade, the foundation of merchantile prosperity, was thus 'something of a dogma

in Berlin and unveiled with much fanfare to a huge crowd on 22 March 1897. Begas created a colossal iron statue of Bismarck, which symbolically refers to his role as leader of the Reichstag, with various allegorical and mythological figures at the base. The Berlin monument, heralded as the 'first Bismarck national monument', was financed entirely by the Reich. Scheffler, for one, found fault with the work, stating that what Begas had captured of Bismarck was the exact opposite of a true conception of the Chancellor.[28] It was reported that the Hamburg Bismarck, on the other hand, 'would become an honorary monument [*Ehrenmal*] to the artistic understanding of the city of Hamburg, raised high above that of Begas in Berlin and similarly styled works', and as such 'the solution to the Bismarck monument nonsense [*Bismarck-Denkmalerei*]'.[29]

Despite the relatively low prize money offered, the Hamburg Bismarck competition drew an initial 219 entries. Of these, nineteen drawings were accepted into the final selection.[30] Since the guidelines for the competition allowed for either architectural or portrait designs, the drawings submitted offered a wide range of styles and subject-matter. According to several critics, the imaginative and forceful qualities of the final entries signalled a breach with 'the faded tradition' of monument design in Germany.[31] As a result, the Hamburg Bismarck competition was deemed by contemporary critics the most significant of the past twenty years.

The site selected for the monument was just west of the old city, directly in line with the 462-foot-high church of St Michael, which commanded the view to the east. Located on a rise near the harbour, the plan indicates that the site was encircled by two major traffic arteries and that an oak wood was planned, which would frame the monument to one side. Since the intended monument could be seen from the harbour, from traffic along the avenues, or encountered by a wanderer through the wood, the selected site had much to offer. Hofmann pointed out further how the oak wood, by serving as a standard of comparison, would 'bring the outlines of the entire monument to a ceremonious height', thereby providing a frame for its monumentality.[32]

The competition drawing 'An Offering of Gratitude' by the sculptor Hugo Lederer and the architect Emil Schaudt of Berlin received first prize.[33] The monument complex, comprised of a 49-foot statue of Bismarck resting on a 62-foot pedestal, rises to 111 feet in height. According to the jury, Lederer and Schaudt's design was appropriate for the setting, since the monument could be viewed from afar, but even more importantly, their conception captured the heroic 'apotheosis of the figure of Bismarck in the consciousness of the *Volk*'.[34] It is telling that the conception of Bismarck in the supposed 'consciousness' of the citizens of Hamburg was not as the

5.2

Georg Koppmann,
Western end of the
Sandthorquai with
the church of
St Michael,
photographed in
1877, from Hans
Meyer-Veden,
*Hamburg:
Historische
Photographien*,
Berlin, Ernst &
Sohn, 1995, p. 35

leader of the Reichstag, nor as the so-called old man in the forest of Saxony, in which Bismarck, owner of a country estate, is shown with his loyal dog. Rather, Bismarck is here metamorphosed into a latter-day version of the legendary Roland, a figure which – precisely in combining Roland and Bismarck – yields a symbolic-historic content referring to an immemorial German spirit predicated upon noble conduct and militant strength.[35] In addition to its noble associations, this design neatly obviates the problem of presenting a timeless image of the Chancellor in time-bound, contemporary dress.

Roland columns, such as the Brandenburg Roland of 1474, were placed on the marketplace – often in front of the town hall – in certain northern cities of the Reich. While the exact origins and meaning of the Roland columns are not entirely known, they were believed to symbolise either a district under royal jurisdiction (*Gerichtsbarkeit*) or the right of a particular city to hold markets (*Marktrecht*). For contemporary Germans, however, the colossal Roland functioned more simply as a popular symbol (*Volkssymbol*) of valiant protection.[36] As the architect Bruno Taut pointed out in a paean to the Roland of Brandenburg in 1916, the 'true monumentality' of the medieval Roland columns separated them favourably from the

127

5.3
Hugo Lederer and
Emil Schaudt, 'An
Offering of
Gratitude', from
*Deutsche
Bauzeitung*, 36,
no. 6 (18 January
1902), p. 38

'cliché monumentality' that had afflicted so many large and small contemporary German structures, including many of the country's colossal monuments.[37]

In the Hamburg monument Bismarck's genealogy is alluded to not only through association with Roland. The effect of the monument is further heightened by the placement on the colossal circular base of allegorical figures representing the eight Germanic tribes (*Volksstämme*) – Niedersachsen, Westfalen, Hessen, Thüringen, Sachsen, Franken, Schwaben, Bayern – which are united symbolically in the figure of Bismarck as Roland.[38] The circular base itself, moreover, appears reminiscent of the mausoleum of Theodoric at Ravenna. In the following years the tomb of Theodoric was to become highly prized as an example of a truly Germanic form.[39]

While the association of the base of the Hamburg monument with the tomb of Theodoric has not been made in the scholarly literature, a case can be made for this historic association if we consider the symbolic relation of Bismarck not only with Roland, but also with Charlemagne. As Charlemagne had brought the statue of Theodoric to Aachen on horseback, so the mausoleum of Theodoric is invoked in the Hamburg monument to establish a genealogical link between the new nation founded by Bismarck and the long, beneficent rule of both Theodoric and Charlemagne. An

5.4
Roland Column,
Brandenberg, 1474,
from *Die
Kunstgewerbeblatt*,
27, no. 6 (March
1916), p. 113

allusion to Charlemagne also connects the monument to the medieval history of Hamburg, since Charlemagne founded a castle there in the ninth century, 'to which was soon added a church, and then a bishop', thus constituting the beginnings of the city.[40] Standing erect atop Theodoric's tomb, Bismarck is poised conceptually between death and immortality through the act of memorialisation. Here the 'national imaging' begins with the death of an old order and transforms this death into a destiny.

In the age of Charlemagne, the figure of Roland served a dual purpose: he underscored the ties between the Christian religion and the Empire. The metamorphosis of Bismarck in the Hamburg monument alludes to both Roland the Christian knight and to Roland the paladin of Charlemagne, to Roland, that is, the valiant knight who sacrificed his life for the cause of the Empire. The shady origins and multiple meanings of the Roland, as well as the contemporary popularity of the figure, made it a malleable *Volkssymbol*. Given the rise of what George Mosse has termed a 'national liturgy', it is not surprising to find a religious knight pressed into the service of a 'religion' of nationalism.[41] For all these reasons the equation of Bismarck and Roland could make symbolic sense despite Bismarck's vigorous endorsement of the *Kulturkampf* against the Catholic Church.

Unlike the majority of the medieval Roland columns, which present Roland with a raised sword and shield, in the Hamburg monument Bismarck rests his hands on a long sword. To this end, the Hamburg Bismarck most closely resembles the purportedly first statue of Roland, the Roland of Obermarsberg. Erected after the conquest of the Saxons, the Roland of Obermarsberg is not shown as a warrior ready for battle but as a Christian knight, a Saint Rolandi, as the inscription on the pedestal suggests. The Roland of Obermarsberg offers a model of a church, a political gesture that underscored the ties of the realm to Christianity, and thus demonstrated to the heathen Saxons how they could integrate themselves into the Empire through the acceptance of the Christian faith.

In the Hamburg monument Bismarck is flanked by the symbols of his realm, the German eagles. With the historical mission of unification achieved, the Hamburg monument of Bismarck as Roland demonstrates the concentrated power of the nation, a power symbolised through the German eagles, the symbolic and syncretic associations of Bismarck with Roland, the reign of Charlemagne, and finally, with the historical figure of Bismarck himself. The power of the German nation arises from the death of an old order, becomes embodied in the Bismarck–Roland, and, like Bismarck's gaze over the harbour of Hamburg, extends beyond the borders of the Reich geographically and temporally.

While it was generally remarked that the Hamburg Bismarck

competition signalled 'a turning point in the history of monumental art',[42] the winning design by Lederer and Schaudt was not unanimously celebrated. Many Hamburg academics, in particular, were opposed to the prize-winning design, arguing from a historical standpoint that the monument required a 'true image of Bismarck's personality for the coming generations'.[43] For these academics the concept of Bismarck as Roland was not only decidedly and detractively modern in style, it was also unfitting, since it did not provide a traditional depiction of the Iron Chancellor. Arguing from an artistic standpoint, those in favour praised 'the great beauty of the form' of the design and lauded it for containing 'nothing of tradition', by which was meant a break with the Wilhelmine tradition of portrait statuary.[44] One important voice in favour came from the Hamburg academic and founder of the Warburg Institute, Aby Warburg, who, unlike his fellow scholars, did not oppose the monument for lacking a more customary realism.

Writing against the grain, Warburg made clear his distaste for the traditional realism of German monuments:

> It marks the lowest stage of aesthetic culture when a work of art is used merely to gain possession of a lost object in effigy. The higher development of taste consists in keeping one's distance and trying to understand the object by means of comparisons within the field of vision. The commercial philistine does not like to be thwarted in his desire to gain possession by a closer approach (my Bismarck, our Bismarck) and if he is disturbed during his artistic feeding time he is irritated and becomes nasty.[45]

Instead of falling prey to an irrelevant realism, the design by Lederer and Schaudt was praised by Warburg as 'simply sublime, sculptural and yet of a transcending visionary quality'.[46] For Warburg the sublimity of the monument rested on its use of a new and modern form of idealism, one that blended old and new, past and present, into a work that necessitated a distance Warburg would define elsewhere as the *Denkraum,* the distance required for reflection and reason.[47]

Along with Behrens and Scheffler, among others, Warburg declared the monument to be modern because of its capacity to arouse strong emotions in the common viewer. For these critics the Hamburg Bismarck achieved what was considered the task of the modern monument: it successfully translated the monumental attitude of modern architecture into an isolated structure.[48] In order to understand better what was meant by this concept of monumentality we might turn to the architect Peter Behrens.

In his 1909 essay, 'What Is Monumental Art?', Behrens writes that monumentality is not determined by size but especially by the ability of the object
to 'stir the masses'.[49] Certain contemporary critics did indeed deem the
Hamburg Bismarck monumental, not because of its colossal size, but
because it contained the crucial element of pathos. As Scheffler explained,
pathos invoked the so-called undisciplined instincts, the 'primitive' emotions
that were thought to have special appeal for the masses.[50] According to this
point of view, the Hamburg Bismarck was a successful modern monument
precisely because of the pathos embodied within it, because of its powerful
emotional effect on those who came to commune with this monumental
shrine to German nationalism.

The stylistic debates over the Hamburg Bismarck hinge on
explicit or implicit notions of 'monumental decorum'.[51] In contrast to what
Warburg termed the 'superficial nature' of the unnecessarily colossal, the
truly monumental is marked by a 'due inner grandeur'.[52] In this sense, to
follow Hofmann, the Hamburg Bismarck is a work in which 'monumentality
of form' coincides with 'monumentality of content'.[53] It was not simply
scale, then, which conferred monumentality, something clearly pointed out
in the case of Begas's Bismarck monument in Berlin. Writing in 1902 for *Der
Lotse*, Hamburg's weekly for German culture, Cornelius Gurlitt makes this
point clear:

> In both monuments the Chancellor is presented as a colossal
> figure. Begas captures him realistically, the young winner of the
> Hamburg competition monumentally. Begas gives him a 'natural'
> pose, Lederer presents him as a cliff-like monument in stone. One
> can learn from Begas the extent to which realism is able to give
> the impression of scale. Indeed, one does not sense the colossal
> dimensions of his Bismarck since every sense of scale is absent.
> He does not appear large – and the Reichstag building behind
> him looks small.[54]

Unlike Begas's gigantic, realistic rendering of Bismarck as leader of the
Reichstag, the characterisation of Bismarck as Roland in the Hamburg
monument brought past and present history together, achieving a monumentality of form and content. The special significance of the Roland for
northern Germany and of Charlemagne for Hamburg, moreover, suffused
the monument with both national and civic associations, with, one could
say, a monumental decorum at perfect pitch.[55]

Monumental decorum, in contrast to sheer size, can thus be
understood in the contemporary German context by successful monumental
effect. This includes not only the coordination of scale, style, subject matter

and location, but also the intended effect of the monument on the beholder. Monumental jewel in the city crown, commemoration of the nation, the design by Lederer and Schaudt offered both monumental decorum and artistic style. As the monument conjoined past and present in the figure of Bismarck as Roland, so it reminded the German citizen of the strong national state of which he or she was a part. 'From Stimulus to Impetus': Warburg's 'title of that chapter of the yet unwritten history of psychological fashions of the twentieth century',[56] could enlist the Hamburg Bismarck as a successful example. Here social memory and monumentality operate both as a 'stimulus' for perception and as an 'impetus' towards 'the very highest' national culture has to offer.

Standing guard at Germany's 'gateway to the world', the Hamburg Bismarck served as an effective and awesome symbol of nation. In this sense German critics often compared their colossal monument with the recently erected Statue of Liberty in America.[57] Like the Lady Liberty, the Hamburg Bismarck was intended as a national landmark. Yet whereas America chose to personify itself with an allegorical figure of freedom, Germany, in opting for 'the doughty Roland giant',[58] presented itself instead in terms of a militaristic omnipotence. For conservative and vehemently nationalist critics such as Georg Fuchs, the Hamburg monument was modern precisely because it embodied the country's new imperialistic spirit. The citizens of Hamburg, he writes, had 'placed on their harbour a monumental symbol of the new German spirit, who extends his powerful wings over the water and calls on one to believe in the world-power and the world-culture'.[59] Or to use the words of the more liberal Scheffler, who stated the obvious rather pointedly in 1907, Lederer and Schaudt's monument was 'not a Bismarck monument, but a lighthouse of national thought'.[60]

Such rhetoric reveals a shift of focus in national identification and representation. Whereas earlier identification had rested on the unification of the nation, and on Bismarck as the architect of that epochal event, national identity is here conceived in terms of the *Machtstaat,* or powerful national state, and its imperialistic claims. In this move Bismarck is no longer merely the mythic founder of the German nation. He is also the hero of a particular brand of national identity that stressed the militarism and imperialism of blood and iron. While the Bismarck–Roland alludes to the history of Hamburg, and to its beginnings in the Middle Ages, a definition of national identity which underscored the concentrated power of the *Machtstaat* was well in keeping with Hamburg's mercantile interests and its position as Germany's most important port city.

Discourses of nationalism are perhaps best illustrated in the statements made on the occasion of the monument's unveiling on Pentecost, 2 June 1906, a date that binds the cultural and the religious with the national. Though the monument was not finished, a fragment of it was nevertheless unveiled to a crowd of 1,600 onlookers, including Princess Marguerite von Bismarck and other members of the former Chancellor's family. To provide the general public with a souvenir of the event, a medallion designed by Ernst Barlach was advertised in the Hamburg newspapers for sale at three marks apiece.[61] The highly choreographed celebration included the singing of the anthem 'Deutschland, Deutschland über alles' accompanied by a male chorus, as well as speeches by mayor Dr Johann Georg Mönckeberg, the president of the monument committee, and Johann Heinrich Burchard, president of the Senate, who presented the city with its monument.

A journalist, commenting on the mood immediately before the ceremonies began, had the following to report. It is worth quoting at length:

> The curtain [veiling the monument] swelled quietly in the gentle breeze. It is as if a form had descended from the world of myth. The swarming humanity stands on their feet ... stands in quivering reverence ... How tiny appear the festive decorations, how dwarf-like, an assembly of pygmies ... But then, like a warm wave ... arose in us an overpowering feeling of release. It came over us like an inspired revelation: indeed, our *Volk* is not as congealed in materialism and empty superficiality [*Äusserlichkeit*] as the hurried daily bustle of the new age often leads the reflective observer to conclude: we are still capable of hero worship ... we are still aglow with the old Germanic enthusiasm for the great and the heroic, a burning love of the fatherland, an intensive pride for the fatherland, still fills our heart ... With God for Kaiser and fatherland ... dominates this extraordinary hour of remembrance![62]

Such writing is redolent of mythomorphosis. This 'report' takes on, in rhetoric and in cadence, the imaged character of that which it speaks. Here the cult of the hero is celebrated as particularly Germanic and set up in opposition to the 'empty superficiality' which had come to shroud the Germanic essence just as the veil had covered the monument to Bismarck.[63]

If the journalist writes to the strains of the nation–state (*Staatsnation*), with its emphasis on unity (felt here as a wave of shared emotion, a rising to a common occasion) and a Germanic essence, the official speeches stress the rhetoric of the *Machtstaat*. According to Illonka Jochum-Bohrmann, these speeches turn on the values of pride, loyalty and constancy, the politics of nationalism, militarism and imperialism, and the artistic tropes of genius, monumentality and authority.[64] The effectiveness of the Hamburg Bismarck is alluded to in the official and unofficial statements made about it on the occasion of its unveiling: the monument, it seems, not only 'stirred the masses', it also symbolised a particular national profile. In so doing it remained within the grip of a newly emerging national identity while not being beyond the grasp of the common viewer. The conclusion of these speeches was followed by the rush of the crowd onto the plaza to admire the enormous laurel wreaths donated by the Senate, which were festooned around the base of the monument – an event which led the same journalist to conclude: 'the pride of Hamburg ... in this monument, which will outlast centuries and millennia, must not be extinguished'.[65]

> For it would be, as Bismarck once noted, 'a most grievous political loss for the nation if its living consciousness of the link to its origins and history were to be extinguished'.
>
> (A. Hofmann, 1894)[66]

A month after the unveiling of the Hamburg Bismarck monument a fire destroyed the church of St Michael, an unchoreographed natural act which effectively removed a competing jewel in the city crown. In *Bismarck-denkmal*, a polemical pamphlet of 1906, Martin Witt remarks: 'The church no longer represents an irritation to the monument now that the Roland towers over everything nearby, and its worshippers can feast their eyes and hearts on an uninterrupted view of him.'[67] At the opening ceremonies for the Hamburg Bismarck not a word was uttered about the church, perhaps in part because it was known that Hamburg's labourers preferred St Michael to his 'mythical opponent', Bismarck, whom they associated with the 'paternalistic turn' taken in the 'suffrage robbery' earlier that year.[68]

With disputes over traditional versus modern style and Warburg-like encomiums on aesthetic distance now a thing of the past, the Hamburg Bismarck could emerge as 'my Bismarck, our Bismarck', as city crown and national monument, as a consolidated image of national culture. Gazing out over the water, the monument associates Hamburg and the nation with travel through the port – whether a pleasure cruise on the Hamburg–Amerika line, a seaward journey towards the colonies, or the launching of the *Imperator* on 22 April 1913. The 'literary' bureau of the Hamburg–Amerika line spoke only in superlatives of the *Imperator*, a fast, four-propeller turbine steamer which was the biggest ship in the world at the time (280 m. long; 52117 G.R.T.): 'a gigantic structure, a gigantic reality, and an even more gigantic presentiment'.[69] Not incidentally the last of three ships of the *Imperator* class was named the *Bismarck*. As in the Hamburg

5.5
Hans Bohrdt,
'Hamburg Verein
zur Förderung des
Fremdenverkehrs.
Auskunftstelle:
Alsterdamm 39',
from L. L. Möller,
*Das frühe Plakat in
Europa und den
USA. Ein
Bestandkatalog*, vol.
3, part 2, Berlin,
Gebr. Mann, 1973,
plate 28, fig. 371

Bismarck monument, so here the port city and the *Machtstaat* are conjoined through reference to Germany's first Chancellor.[70]

By the end of the twentieth century the Hamburg monument had been effectively transformed into an image, an easy landmark of Germany's premier port city: 'Prost auf alles, was im Hamburg Spitze ist!' (Cheers, to everything tops in Hamburg!). In this recent advertisement, monuments – drained and flattened into a surface effect – enter Roland Barthes' world of

5.6
'Prost auf alles, was in Hamburg Spitze ist!', advertisement by Gitschel-Werbung, Hamburg, from *Hamburger Stadtvisionen*, Hamburg, Ellert & Richter, 1993, unpaginated

myth – an economy of unabashed exchange value where the architectural jewels in the city crown are strung alongside brands of beer in an image devoid of all contradiction.[71] Effacing the historical particularity and actual placement of the Hamburg Bismarck, the church of St Michael and the city hall, for instance, the advertisement aligns the jewels in the city crown for the glance of consumer distraction. Now a successful landmark – which is to say a monument become image – the Hamburg Bismarck is at once geographically fixed and semiologically capacious.[72]

'Prost auf alles, was im Hamburg Spitze ist!' underscores the power of contemporary capital to transform monuments into images. Yet it also demonstrates Scheffler's understanding of the successful national monument as both an advertisement for the present and a useful representation in future. Perhaps Emil Schaudt captured this best when he defined what his partner had achieved in the Hamburg monument:

> It is to Lederer's great credit that he found a means of creating a spiritual [geistiges] portrait of Bismarck; not the man but the image of him striding across the stage of his era. Future generations will hear the language of its forms.[73]

While the texture of history might be effaced in the move from monument to image, as an image the Hamburg Bismarck continues to serve national culture and the culture of capital.[74]

Acknowledgements

I would like to thank Stacey Loughrey for research assistance and Iain Boyd Whyte for editorial suggestions. Unless otherwise noted, translations are mine.

Notes

1 J. Meier-Graefe, 'Peter Behrens–Düsseldorf', Dekorative Kunst, July 1905, vol. 13, p. 382.
2 E. Gellner, Nations and Nationalism, Oxford, Blackwell, 1983, p. 36.
3 On this point in relation to Gellner's argument see J. Evans, 'Introduction: Nation and Representation', in D. Boswell and J. Evans (eds) Representing the Nation: A Reader – Histories, Heritage and Museums, London and New York, Routledge, 1999, p. 1.
4 K. Scheffler, Moderne Baukunst, Berlin, Julius Bard, 1907, p. 136.
5 The term 'imagined community' comes from B. Anderson, Imagined Communities: Reflections on the Origin and Spread of Nationalism, London and New York, 1991; originally published in

1983. Although Anderson discusses how the novel and the newspaper 'provided the technical means for "re-presenting" the kind of imagined community that is the nation' (p. 25), he does not specifically examine the role of monuments in national identity formation. On this see K. Lang, 'Monumental Unease: Monuments and the Making of National Identity in Germany', in F. Forster-Hahn (ed.) *Imagining Modern German Culture: 1889–1910* (Studies in the History of Art, 53), Washington, DC, National Gallery of Art, 1996, pp. 274–98.

6   R. Muther, 'Ästhetische Kultur', *Aufsätze über bildende Kunst*, Berlin, Ladyschinkow, 1914, vol. 2, p. 154.

7   T. Nipperdey, 'Nationalidee und Nationaldenkmal in Deutschland im 19. Jahrhundert', *Historische Zeitschrift*, June 1968, vol. 206, p. 533. Nipperdey's essay remains the foundational text on the German national monument.

8   Ibid., pp. 538–9. See also W. Hartwig, 'Bürgertum, Staatssymbolik und Staatsbewußtsein im Kaiserreich 1871–1914', *Zeitschrift für Historische Sozialwissenschaft*, 1990, vol. 16, pp. 269–95.

9   E. Hobsbawm, 'Mass-Producing Traditions: Europe, 1870–1914', in E. Hobsbawm and T. Ranger (eds) *The Invention of Tradition*, Cambridge, Cambridge University Press, 1983, p. 268. See also R. Handler and J. Linnekin, 'Tradition, Genuine or Spurious', *The Journal of American Folklore*, 1984, vol. 97, no. 385, pp. 273–90; and M. Steinberg, *The Meaning of the Salzburg Festival: Austria as Theater and Ideology, 1890–1938*, Ithaca, NY, and London, Cornell University Press, 1990, where representation is considered 'constitutive rather than reflective of cultural and political identity and power' (ibid., p. 9).

10 Hobsbawm and Ranger, *The Invention of Tradition*. As Hobsbawm points out, the invention of traditions occurs more frequently under conditions of rapid social change. Therefore, the years 1870–1914 'saw them spring up with particular assiduity', since 'new or old but dramatically transformed, social groups, environments and social contexts called for new devices to ensure or express social cohesion and identity and to structure social relations' (ibid., p. 263).

11 Like Kaiser Wilhelm I, Bismarck did not want monuments erected to him during his lifetime. Before his death in 1898, a mere forty monuments to Bismarck stood on German soil. Within one year of his death, however, 470 municipalities had elected to erect Bismarck towers. Unlike the monuments commemorating the Kaisers Wilhelm, monuments to Bismarck enjoyed support among large segments of the population. See in particular V. Plagemann, 'Bismarck-Denkmäler', in *Vaterstadt, Vaterland, schütz Dich Gott mit starker Hand: Denkmäler in Hamburg*, Hamburg, Hans Christians Verlag, 1986, pp. 102–6; H.-W. Hedinger, 'Bismarck-Denkmäler und Bismarck-Verehrung', in E. Mai and S. Waetzoldt, *Kunstverwaltung, Bau- und Denkmal Politik im Kaiserreich*, Berlin, Gebr. Mann, 1981, pp. 277–314.

12 On the contemporary notion of 'city crown', see B. Taut, *Die Stadtkrone*, Jena, E. Diedrichs, 1919; R. Haag Bletter, 'The Interpretation of the Glass Dream – Expressionist Architecture and the History of the Crystal Metaphor', *Journal of the Society of Architectural Historians*, March 1981, vol. 40, pp. 20–43; and R. Haag Bletter, 'Expressionism and the New Objectivity', *Art Journal*, Summer 1983, vol. 43, no. 2, pp. 108–20.

13 W. Jochmann, 'Handelsmetropole des Deutschen Reiches', in W. Jochmann and H.-D. Loose (eds) *Hamburg: Geschichte der Stadt und ihrer Bewohner*, Hamburg, Hoffmann und Campe, 1986, p. 29. See also p. 35.

14 See for instance I. Jochum-Bohrmann, *Hugo Lederer: Ein deutschnationaler Bildhauer des 20. Jahrhunderts*, Frankfurt am Main, Peter Lang, 1990, p. 171. I should add that T. Nipperdey, 'Nationalidee' and L. Titel, 'Monumentaldenkmäler von 1871 bis 1918 in Deutschland: Ein Beitrag zum Thema Denkmal und Landschaft', in E. Mai and S. Waetzoldt (eds) *Kunstverwaltung*, pp. 215–75, do not view these national monuments as merely celebratory, but instead allude to the fraught political and social contexts under which they were

produced. On the relation between unease in national culture and monument production see K. Lang, 'Monumental Unease'; and K. Lang, 'The Hamburg Bismarck monument as "Lighthouse of National Thought"', in W. Reinink and J. Stempel (eds) *Memory and Oblivion: Acts of the XXIXth International Congress of the History of Art*, Amsterdam, Kluwer, 1999, pp. 567–79. M. Russell takes up this relation in his recent essay, 'The Building of Hamburg's Bismarck Memorial, 1898–1906', *The Historical Journal*, 2000, vol. 43, no. 1, pp. 133–56.

15 While I would agree with K. Belgum, 'Displaying the Nation: A View of Nineteenth-Century Monuments through a Popular Magazine', *Central European History*, 1993, vol. 26, no. 4, p. 468, that the 'insistence on the immensity of such monuments and the difficulties associated with their construction glorified the potential of industrial technology as well as commercial cooperation', this formulation considers neither other motives for the production of these monuments nor contemporary disputes over an appropriate monumentality. See also K. Belgum, *Popularizing the Nation: Audience, Representation, and the Production of Identity in Die Gartenlaube, 1853–1900*, Lincoln, NE, University of Nebraska Press, 1998.

16 Cited in J. Bracker, 'Michel kontra Bismarck', in Freie Akademie der Künste in Hamburg (ed.) *Zurück in die Zukunft: Kunst und Gesellschaft von 1900 bis 1914*, Hamburg, Frölich & Kaufmann, 1981, p. 14.

17 R. J. Evans, *Death in Hamburg: Society and Politics in the Cholera Years 1830–1910*, Oxford, Clarendon Press, 1987, p. 10.

18 Ibid., p. 11. Evans continues:

> Just as historians have persistently underestimated the strength and vehemence of particularist sentiment in Germany in the second and third quarters of the nineteenth century, so too they have commonly overestimated the degree and extent of centralization and uniformity in the German Empire in the last quarter. Whatever they thought were the needs of the German Empire as a great power, the rulers of Hamburg remained firmly wedded to the principle that they, rather than the Prussians, were the best judges of what was good for Hamburg.
>
> (Ibid., p. 11)

See also J. Grolle, 'Das Hamburgbild in der Geschichtsschreibung des 19. Jahrhundert', in I. Stephan and H.-G. Winter (eds) *'Heil über dir, Hammonia'. Hamburg im 19. Jahrhundert: Kultur, Geschichte, Politik*, Hamburg, Dölling und Galitz, 1992, pp. 17–46; E. Klessmann, *Geschichte der Stadt Hamburg*, Hamburg, Hoffmann und Campe, 1981, esp. pp. 469–559; Jochmann, 'Handelsmetropole', pp. 15–107; and H. Hipp, *Freie und Hansestadt Hamburg: Geschichte, Kultur und Stadtbaukunst an Elbe und Alster*, Cologne, DuMont, 1990.

19 A. Hofmann, 'Der Wettbewerb zur Erlangung von Entwürfen für ein Bismarck-Denkmal', *Deutsche Bauzeitung*, 18 January 1902, vol. 36, no. 6, p. 34.

20 *Hamburger Korrespondent*, 2 June 1906. Cited in Jochum-Bohrmann, *Hugo Lederer*, p. 63.

21 Cited in R. Muther, 'Das Hamburger Bismarck-Denkmal' in *Aufsätze über bildende Kunst*, Berlin, Ladyschinkow, 1914, vol. 2, p. 11. The appeal was signed by over 1,000 of the Hamburg 'Honoratiorenschaft aus Politik, Wirtschaft und Kultur'. R. Alings, *Monument und Nation: Das Bild vom Nationalstaat im Medium Denkmal – zur Verhältnis von Nation und Staat im deutschen Kaiserreich 1871–1918*, Berlin, Walter de Gruyter, 1996, p. 250.

22 The donations from the citizens are reported to have very soon reached the incredible sum of 453,063 Marks per month. 'Der Aufbau des Bismarckdenkmals in Hamburg', *Deutsche Bauzeitung*, 11 April 1906, vol. 40, no. 29, p. 199.

23 A. Lichtwark and W. Rathenau, *Der Rheinische Bismarck*, Berlin, S. Fischer, 1912, pp. 10–11. See also A. Lichtwark, 'Denkmäler', 1897, p. 105 and *passim*.

24 M. Hurd, *Public Spheres, Public Mores, and Democracy: Hamburg and Stockholm, 1870–1914*, Ann Arbor, MI, University of Michigan Press, 2000, p. 89.

25 Hurd, *Public Spheres*, p. 89. See also H. W. Eckardt, *Privilegien und Parlament: Die Auseinandersetzungen um das allgemeine und gleiche Wahlrecht*, Hamburg, Hamburg Veröffentlichung der Landeszentrale für politische Bildung, 1980.

26 On the socialist demonstrations see R. J. Evans, ' "Red Wednesday" in Hamburg: Social Democrats, Police and *Lumpenproletariat* in the Suffrage Disturbances of 17 January 1906', in *Rethinking German History: Nineteenth-Century Germany and the Origins of the Third Reich*, London, Allen & Unwin, 1987, pp. 248–90.

27 Russell, 'The Building of Hamburg's Bismarck Memorial,' pp. 135–9.

28 K. Scheffler, 'Begas and Bismarck', *Der Lotse*, 29 July 1901, vol. 1, no. 39, pp. 411–15. In 'Denkmäler' (*Pan*, 1897, vol. 2, no. 2, pp. 105–7), A. Lichtwark likewise complained bitterly about the Berlin Bismarck, noting how the size of the monument was out of proportion to the setting.

29 *Hamburger Correspondent*, January 1902. Extended passage cited in Jochum-Bohrmann, *Hugo Lederer*, p. 55.

30 The jury members included Bürgermeister Dr Mönckeberg, Bürgermeister Dr Burchard, President Hinrichsen, the architects Martin Haller, Camillo Sitte, and Paul Wallot, and the sculptors Robert Diez and Rudolf Maison, as well as Georg Treu, director of the Dresden sculpture gallery. Treu was selected because of his prominent position in the art world, but more importantly because it was thought that he would be open to an unconventional design. Hofmann, 'Der Wettbewerb', p. 34. The interest in the competition was so keen that, in the interest of space, the viewing of the entries had to take place in the Velodrom Rotherbaum rather than in the Kunsthalle, as originally planned. Hofmann, 'Der Wettbewerb', p. 36.

31 Ibid., p. 34. For illustrations of the drawings accepted into the final selection, see A. Hofmann, 'Der Wettbewerb zur Erlangen von Entwürfen für ein Bismarck-Denkmal in Hamburg (Fortsetzung)', *Deutsche Bauzeitung*, 22 January 1902, vol. 36, no. 7, pp. 45–50, 53, 55; and G. Fuchs, 'Zeitgemässe Betrachtungen zum Wettbewerb', *Deutsche Kunst und Dekoration*, April 1902, vol. 5, no. 7, pp. 347–62.

32 Hofmann, 'Der Wettbewerb (Fortsetzung)', p. 42.

33 For their first prize entry, Lederer and Schaudt received 10,000 Marks. As reported in *Deutsche Bauzeitung*, 29 January 1902, vol. 36, no. 9, p. 56, this design won by a jury vote of 28 to 2. Not all citizens were in accord with the first prize-winning design, although more were for it than against it, as demonstrated by the spate of daily letters published in the Hamburg newspapers.

34 Hofmann, 'Der Wettbewerb (Fortsetzung)', p. 41. In the conclusion to this article, Hofmann even went so far as to compare the design to Schopenhauer's *Die Welt als Wille und Vorstellung*: 'World and will, will and idea, that is the Hamburg Bismarck monument.' H. [A. Hofmann], 'Der Wettbewerb zur Erlangung von Entwürfen für ein Bismarck-Denkmal in Hamburg (Schluss)', *Deutsche Bauzeitung*, 1 February 1902, vol. 36, no. 10, p. 57.

35 Jochum-Bohrmann, *Hugo Lederer*, also points out that (p. 55 and fn. 104, p. 206):

> Parallel to the public debate over the Roland-Bismarck there arose a dispute among the 'experts', seeking to establish the true meaning of the 'Roland'. This argument, which was also reported in the press, asked whether it was of French or Breton origins, and whether it should be rejected on these grounds alone.

36 On this point see, for instance, 'Das Bismarck Denkmal in Hamburg', *Deutsche Bauzeitung*, 13 June 1906, vol. 40, no. 47, p. 327. A useful text on the history of the Roland columns in

Germany is T. Goerlitz, *Der Ursprung und die Bedeutung der Rolandsbilder*, Weimar, H. Böhlans Nachf., 1934. Recent literature includes W. Grape, *Roland: Die Ältesten Standbilder als Wegbereiter der Neuzeit*, Hürtgenwald, Guido Pressler, 1990; N. Popov, *Das magische Dreieck. Bremen – Riga – Dubrovnik: Rolandfiguren im europäischen Raum*, Oschersleben, Dr. Zeithen, 1993; and H. Rempel, *Die Rolandstatuen: Herkunft und geschichtliche Wandlung*, Darmstadt, Wissenschaftliche Buchgesellschaft, 1989.

37   Bruno Taut, 'Der Roland von Brandenburg', *Das Kunstgewerbeblatt*, March 1916, vol. 27, no. 6, p. 112.

38   The eight pilasters around the base of the monument were originally intended to bear heraldic shields of the German states. For reasons of cost this plan was jettisoned and the Germanic tribes were designated instead. These were not completed until the summer of 1908. Alings, *Monument und Nation*, pp. 247–8. For the alterations between the original and final conceptions of the monument, and a chronology of its construction, see I. Jochum-Bohrmann, *Hugo Lederer*, pp. 59–61.

39   In the early years of the century the mausoleum of Theodoric was reverently discussed and illustrated in *Deutsche Bauzeitung*. See, for instance, *Deutsche Bauzeitung*, 23 June 1906, vol. 40, p. 50. In support of his own design for the 1907 Bismarck national monument competition at Bingerbrück on the Rhine, Wilhelm Kreis joined the present with the past with a deft sleight of hand: Theodoric, he writes,

> was a hero somewhat in the manner of Bismarck, and . . . this, his building, arising in the culture of the antique and produced from the nature of the strong *Germanen*, can serve us as a model for the expression of every art with which we honor Bismarck.
>
> (Kreis in A. Hofmann, 'Der zur Ausführung gewälte Entwurf für ein Bismarck-National-Denkmal auf der Elisenhöhe bei Bingerbrück', in *Deutsche Bauzeitung*, 2 November 1912, vol. 46, no. 88, pp. 772–4)

40   K. Baedecker, *Northern Germany as Far as the Bavarian and Austrian Frontiers*, Leipzig, K. Baedeker, 1910, p. 119.

41   G. Mosse, *The Nationalization of the Masses: Political Symbolism and Mass Movements in Germany from the Napoleonic Wars through the Third Reich*, New York, Howard Fertig, 1975.

42   A. Warburg, 'Contemporary Art: Lederer', unpublished notes by Warburg from 1901, trans. in E. H. Gombrich, *Aby Warburg: An Intellectual Biography*, Chicago, University of Chicago, 1986, p. 153. See also K. Scheffler, *Moderne Baukunst*, pp. 134–5.

43   Körber, *Deutsche Bauzeitung*, 25 January 1902, vol. 36, no. 8, p. 51.

44   Ibid., pp. 51–2. Debates over traditional versus modern style are typical in the first decade of the twentieth century in Germany, as the country grappled to define suitable modes of representation for the new nation. While art and architectural historians might be keen to place German culture of this period into the neat categories of the historical and the avant-garde, in fact many contemporary artists and architects drew on the past and present simultaneously. A useful example is provided by Peter Behrens, whose pavilions for the Oldenburger Landes- Industrie- and Gewerbe-Ausstellung of 1905 display a reliance on the ideal geometric form which would mark his architectural style. Behrens's design for a Bismarck monument on the nearby Bookholzberg of 1908, on the other hand, is nothing short of the 'Germanic' in terms of style and choice of materials. For a multi-faceted history of these projects see the comprehensive article by Peter Springer, 'Peter Behrens' Bismarck-Monument. Eine Fallstudie', *Niederdeutsche Beiträge zur Kunstgeschichte*, 1992, vol. 31, pp. 129–207, who nevertheless considers Behrens's design for the Bismarck monument as marking his metamorphosis 'from painter to architect'. I thank Sherwin Simmons for bringing this essay to my attention.

45   Warburg in Gombrich, *Aby Warburg*, p. 154. Warburg is here implicating what has been termed a 'monument proletariat'. Though the class connotations of this term are obvious, Warburg's use of the term refers more to an aesthetic than an economic proletariat. As such, it may be likened to the contemporaneous term '*Hurrapatriotismus*', which likewise refers to a superficial celebration of nation, one that turned on easily graspable representations, bombastic symbols, and kitsch.

46   A. Warburg, unpublished diary entry of 2 June 1906, written on the occasion of the public unveiling of the Hamburg Bismarck. Translated in Gombrich, *Aby Warburg*, p. 155.

47   The distinction Warburg is making here, and which is further elaborated upon in many of his published writings, is that between *greifen* and *begreifen*, or between the physical and the conceptual grasp. The conceptual grasp *of* an object marks a higher stage of development than a physical grasp *on* an object, since the former requires conceptualisation and thus an intellectual distance from the actual, physical object.

48   Scheffler, *Moderne Baukunst*, p. 133; Hofmann, 'Der Wettbewerb (Fortsetzung)', p. 42.

49   P. Behrens, 'Was ist monumentale Kunst?' *Das Kunstgewerbeblatt*, 1909, N. F. 20, pp. 45–48. The contents of this essay first appeared as a paper, 'Vom Kirchenbau', delivered on 7 April 1908 to the Kunstgewerbeverein, Museum für Kunst und Gewerbe, Hamburg. Excerpts of the lecture also appeared in *Weserzeitung*, 15 December 1908, and in A. Lindner, 'Peter Behrens in Hamburg', in the *Neue Hamburger Zeitung*, 9 April 1908.

50   Scheffler, *Moderne Baukunst*, p. 130.

51   A. Warburg, 'The Mural Paintings in Hamburg City Hall' (1910), in *Aby Warburg: The Renewal of Pagan Antiquity: Contributions to the Cultural History of the European Renaissance*, Los Angeles, Getty Research Institute for the History of Art and the Humanities, 1999, pp. 711–16. Originally published in *Kunst und Künstler*, 1910, vol. 8, pp. 427–9. Evaluating Hugo Vogel's murals for the great Festsaal in Hamburg's city hall, Warburg (p. 4) notes how history painting is presently

> caught up in the stylistic transformation overtaking the writing of history itself: in both, the tendency now is to move away from the confines of a single antiquarian and political narrative and toward a typological approach, spanning whole cultural epochs on a 'grand scale'.

Monumental decorum was central to stylistic transformation in this regard. As in the case of the Hamburg Bismarck, here too the issue was how to negotiate historical distance and presence, as well as the stylistically old and new, into a suitable monumentality.

52   Warburg, 'The Mural Paintings in Hamburg City Hall', p. 712.

53   A. Hofmann, *Denkmäler*, Stuttgart, Alfred Kröner, 1906, vol. 1, p. 247. See also P. Behrens, 'Was ist monumentale Kunst?' and J. Meier-Graefe, 'Peter Behrens', *Dekorative Kunst*, October 1899, vol. 3, p. 204.

54   C. Gurlitt, 'Bismarcks Denkmal in Hamburg', *Der Lotse*, 18 Jan. 1902, vol. 11, no. 16, p. 31. It is interesting to note that *Der Lotse*, published between 1900 and 1902, was created in order to draw attention to Hamburg's particular cultural and economic achievements. At the same time, it was hoped that focusing on these achievements might lessen the cultural worth of the merely industrial and material. Not surprisingly, several members of the monument committee, including Lichtwark and Warburg, were involved in the founding of the weekly. See R. Schütt, *Bohemiens und Biedermänne: Die Hamburger Gruppe 1925 bis 1931*, Hamburg, fliehkraft, 1996, pp. 143–7ff.

55   See, for instance, G. Muschner, 'Das Hamburger Bismarck-Denkmal', *Deutsche Kunst und Dekoration*, Oct. 1906–March 1907, vol. 19, pp. 113–21. According to Muschner (p. 121), 'The work is the first realisation of a truly modern monument in monumental form.'

56   Warburg, 'The Mural Paintings in Hamburg City Hall', p. 716.

57 See, for instance, F. Naumann, 'Das Bismarckdenkmal in Hamburg', *Form und Farbe*, Berlin, Buchverlag der Hilfe, 1909, p. 171; Hofmann, 'Der Wettbewerb (Fortsetzung)', p. 41.

58 This is how Lederer and Schaudt's conception was described by the jury. A. Hofmann, 'Der Wettbewerb (Fortsetzung)', p. 41.

59 Fuchs, 'Zeitgemässe Betrachtungen', p. 351. Two years later Fuchs would write his patently nationalist and virulently anti-Semitic tract, *Der Kaiser und die Zukunft des deutschen Volkes*.

60 Scheffler, *Moderne Baukunst*, p. 136.

61 The medallion contained the following inscription:

> May you stand like a tower
> in the current of time
> May your name shine eternally
> In this monument of the future.

For an illustration of the medallion see W. Hofmann, G. Syamken, and M. Warnke (eds) *Menschenrechte des Auges: Über Aby Warburg*, Frankfurt am Main, Europäische Verlagsanstalt, 1980, p. 17.

62 *Hamburger Correspondent,* 2 June 1906. Cited in Jochum-Bohrmann, *Hugo Lederer*, p. 63.

63 The association of 'superficiality' (*Äusserlichkeit*) with the truly Germanic and 'outwardness' with the empty, the false, and the ersatz (in this case with the commodity culture of the Wilhelmine period), was a well-worn paradigm by the beginning of the twentieth century. For an interesting and wide-ranging discussion of this trope in relation to German literature, see S. Jonsson, *Subject without Nation: Robert Musil and the History of Modern Identity*, Durham, NC, and London, Duke University Press, 2000, Chapter 1, 'Topographies of Inwardness'.

64 Jochum-Bohrmann, *Hugo Lederer*, pp. 64–5.

65 *Hamburger Correspondent,* 2 June 1906. Cited in Jochum-Bohrmann, *Hugo Lederer*, p. 63. After having declined an invitation to the unveiling, on a visit to Hamburg two weeks later Wilhelm II failed to visit the monument, a gesture which demonstrates the fault-line between official politics and the unoffical cult of Bismarck.

66 A. Hofmann, 'Die Gestaltung von National-Denkmälern', *Deutsche Bauzeitung*, 11 April 1894, vol. 28, p. 194.

67 Cited in J. Bracker, 'Michel contra Bismarck', p. 17. Bracker continues with an amusing anecdote:

> The sailor Carl Holst turned to 'Plattdeutsch' in order to spread among the public this counter-myth, using verse form on a postcard: 'The old Michael gave up his ghost when Bismarck took over his post'. ('De ole Michel mag nich mehr, denn Bismarck käm em in de Quer . . .').

68 J. Bracker, 'Michel kontra Bismarck,' p. 17. If Roland was considered a *Volkssymbol* by those in favour of the Hamburg monument, the patron saint of the rival church is here suffused with shades of the 'German Michel,' who was likewise heralded as a symbol of the people and of a united and free Germany, particularly during the revolution of 1848. Unlike the Roland, the German Michel was not so much a heroic figure as a personification of the character traits of the *Volk*. See K. Riha, 'Der deutsche Michel. Zur Ausprägung einer nationalen Allegorie im 19. Jahrhundert', in K. Herding and G. Otto (eds) *Karikaturen: 'Nervöse Auffangsorgane des inneren und äusseren Lebens'*, Giessen, Anabas, 1980, pp. 186–205; and K. von See, *Deutsche Germanen-Ideologie: Vom Humanismus bis zur Gegenwart*, Frankfurt, Athenäum, pp. 47ff.

69 Hans Meyer-Veden, *Hamburg: Historische Photographien 1842–1914*, Berlin, Ernst & Sohn, 1995, p. 150.

70 The shift from national unity to the powerful national state in the rhetoric of German

nationalism, and the linking of the *Machtstaat* to industrial and military might, continued unabated until at least the beginning of the First World War. See in this regard the thought-provoking series of essays in J. Dülffer and K. Holl (eds) *Bereit zum Krieg: Kriegsmentalität im wilhelminischen Deutschland 1890–1914*, Göttingen, Vandenhoeck & Ruprecht, 1986.

71 See R. Barthes, *Mythologies*, Paris, Editions du Seuil, 1957.

72 My understanding of a national landmark as at once semiologically fixed and fluid is inspired by R. Barthes's magisterial essay on 'The Eiffel Tower', in Susan Sontag (ed) *A Barthes Reader*, New York, Hill and Wang, 1987, pp. 236–50.

73 Emil Schaudt, 'Das Bismarck-Denkmal in Hamburg', *Zentralblatt der Bauverwaltung*, 16 June 1906, vol. 26, no. 49, p. 309.

74 The German daily newspaper *Die Welt* characterised the monument in 1985 as the epitome of 'bourgeoise-republican identity'. Cited in R. Alings, *Monument und Nation*, p. 254. While the present chapter does not examine heritage, my argument about a successful image of national culture as at once fixed and capacious can be extended to include heritage. Both national culture and heritage entail the attempt to enfold an individual response into a collective idea. John Brewer puts this well in *The Pleasures of the Imagination: English Culture in the Eighteenth Century*, Chicago, University of Chicago Press, 1997, p. 476, when he describes heritage as a 'way of thinking, which treats culture as a special sort of property owned by the public or nation'. Cited in David A. Brewer, 'Making Hogarth Heritage', *Representations*, Fall 2000, vol. 72, p. 55.

Chapter 6

The lantern and the glass

On the themes of renewal and dwelling in Le Corbusier's Purist art and architecture

Dagmar Motycka Weston

> Let this lamp be lit to-day and folly be confounded.
>
> (Le Corbusier)[1]

The blending of instrumental and symbolic representation has been a problematic feature of twentieth-century architecture. Since the failure of the postmodernist project, instrumental reason continues to dominate architectural practice. This is usually to the exclusion of an authentic symbolic representation such as is found in myth and poetry, and which can emerge only from a creative interpretation of tradition. One of the most illuminating examples of this modern dilemma in the early twentieth century is the work of Le Corbusier. His reductivist, Utopian urban visions are still justly seen as a key impetus behind the urban planning policies which inflicted such damage on our cities in the name of modern progress. Yet as a counterpart to his urban work, Le Corbusier saw an urgent need for the regeneration of the culture of dwelling.[2] Through his intuitive creative process, he addressed this problem more successfully than most others in the modern period. When working at the scale of a single painting or a house, he was often able to create a work of art meaningfully rooted in deep archetypal undercurrents and able to sustain a vital world of meaning.

Le Corbusier's Purist work is still often understood in terms of a superficial reading of the numerous polemical statements which he and Ozenfant disseminated during the *L'Esprit Nouveau* years.[3] A fuller understanding, however, must address the less explicit themes which run through Le Corbusier's Purist work, and which are oriented towards physical and spiritual renewal. One of the distinctive features of modern urbanist polemic is the way in which its language adopted a quasi-religious tone, drawing into a secular discourse much of the imagery and proselytising urgency belonging to theological doctrine, and especially to the thematics of soteriology.[4] Le Corbusier's work of this time contains numerous cryptic allusions to imminent apocalypse followed by potential redemption. This phenomenon raises the open question of what meaning, if any, does such metaphoric language hold in the context of a predominantly secular, rationalist culture. It also draws attention to the strong messianic dimension of the role of the artist-architect. The first part of this chapter provides a brief overview of some of the redemptive themes underlying Le Corbusier's urban visions. The second part contains a more detailed discussion of his development of the thematics of dwelling in his painting and architecture.

'A new city to replace the old'[5]

> The city of light that will dispel the miasmas of anxiety now darkening our lives, that will succeed the twilight of despair we live in at the present, exists on paper. We are only waiting for a 'yes'[6]

This is one of many pronouncements made by Le Corbusier on the subject which so absorbed him during the early decades of his career – the new, redeemed Radiant City. While the Utopian aspirations underlying modern architecture – and especially the architecture of the twentieth-century city – are well known, the heroic sweep of Le Corbusier's vision still remains a source of marvel. It is one of the strongest expressions of millennial sentiments among the protagonists of modern architecture.[7] Their visions were fuelled by a conviction, shared by all of the avant-gardes, of the decadence of the old, nineteenth-century order of European society, of a bourgeois culture that had come to be seen as irredeemably diseased, corrupt and irrelevant. In the wake of Futurist fantasies, and of the destruction of the

Great War, it seemed imperative to start anew by sweeping away the decaying fabric of the old order, by creating a *tabula rasa* and then constructing on unpolluted land a Utopian vision, a species of earthly paradise.[8]

Le Corbusier's vision of the new city is oriented towards the twin symbolic paradigms of an Arcadian, primordial garden, on the one hand, and that of the Heavenly City of salvation on the other. The significance of primitive, atavistic nature as a vehicle to cosmic reconciliation has sometimes been noted. Le Corbusier's desire to make the city itself into a garden or a park is symptomatic of a widespread yearning among the modern visionaries, when confronted with the existing, terrible conditions of the industrial city, for a kind of 'Golden Age' of primordial innocence and harmony.[9] In *The Radiant City* Le Corbusier, influenced by the vision of Rousseau, bemoans modern man's 'stray[ing] from the paths of nature' and proposes a way in which this fateful lapse can be remedied and harmony restored. The traditional street and urban square will be swept away. The city will all but disappear,[10] making space for the endless atavistic celebration of the athleticism of the body (preferably in its primordial nakedness), in the new parks and sports facilities. In addition to the flowing parkland surrounding the buildings, each dwelling is to have a direct relationship with its own plot of nature in the form of a suspended garden or roof terraces. Man will again dwell in a close pact with nature, to the benefit of his spiritual well-being.[11] Here one can trace the origins of Le Corbusier's search for a modern interpretation of the archetypal house-and-garden unit.[12] This configuration often includes a hearth, oculus and tree, each with implicit cosmological connotations for Le Corbusier, which will be explored later in this chapter. This dwelling, strongly informed by the image of the primitive hut or temple, is to be the standard building block of the new city. Le Corbusier's attraction to the paradisal image of the Golden Age or garden is the counterpart of his allusions to the redeemed city.

While the ethical imperatives of the new city were already present in the earliest writings, Le Corbusier's salvational programme reached its most developed expression in *The Radiant City*. In this work, the benighted traditional city (be it Paris or New York), is described in vivid purgatorial imagery as a dehumanising place cursed with filth, suffocating gases, perpetual gloom and human despair.[13] By contrast to this 'bubbling poison brew', the Radiant Modern City, shimmering on the horizon, is full of light, air and joy, resplendent with 'immense, radiant prisms' and 'geometric façades of glass reflecting the blue glory of the sky'.[14] Its very name implies a redeemed society not only permeated by geometrical order and light, but one which is itself brilliant, emitting the light of harmony, justice and well-being.[15] From his imagery of the good, of light, glass and crystal,[16] one is led to suspect that Le Corbusier wishes to suggest a metaphorical parallel between his *Ville radieuse* and the Celestial City of Revelation, descending to earth at the end of time. Both hold a promise of a kind of eternal salvation for its blessed inhabitants. To make the point more explicit, Le Corbusier reproduces in the book a late medieval painting of 'the chariot of death', with the caption 'In life after death, justice will come.'[17] Later, in urging the building of 'the places where mankind can be reborn', he uses an image of a biblical patriarch from the Last Judgement portal of Chartres Cathedral, embracing the souls of the righteous in Heavenly Jerusalem.[18]

Purification

An essential element in the transformation and redemption of the old city and society is purification. This is a complex theme within the salvational thematics of Purism. It draws on the role of purity and purification in many traditions as a prerequisite for sacrifice, renewal and redemption. While a more detailed discussion is beyond the scope of this chapter, one might point to various manifestations of this concern in Purism, as, for example, in its demands for economy, asceticism and whitewash,[19] or in the crystalline qualities of its architecture. It is also implicit in the highly developed iconography of water and ritual body cleansing, alluding to the thematics of baptism.

Creativity

Le Corbusier's frontispiece for *The Radiant City* is a full-page reproduction of his enigmatic 1930 painting *Hand and Flint*. While he insists that the picture is not symbolic, it is difficult not to see its somewhat arcane configuration of fragments as expressive of the author's aspirations for the city whose virtues the book celebrates.[20] Corbusian iconography of the hand is very complex, encompassing the reconciliation of opposites (such as matter and spirit), human and cosmic creativity, and the bestowal of wisdom and salvation.[21] One may surmise that the stroking and probing by the artist's hand of the smooth, feminine flint in this painting alludes to sexual contact.[22] The image parallels that of 'the hand and the seashell [that] love each other' in the *Poème de l'angle droit*.[23] This, in Corbusian iconography, implies the reconciliation of opposites, as in the conjunction of the vertical and the horizontal in the making of the Right Angle. The image here seems to be related to the analogy, reiterated in the *Poème*, which Le Corbusier perceived between human procreation and creative action.[24] The other recognisable objects in the painting, the pen and the box of matches (both also very 'handy'[25]), further allude to acts of creativity (the matches perhaps referring to the spark of imaginative fire which initiates creation, as well as to the illumination which results from it). The other dimension of the content is the flint's ancient affiliation with human making and especially with tools.[26] It is this quality of what might be called 'use value' which Le Corbusier particularly prized in the humble Purist *objets-type*, and which the pen and the matchbox embody. If this reading is correct, then the painting may be understood as an emblem of the personal creativity which Le Corbusier had often emphasised,[27] and which was expected of the worthy inhabitants of the new society in imitation of nature (and of their architect).[28] Le Corbusier's stress on personal creativity is an example of the way in which Utopian visions, with their insistence on certain ideal standards of behaviour (to the point, sometimes, of the suppression of individuality), tend towards coercion. This problem is perhaps implicit in the Purist stress on the virtues of typicality (of which he, himself, was ironically such a poor specimen). Paradoxically also, while everyone is going to be equal, to

6.1
Le Corbusier, *Hand and Flint*, 1930, frontispiece to *The Radiant City*. Painting FLC 345. © FLC/ADAGP, Paris and DACS, London, 2002

overcome all the practical problems of realisation (such as laws of private ownership), the city will have to be built by a dictator.[29]

Clearly, Le Corbusier's proposals for the new city, with their rational, *tabula rasa* planning, and lack of meaningful public life, are somewhat abstract, perspectival constructs. The idea that something as rich and complex as a living city can spring fully formed from the mind and drawing board of a single prophetic individual is doomed to failure. Similarly, the idea that the ethical, participatory order of a traditional city could be translated into a set of geometrical rules is an instrumental delusion. Le Corbusier's borrowing of the imagery of a religious tradition reveals modern man's searching for the deep meaning of the sacred, yet remains on the rather superficial level of a sign. The urban visions represent the most problematic part of Le Corbusier's performance. In the remainder of this chapter, I shall turn my attention to a more fruitful area of his prodigious creative output, his efforts to rediscover the poetics of dwelling.

The theme of Purist still life as magic niche of transformation

Amédée Ozenfant and Charles Edouard Jeanneret launched Purism soon after the latter had settled in Paris in 1917. The stated aims behind Purist painting are familiar from the authors' prolific writings. Through their assemblages of humble *objets-type* in ambiguous Cubist space, they sought to validate machine production as a legitimate and liberating part of modern life. The subtle play of relationships set up within the non-perspectival spatial structure of the canvases, however, also engendered a rich thematic content. This was oriented not simply towards physical renewal, but also, through symbolic means, towards spiritual regeneration. One finds within Le Corbusier's paintings, photographs and early architecture an attempt to reinvent and regenerate the whole of the culture of dwelling.

Ornament as microcosm

From his earliest education at the School of Art in La Chaux-de-Fonds, where he studied the writings of Ruskin and Owen Jones, Le Corbusier came to understand architectural ornament as an integral part of the meaning of architecture, in its traditional role as a *microcosm* of the order of the whole.[30] This understanding of ornament, with its forms drawn from nature, and particularly from rock formations and trees, is evident in a number of the earliest buildings with which Le Corbusier was involved.[31] As he became increasingly concerned with the application of modern technological means to the problem of affordable, decent housing, the use of traditional applied ornament became untenable for Le Corbusier. He then sought to find ways of engaging with some of the traditional symbolic themes of dwelling in a modern idiom. The Purist paintings (accompanied by a select group of other objects) became for him the new acceptable form of decorative art. They were deemed a suitable vehicle for the meditation expected of one within the 'vessel of silence and lofty solitude'[32] that was to be the modern dwelling. As with traditional ornament, the paintings had an ethical function: to provide what might be called existential orientation. They were objects of instruction and reverent contemplation, offering arcane meaning to 'those who deserve it'.[33] This was clearly the intention behind, for example, the Purist paintings concentrated at the culmination of the meditative journey through the maison La Roche in the owner's austere bedroom.[34] The necessary spiritual initiation was to be achieved through purification, which would lead to the attainment of harmony. Through harmony, as Le Corbusier later asserted, earthly paradise could be brought within reach.[35] His microcosmic aspirations – the desire to evoke in his works a symbolic field needed for authentic dwelling – are perceptible in many of the paintings and photographs. These often display a desire to compensate for the loss of a coherent, generally accessible symbolic background by a tendency towards an excessive iconographic complexity and completeness. As we shall see, the pieces are often extremely ambitious, attempting to situate human dwelling and ethical action in a cosmic context.

Perception and spatiality

A salient aspect of the Purists' interest in the primitive is their preoccupation with man's primordial condition of embodiment, and especially with the phenomena of perception.[36] Ozenfant and Jeanneret adopted dimensionally ambiguous Cubist space – especially as it came to be interpreted by Juan Gris around 1918 – and developed it into their own species of 'implicit' space.[37] Here, depth is rendered indeterminate and mysterious, and virtual spatial relationships – such as implied continuities and visual echoes – between assembled object/fragments are honed into metaphoric content. As with many of the avant-gardes, the Purists challenged the sterile formality of the perspective illusionism of Academic painting. Le Corbusier can be seen as one of the most important early proponents of 'situational space' in his architecture and painting. This generally involved a rejection (in his buildings, if not his city plans) of the formal space of Beaux-Arts planning, and an interest in structuring space in response to situational factors, such as the features of the physical and cultural context of the building. The poetic observation of concrete daily situations comes to inform the making of architectural places. Le Corbusier's interest in a primary, situationally structured space is memorably exemplified by a remarkable early passage, when he describes the spontaneous arrangement of utensils on the table of a small restaurant at the end of a meal. The 'inevitable order which relates these objects to each other', even after the diners have departed, an order stemming from the body and from tradition, is an embodiment of the situation of dining, and 'the distances that separate them are a measure of life'.[38] The subtle lyricism of such situational spatial relationships between objects is celebrated by Purist still lifes. The other aspect of spatial structuring involves the manipulation of fragments in a way first developed in Cubist collage. Working with *objets-type* (or the later *objets à réaction poétique*) in painting, and with evocative architectural fragments in buildings, Le Corbusier was able to create a 'communicative space',[39] in which metaphorical meanings are generated through thematic juxtaposition.

The implicit niche

At the same time, Ozenfant and Le Corbusier were interested, in a way which had much in common with the outlook of the Surrealists, in the phenomenal structure of lived vision. Their goal was to see something in a direct, pre-reflective mode, one not yet conditioned by the ingrained conceptual framework of perspectival representation. The implicit Purist space is deployed in the paintings and photographs of the buildings to amplify the mystery of vision and to aid thematic content.

One of the key characteristics of Purist space, its two- and three-dimensional ambiguity, has the effect that many of the paintings can be read as variably concave and convex spaces: in other words, as either a recess or projection.[40] This is a theme which one often finds, with greater or lesser explicitness, in Cubist still life. As part of their efforts to break away from the old idea of illusionistic space behind the perspective 'window', Picasso and Braque sought ways of neutralising the boundary of the frame, and allowing their still life to spill out of its enclosure. This is evident in a number of works of the Synthetic phase, where the 'frame' of the picture doubles as the edge of the table top on which the objects are displayed. The next step of emancipation occurs as the still life begins literally to break through the picture plane and to assume a position in the real space of the beholder. This is the case with the numerous, mostly ephemeral reliefs made by the Cubists around 1912–14, such as Picasso's *Glass, Newspaper and Dice*.[41] Interestingly, the objects in this work are framed in a shallow, niche-like box. The emphasis in these painting-sculptures was, on the one hand, on the *construction* of tactile objects made of real materials in real space, creating a world more immediately relevant than that of the traditional bourgeois work of art.[42] Picasso was attracted to the process of assembly and construction as part of the meaning of the piece, as for example with the cardboard model of the 1912 guitar which was kept in pieces in a box and assembled when needed.[43] On the other hand, and as a corollary of this concern with construction, these Cubist sculptures, in their abandonment of continuous volumes and the fragmentation of objects, were investigations into the phenomenal interpenetration of things and space, a concern shared by a number of the other avant-garde movements. Another variation on this theme in Cubism is painting which creates a strong illusion of positive and negative space. In Picasso's 1918 painting *Guitar and Fruit Bowl on a Table*, the painted 'frame' (which, unusually, circumscribes the whole of the picture) produces, through the manipulation of virtual light and shade, a powerful sense of both a niche – a shallow room within which the still life objects are standing – and a projection.[44]

Something similar can be detected in Purist painting. Some of Amédée Ozenfant's works are explicitly structured as niches. These include his *Carafe, Bottle and Guitar in a Cellar* of 1919, and *Cup, Glass and Bottles in front of a Window* of 1922. The 'niche' paintings were sometimes used as implicit alcoves in the interiors and can be seen as such in the published photographs. This is the case in the well-known photo of the Ozenfant studio,[45] in which the latter painting's 'window' reads as an implicit opening in the front wall below the library, while also echoing the niche of the nearby fireplace. Le Corbusier's paintings tend to operate on a more implicit level. This is confirmed by a detailed examination of the spatial structure of his 1922 painting *Pale Still Life with a Lantern*. The canvas appears to be a rectangular table top laid with some sixteen objects, including a book, a box lantern, a carafe, wine bottles and glasses. These theme-objects, arranged in subtle and complex relationships within a shallow space, are seen from a variety of viewpoints (mostly, but not exclusively, in a synthesis of orthogonal projections). This 'simultaneity of vision' is suggestive of the sense of tactile familiarity and phenomenal constancy which one experiences with respect to things one handles in daily life.[46] There is also a strong sense of the poetry of the situational relationships between these evocative fragments, which take on a thematic content (to which I shall return shortly).

6.2
Amédée Ozenfant,
Cup, Glass and
Bottles in front of a
Window, **1922.**
Kunstmuseum,
Basel.

There is a stress on transparency, so that apparently overlapping objects can be seen 'behind' or through each other in new and surprising relationships. The right side of the lantern, for example, continues behind the wine bottles, fusing with their outlines. The reflective, bevelled inner wall of the lantern, standing behind the bottles, is visible as a veil over them, suggesting both a sense of illumination and of containment. The relationships between the individual objects are similarly suffused with spatial ambiguity, making a logically consistent reading impossible. For example, the volumes of the teapot and the wine glass to its right, sharing the arc of the teapot handle, present a spatial conundrum, as does the relationship between the small fluted glass and the pipe. Logic is thus suspended as one is carried along in a quasi-Surrealist, oneiric play of visual rhymes and conjunctions.[47] The objects in the bottom left corner – the low podium of the book and the fluted glass in particular – appear to stand up from the corner of the canvas/base. The small milk jug appears as a thin layer in front of its black background. The two wine glasses (centre and right) are modelled with some *chiaroscuro* and thus appear more solid and bulging. Many of the other objects, seen in pristine and timeless orthogonal projection, appear paper-thin and layered over each other. The lighting, as in Cubist still life, is deliberately inconsistent, appearing, in another subversion of the logical unity of perspective representation, to come from conflicting directions.

6.3
Le Corbusier, *Pale Still Life with a Lantern*, 1922, Painting FLC 209.
© FLC/ADAGP, Paris and DACS, London, 2002

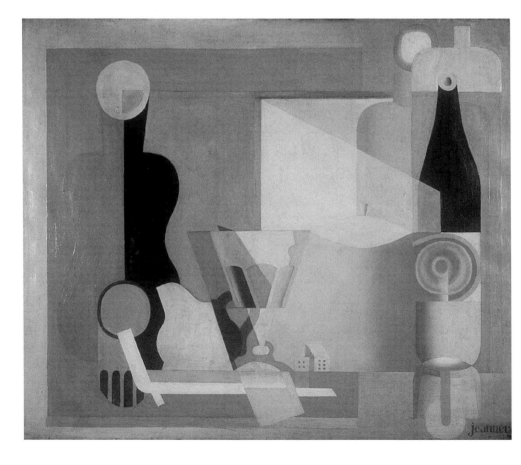

This inconsistency of light source is most clearly evident in the teapot (apparently illuminated from the left) and the adjacent wineglass (illuminated from the right side). Lighting is used instead to highlight areas of the composition in order to enhance the visual harmony within the painting. The traditional iconography of sacred light, associated with geometry, purity, truth and the good, was adapted by the Purists and will be discussed later.

The 'projecting' elements in the picture are carefully counterbalanced by several strong suggestions of concavity. Most notably, the grey book, especially where it meets the canvas table at the top left, tends to be perceived as a recess in which the carafe and glasses are sheltered. This reading is in constant tension with that of the same book's positive lower edge, lying on the table.[48] This, however, also doubles as a niche or even a window with a projecting brown sill at the left. The enclosure of the box lantern, here unusually dematerialised, provides another concavity. The dominant dark areas in the picture – the right half of the carafe, the top half of the wine bottle, and the jug handle – tend also, because of their receding colour, towards a deeper position in the implicit pictorial depth. Within this oscillating spatial fabric, the two dice are both flat (the left one) and volumetric (the right). They double also as miniature houses (with dot-windows), alluding both to play (the game of dominoes) and to the Domino frame. While the dotted faces resemble fenestrated walls, their sum of ten is suggestive of the possibilities of mathematical permutations. Such calculated ambiguity between flatness and depth, convex and concave space, is suggestive of Le Corbusier's thinking about his paintings as potential three-dimensional objects or sculptures.[49] And indeed the Purists insisted that their paintings were to be understood as spaces rather than as pictures. This is suggestive, I think, of the fact that the pictures were thought of by Le Corbusier as miniature representations of inhabited architecture.

The thematic content of Purist still life

There is a world in a painting or a building . . . Seek and you shall find. Look into the depths of the work and ask yourself questions. There are illuminations and scenes; there are hours of fullness, agonies, radiant or menacing skies, houses and mountains, seas and lagoons, suns and moons. And there are besides all the cries of the subconscious, sensual and chaste; and everything that you can imagine.

(Le Corbusier)[50]

As this quotation confirms, Purism, like Cubism before it, was never a formal or abstract art. Akin to some works of the Metaphysical school, the poetics of Purism is based on the proposition that a deeper and mysterious dimension of reality can sometimes be glimpsed through the contemplation of their familiar, mundane appearance. It is also an art concerned with the metaphorical transformation of related fragments. The structure of Purist space, while celebrating the mystery of embodied vision, served to highlight the way in which seeing as an act of perception is inherently metaphorical.[51] It is a basic condition of our embodied, situated nature that the world is always given to us as meaningful. It is to this domain of metaphoric content that we now turn our attention.

The house

A notable feature of Le Corbusier's iconography is his interest in the notion of the primitive hut or first house. He saw this as a model for the *maison-type* which he was seeking and which would help to regenerate dwelling, especially in the aftermath of the Great War. This theme under-lies his more functionalist and technological discourse on the subject of mass-produced housing. In the symbolic tradition, the near-universal theme of man's mythical original house refers to the persistent idea that there once existed an archetypal, natural or divinely revealed work of architecture, a paradigm of all building.[52] Speculations about this primi-tive dwelling tend to intensify whenever the need for renewal in archi-tecture is felt. In both the Christian and Jewish traditions, this first house (the tabernacle) connotes moral righteousness, and is recognised as the dwelling of the redeemed in the Messianic kingdom. Having the form of a rudimentary architectural canopy (a notional symbolic shelter), it serves, as for example in the Jewish wedding ceremony, as a paradigm of mar-riage and dwelling. The first house is closely related to the human body, partaking of its scale and proportions. Throughout history, the theme of the primordial house has been linked to the promise of renewal, and of paradise.[53]

All of these motifs were taken on board by Le Corbusier. His thinking about the first house becomes, however, fused with the imagery of the temple.[54] In his first article on the *tracés régulateurs*,[55] Le Corbusier, referring to the Vitruvian tradition, presented his own interpretation of the making of the first house, immediately followed by the analogous making of the primitive temple. In the ancient understanding, the temple (which had developed out of the house paradigm), embodied the *imago mundi*, a micro-cosmic recapitulation of the transcendent order of the cosmos. As the sacred house of the gods on earth, it had the power to purify, cleanse and resanctify the world and the earthly city. It is likewise identified with the human body, partaking of the same ideal geometry and proportions. When repeated, as in the Gothic cathedral, the aedicular motif becomes a 'multi-plication of shrines',[56] revealing the hierarchical structure of the Heavenly City. In Antiquity, the goddess of the benign and fecundating domestic fire (Hestia in Greece, corresponding to Vesta in Roman culture) was wor-shipped in every household and also (by sexually pure priests and initiates) in special civic shrines.[57]

Temple paradigm in Le Corbusier

'I have brought the temple to the family, to the domestic hearth, I have re-established the conditions of nature in the life of man,' wrote Le Corbusier at the end of his life, summarising a perennial theme.[58] This somewhat startling assertion is symptomatic of the wide-ranging modern phenome-non of the 'secular sacred'.[59] It is characterised by the blurring of distinc-tion between the traditional sacred and private secular experience in nineteenth- and twentieth-century culture. With the disintegration of a shared faith, traditional social orders and public life, cultural experience becomes introverted, focusing by the end of the nineteenth century increasingly on the private domain of the individual. This daily life, with its mundane 'rituals', takes on an unwarranted significance, as the house is transformed – through the agency of art – into a temple. The intimate domestic interior, a repository of self-defining private possessions, is raised to an absurdly lofty status. Simultaneously, the city, which traditionally had been the theatre for public and sacred ceremonies, and an embodiment of the ethical order of society, loses its former signifi-cance.

Much of Le Corbusier's Purist and later work is informed by the theme of the house–temple. The Purist still-life paintings and niches in his early architecture can be seen in terms of this aedicular motif and all its symbolic implications. Le Corbusier's 1918 painting *La Cheminée* shows some horizontal books and an imposing cubic mass on a mantelpiece. The work, which he called his first painting, held a deep personal and icono-graphic significance for him. In one of his books, Le Corbusier juxtaposed a full-page reproduction of his pencil study for *La Cheminée* with a page of images of the Jewish tabernacle from *Towards a New Architecture*. The caption conveys the iconic significance of the drawing, as well as hinting at the artist's view of the necessity of arduous striving and personal sacri-fice in a process of initiation. It reads: 'L-C lost the use of his left eye when doing this drawing at night: separation of the retina. This first picture is the key to an understanding of his approach to plastic art.'[60]

This example provides an important insight into the linking of the house and the temple. As Carl has noted,[61] this image was related by Le Corbusier to his early sketch of the distant Acropolis, with the Parthenon (which he had called 'a sovereign cube') floating on its plateau against the constant sea horizon. The French term *cheminée* has the connotations not only of chimney-piece, but also of hearth and home (*foyer*). The conjunction of the hearth and temple recalls the worship of the household fire goddess Hestia, and can be taken here to signify dwelling. *La Cheminée* also already contains the seeds of most of the essential elements of Purist still life: the purified theme objects, the horizon, rudimentary enclosure, a play of light and shade. All these features link its world to the iconography of the temple.

There are numerous examples in Le Corbusier's *œuvre* of the primal house–temple theme, of which one will suffice here. His early design for the Domino frame, his 'conception pure et totale',[62] was seen as an ideal, almost dematerialised house-*type*, a kind of primitive temple. Made of the

6.4
Le Corbusier, Study for *La Cheminée,* **1918. Pencil drawing FLC 2304.**
© FLC/ADAGP, Paris and DACS, London, 2002

humble modern material of reinforced concrete, and embodying ideal geometrical laws, this purifying type was to be reincarnated in every new dwelling.[63] With its rather reductionist understanding of geometrical order, the Domino frame was, however, a largely instrumental construct aspiring to the transcendent.

Meaning in *Pale Still Life with a Lantern*

The imagery of dwelling in the Purist niche

The field of the Purist canvas, the laid table, with its simultaneously aedicular properties, can be seen on one level as the stage of human action, populated by human-surrogate objects. More specifically, in Corbusian as in Cubist iconography, the space of the picture can often be seen as a metaphor for human dwelling. In Picasso's *Still Life with a Bottle, Fruit Bowl and Violin*,[64] for example, the ambiguity of Cubist space facilitates the metamorphosis of a fruit still life into a reclining female nude. The resulting metaphor of 'laid table' and 'woman' or 'marital bed' provides a strong evocation of home, fecundity and abundance.[65] And indeed the affinity in our subconscious between the two paradigms has been noted by psychoanalysis.[66] The iconography of the set table in Purist still life, I would argue, has a similar basis.

The still life is constructed of our daily domestic companions (the mystically purified *objets-type*), many of which carry residues of sacred meaning (the book, the vessels, the lantern, the fragments of architecture). The setting is the site of the reconciliation of opposites (darkness and light, orthogonal and curved geometries, male and female, and so on) in a symbolically charged visual harmony. And although the human figure appears in Le Corbusier's painting only in the late 1920s, many of the objects here have strong, intentional anthropomorphic qualities. Those tools such as jugs, glasses and pipes, which Le Corbusier saw as 'the true extensions of human limbs', also dreamily mirror the forms, scale and proportions of the human body.[67] As in Cubism, musical instruments – having a voice and an intimately tactile presence – act as analogues for the human body. This is especially true of guitars and violins, which become surrogates for the female form, often with erotic overtones.[68]

In the *Pale Still Life with a Lantern* (6.3), two vertical axes are set up – one (on the left) around the feminine carafe, the other (on the right) dominated by the dark phallic wine bottle. These connotations of the wine bottle, latently present in Purist works, are made explicit in a group of works Le Corbusier executed in the late 1950s and early 1960s, such as *Le Soir*.[69] Fusing again the table and bed, these depict a female nude crouching over a still life in such a way that the upright wine bottle seems to intersect with her genital area. In another collage, *The Green Bottle*, the oval shape of the wine surface in the bottle appears to pulsate against its green background at this point of penetration. In other variations on this theme, the woman's genital area becomes the matrix of the conciliation of opposites in the 1960 drawing *Chez moi*, in which the thematic icon of the glass and its inverse[70] is superimposed over her raised thighs. To return to *Pale Still Life with a Lantern*, at the base of the carafe (whose double curves recall those of a guitar) stands a cylindrical glass. This is simultaneously a borrowing from the Cubist device of representing a void with a positive volume, as the sound hole of the 'carafe-guitar' is represented by an apparently upright cylinder. As in Cubist imagery, the hole of the guitar alludes to female genitals, and is in this painting encroached upon by the clay pipe, the foremost masculine object in Purist still life. The erotic imagery is further amplified by the functional relationship between the wine bottle and the carafe: the latter receiving Dionysian liquid from the former. Thus, Le Corbusier establishes the theme of marriage as an essential component of dwelling. If we recall his affiliation of the sexual union between a man and a woman with the marriage of the vertical and the horizontal (that is, the making of visible order through the Right Angle) and with human creation in general, the still life can be seen as oriented towards creativity.[71] The image of earthly marriage always alludes to hierogamy (primordially, the marriage between heaven and earth), and thus to cosmic creation, the making of order out of chaos.[72] Thus Le Corbusier attempts to resituate human dwelling within a traditional cosmic context. This illustrates the proposition that his paintings aspire, within his architecture, to the role of microcosmic ornament.

The meaning of the lantern

The carafe and the dark bottle form two poles around the group, like a pair of caryatids supporting a notional entablature or proscenium arch. They stand in front of the box lantern (a humble, mass-produced tool and *objet-type*), which is another thematic object for Le Corbusier, carrying numerous meanings. On the first level, the lantern is a source of light. Traditionally, being the purest and least material of elements, light was considered the most ideal and ethical, allied with truth and the good. It was closely linked with geometry and mathematics as a transcendent giver of form and order.[73] The lamp is a beacon illuminating the path towards enlightenment, a guide to the life of *L'Esprit Nouveau*.[74] It is in these senses that Le Corbusier deploys the image in his reported

6.5

Le Corbusier, *Le Soir*, 1958, Nordjyllands Kunstmuseum. Collage FLC 152. © FLC/ADAGP, Paris and DACS, London, 2002

exhortation 'Let this lamp be lit to-day and folly be confounded.'[75] In nine-teenth-century art, the lantern is often associated with Christ. Since Le Corbusier saw himself as a prophetic bringer of the teachings of Purism within his salvational programme, and his iconographic world is often strongly autobiographical; one may even venture to affiliate the lantern with his own persona.[76] As a geometrically configured aedicule and an agent of transformation (purification) through light, the lantern echoes the structure of the still-life 'niches' themselves. The mass-produced lantern – orthogonal and enclosive – can be seen in Le Corbusier's work as a notional shelter (primitive hut) or standard house. The box of the lantern, open on one side and surmounted by a cylinder, recalls the sus-pended gardens and virtual rooms of the Pavillon de l'Esprit Nouveau and the Villa Stein, both of which at one time had an oculus. This reading is reinforced by its square or cubic geometry, an ideal form which Le Cor-busier considered, due to the square's stability and traditional links with

163

the earthly domain, particularly well suited to the house.[77] It features in this way in the paintings, acting as a setting or shelter to assorted objects. In this regard, it is related to the many prefabricated *casiers*, the housing for all kinds of things, which so enraptured Le Corbusier, and which furnish his architecture of the 1920s. Some of Le Corbusier's later variations on the theme suggest an interesting link between the lantern-house and the female figure. In *Le Soir*, for example, the crouching female nude assumes a sheltering, embracing position with respect to the still-life table. The figure echoes the form of the aedicular lantern in the picture, suggesting a thematic parallel. This is reminiscent of the archaic analogy

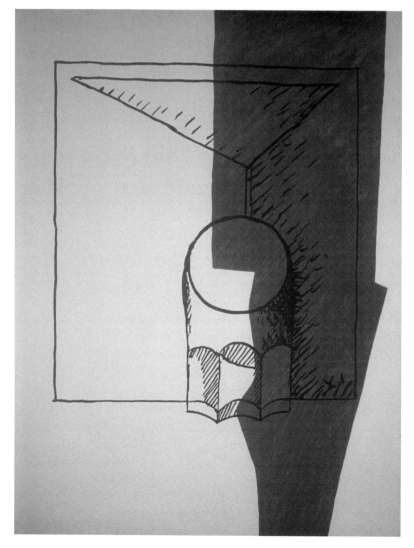

6.6
Le Corbusier, The Lantern and Glass sign, first plate of Le *Poème de l'angle droit*, 1955.
© FLC/ADAGP, Paris and DACS, London, 2002

between the female principle and the concave house (both also allied with home and shelter).[78] Keeping all of these meanings in mind, the lantern, with the anthropomorphic tumbler inside it, becomes an image of inhabited architecture or dwelling. Furthermore, the concave house-lantern and the cylindrical, phallic glass reiterate the image of the marriage of opposites, and thus of creativity, the essential component of the Corbusian understanding of dwelling. The merging of the orthogonal, 'droit' and ideal order of the architectural frame with the curved and human quality of the glass can be seen as a representation of the marriage of cosmic and human order to which Le Corbusier sometimes alluded. It is in this sense of earthly dwelling, I believe, that Le Corbusier uses the lantern and glass sign as the opening plate of his *Poème de l'angle droit*.[79]

The Purist niche as a magic box of transformation

The fluid, metamorphic character of Purist still life enables the shallow box of its pictorial space to be read as a magic theatre of transformation. A cross between a shop window (a source of fascination for the Purists and Surrealists) and an alchemical laboratory, such paintings speak of the power of 'l'Esprit Nouveau' to transform life. The humble utensils assembled are a kind of base matter which, through the artist's efforts, can be refined and transformed into the gold of 'harmony'. The fact that most of the objects are vessels reinforces this proposition.[80] While he was not the kind of determined alchemist that some commentators have suggested,[81] the secret mystical discipline of alchemy permeated Parisian culture at this time, and offered him numerous metaphorical allusions – such as his references to 'crystals' and 'quintessence' (the philosopher's stone) in connection with the Villa Stein – for his own enterprise. The palpable visual harmony achieved in some of the best Purist works is the kind of higher reality, the philosophers' gold, sought also for example by the Surrealists in their poetry. Akin to such themes is the iconography of wine, popular in both Cubist and Purist works. Traditionally, wine is linked to ecstasy and cosmic fecundity, to sacrifice and regeneration. Suggestive of the Dionysian realm, wine in still life evokes the earthy, primary dimensions of experience and of the imagination. As thematized in these paintings, wine also carries another layer of significance. The transformation, through fermentation, of humble grape juice into wine, becomes a metaphor for the quasi-alchemical transformation which the Purist subject matter undergoes in the mysterious niche, cum-alchemical laboratory of the painting. A similar transformation, involving the interplay of vessels, reconciliation of opposites and secret discipline, was envisioned in the purified life of *L'Esprit Nouveau*.

*The aedicule or virtual house in Le Corbusier's architecture: Villa
Stein de Monzie*

The implicit 'niches' of the Purist still lifes were an important form of ornament in Le Corbusier's early architecture. In parallel and thematically
related to this phenomenon, the aedicular motif developed into an interesting architectural theme as well. The examples of such niches, virtual houses
or miniature 'temples' in the work are numerous. Among the most highly
developed are those at the Villa Stein de Monzie at Garches. The villa represents one of the summits of the development of Le Corbusier's thinking on
the renewal of the culture of dwelling through the secular sacred and
through creativity in the Purist period, and a paradigm for life in the new
city. The house contains a number of niche–virtual house configurations at
different scales both inside and out. Often, these implicit 'houses' are
equipped with their own miniature version of a garden, tree and oculus,
elements traditionally belonging to the temple. Le Corbusier had rehearsed
this configuration at the Pavillon de l'Esprit Nouveau, where the tree of the
'suspended' garden had penetrated the oculus. It is a situational grouping
which, in addition to its congenial qualities, comes for him to constitute a
miniature re-enactment of a temple, a kind of *imago mundi*. The first level
of this hierarchical representation at Garches lies in the main suspended
garden, which is inseparably linked to the house by its proportional structure.[82] The metaphoric house is characterised by the ambiguity of inside and
outside which plays such a pervasive role in Le Corbusier's poetic
representation.[83] It is constituted by basic elements of enclosure, and has its
own set of articulated elevations, its own 'roof garden' and its horizon of the
balustrade. In both the photos of the inside of this terrace in the *Œuvre
complète* I, careful use has been made of shadows to amplify its secondary
reading as a self-contained room/house. The small photo of the space
looking towards the south garden is taken in the morning, before the sun
begins to penetrate it.[84] As a result, the line of the shadow still almost aligns
with the boundary between the 'inside' and 'outside', marked by the transition in the floor finish from ceramic tiles to concrete paving slabs. The
space of the terrace is thus a 'room' of shadow, thematically reminiscent of
the various other dark recesses and niches of the *casiers* and of his architecture. The shadowy foreground area below the dark underside of the
intermediate terrace is spectrally inhabited by a grouping of characteristically animate outdoor furniture, while in the background the small, two-
shelved niche holding objects is visible. The quasi-sacred iconography of
this archetypal house/temple was reinforced by the small hearth-niche, the
oculus of the secondary terrace above, and a concrete altar-like table (which
was not realised).

The second restatement of this theme occurs in the house-within-a-house below the secondary, lower terrace. The integrity of this 'room' within the main terrace is articulated by its roof, and by the cut-out in the west wall above it. This 'room' originally had a large oculus in its roof beside the area of glass block floor.[85] The third restatement occurs with the small niche built into the chimney on the east wall of the suspended garden.

6.7
Le Corbusier, Villa
Stein de Monzie,
Garches, 1927.
Rear, garden
elevation © FLC
L1(10)41.
© FLC/ADAGP, Paris
and DACS, London,
2002

It has a narrow middle shelf and a wider bottom shelf which extends beyond the niche, echoing in miniature the form of the larger terrace space in which it is situated. Being associated with the chimney stack behind it, this little alcove has the connotations of a hearth. This recess is also a variation of a Purist still life, its shallow box of space framing a grouping of *objets-type*. It is somewhat reminiscent of an aedicular household shrine (the *lararium* of the Roman house, for example) where offerings were laid during domestic ceremonies. There are several more instances of such niches in the house, each such part a miniature recapitulation of the whole. These include the central top-floor bathroom loggia on the north façade – a little outside aedicule dedicated to purification, proportionately equivalent to the whole elevation and surmounted by its own oculus – and the temple-like roof gazebo. The hierarchical series of restatements of the theme of dwelling were presumably intended to encourage the cultured inhabitants of the house to engage in daily microcosmic re-enactments of certain paradigmatic events and, through their actions, to reflect on the greater cosmic drama. This makes the house an eloquent expression of the kind of meditative self-awareness essential for the radiant new society. As in so much modernism, the architectural drama is played out within the intimate private domain, leaving little for the public sphere of the city.

The thematics of niches and implicit houses in Le Corbusier's work can thus be seen as an attempt to re-infuse architecture with the kind of deep culture which he found, for example, in the Pompeiian houses he had so admired as a young man. The hierarchical restatement of this theme in his architecture (a kind of 'multiplication of shrines'), was a way of suggesting a sense of hoped-for renewal, and of reinterpreting the ancient tradition of ornament for the modern architecture of the twentieth century.

Le Corbusier's grave at Cap Martin
Finally, the sepulchral monument that Le Corbusier designed for his wife Yvonne and himself at the time of her death in 1957, comprises a rudimentary, aedicular house or temple, a cylinder holding a miniature cactus 'tree', and a tiny garden in the slab of the four-quartered podium. Built on the plateau of the Roquebrune cemetery, this podium appears to float, Acropolis-like, above the distant horizon of the Mediterranean Sea, where the architect was to meet his own death some eight years later. The configuration can be seen as another variation of the lantern and glass theme, and a final evocation of dwelling. Echoing the house-shaped and phallic-post grave markers of ancient Mediterranean burials, the two miniature structures also have the connotations of female and male respectively (thus suggesting dwelling together in the afterlife). The painting on the enamel-

plaque door to the ash-urn container reiterates the iconographic theme of the union, at the level of the horizon, of male (the sun) and female (the sea), of heaven and earth, as a beginning of a new cosmic cycle.

Le Corbusier's meditations in his work on the theme of dwelling are oriented towards some of the same ideas which also animated his urban thought. And while his work undoubtedly sometimes suffers from the excessively private, arcane, and all-encompassing nature of his iconographic system, his meditations at the smaller scale are richly imaginative and metaphorical. They reveal a fruitful use of tradition, deeply rooted as they are in a number of timeless symbolic themes, most notably the archetypal acts of dwelling and building. The lantern and glass configuration is an example of a theme which retains a strong, recognisable residue of primary meaning. Le Corbusier's treatment of the ethical dimension of dwelling as a vehicle towards the regeneration of modern society has an authenticity and richness extremely rare in twentieth-century architecture.

Notes

1 Le Corbusier, *Creation is a Patient Search*, New York, Praeger, 1960, p. 14.

2 The term 'dwelling' is used throughout in the Heideggerian sense of being situated within the world, and within certain constant cosmic conditions.

3 While undoubtedly illuminating about both the new movement and the sensibilities of its authors, these writings cannot always be taken at face value, as some things (such as the logical basis of the new art) were overemphasised, while others (the more metaphorical, quasi-mystical aims) remained implicit. To get a truer view of the full Purist agenda, it is necessary to examine the paintings, buildings and published photographs in conjunction with the texts.

4 On this phenomenon, see C. Rowe's writings, especially *The Architecture of Good Intentions*, London, Academy, 1994. The importing of quasi-theological imagery into the polemics of architecture is rooted in late nineteenth-century preoccupation with reinjecting the spiritual into art. Many of these efforts are charted in the LACMA, *The Spiritual in Art: Abstract Painting 1890–1985*, Exhibition Catalogue, New York, Abbeville, 1986. A similar interest in the spiritual is evident in much German theory of the early twentieth century. In Purism, these ideas resonate, for example, in the polyvalent term *esprit*. The Purist terms *bonheur*, harmony, or later *unité* also carry something of this quasi-mystical content.

5 This is the title of Chapter 8 of Le Corbusier's *The Radiant City*, London, Faber, 1967. Originally published as *La Ville Radieuse,* Paris, Vincent, Fréal & Cie, 1933.

6 Le Corbusier, *The Radiant City*, p. 94.

7 Colin Rowe was an important early commentator on the implicit aims behind modern architecture in his influential teaching in the 1960s. His work was often published only later, as in *Collage City* (written with Fred Koetter), Cambridge, MA, MIT, 1978, and *The Architecture of Good Intentions*. Iain Boyd Whyte's valuable work on the Expressionist Utopias addresses related issues in the contemporaneous German context: *The Crystal Chain Letters: Architectural Fantasies of Bruno Taut and his Circle*, Cambridge, MA, MIT, c.1985. See also his 'Expressionist Sublime', in T. Benson *et al.*, *Expressionist Utopias: Paradise, Metropolis, Architectural Fantasy*, Los Angeles, LACMA, 1993, pp. 118–37, and 'The Expressionist Utopia', *Macjournal* 4, 1999, pp. 76–84.

8 The idea of a *realisable* earthly paradise can be traced back to the Utopian visions and ideal cities of the Renaissance. It is, however, clearly expressed as a vehicle of social reform by Enlightenment thinkers, the Garden City, and the Arts and Crafts movements. In medieval imagery, Heavenly Jerusalem is usually represented as a walled city of towers, laid out according to an ideal geometric order. However, the symbolic, ethical order underlying this paradigm is much deeper than the perspectival order which shaped the Radiant City.

9 This is implicit in Le Corbusier's earliest urban writings. In *The Home of Man* (written with F. de Pierrefeu, London, The Architectural Press, 1948), he restates it with clarity:

> For it is essential in the final reckoning, that the town planner and the architect should again erect the settings of the golden age. Man-nature, social relations between men: ... manifestations of a consciousness illuminated by the 'essential joys.' A symphony, a harmony.
>
> (p. 102)

This passage is illustrated by a print of a golden age ('an age in which chaos was banished, before the birth of present covetousness'). This print (after J. B. Huet) decorated, as Le Corbusier says, his office at the time. Interestingly, Le Corbusier's golden age has a geometrical order (since chaos is banished), as does his Radiant City.

10 'Great blocks of dwellings run through the town. What does it matter? They are behind a screen of trees.' Le Corbusier, in connection with his plan for Rio de Janeiro in *The Home of Man*, p. 91. This book also contains a long illustrated passage on the interaction of nature (especially trees) and the new city. The issue is already amply illustrated in *The City of Tomorrow and its Planning*, London, John Rodker, 1929, originally published as *Urbanisme*, Paris, Crès et Cié, 1925, for example, p. 200, and *The Radiant City*, p. 205.

11 See, for example, *The Home of Man*, p. 97: 'And the "essential joys" have entered the dwelling . . . Trees are present in the room of the dwelling.'

12 This appealing motif, seen as ideal for the new standard dwelling, was apparently in part inspired by the self-contained monk's house and garden of Carthusian monasteries. Le Corbusier wrote to his parents in 1907: 'Ah, les Chartreaux! Je voudrais toute ma vie habiter ce qu'ils appellent leur cellules. C'est la solution de la maison ouvrière, type unique ou plutôt du Paradis terrestre.' P. Saddy and C. Malécot (eds) *Le Corbusier: Le Passé à réaction poétique*, Paris, Caisse Nationale des Monuments Historiques et des Sites, 1988, p. 79.

13 Le Corbusier, for example, refers to the 'devil's air' (p. 41) which fills the dark and narrow streets of these 'cities of despair' (p. 44).

> The city is swelling . . . The street becomes appalling, noisy, dusty, dangerous . . . The pedestrians herded together on the sidewalks, get in each other's way, bump into each other, zigzag from side to side; the whole scene is a glimpse of purgatory . . . torrid canyons of summer heat . . . air tainted with dust and soot . . . streets so full of mortal peril. How can anyone achieve the serenity indispensable to life . . . or feel drunk with sunlight? How can anyone *live*?
>
> (Le Corbusier, *The Radiant City*, p. 91, original emphasis)

14 Le Corbusier, *The Radiant City*, p. 91.

15 The ethical content of the new city had already been expounded by Le Corbusier in *The City of Tomorrow* (see, for example, pp. 177–8). In *The Radiant City*, among references to light and geometric clarity, he for example extols the virtues of 'Liberty, Equality, Fraternity' (p. 11), urging the creation of a new, egalitarian society, in which 'it is better to give than to receive' (p. 15), and where 'spiritual values' will triumph over greed and corruption' (p. 14). The city is seen in terms of the perfect balance between a private meditative experience (the dwelling, 'a vessel of silence and lofty solitude') and citizenship or civic activity 'achieved by the harmonious grouping of creative impulses directed towards the public good' (p. 67).

16 The imagery of the crystal, a popular theme in late nineteenth and early twentieth-century artistic circles, plays a complex and interesting role in Le Corbusier's thought. To summarise some of its meaning: the crystal, as an icon of purity, truth, perfection and harmony, has a strong ethical content for Le Corbusier. See, for example, his 'Architecture d'époque machiniste', *Journal de Psychologie Normale et Pathologique*, Paris, 1926, p. 22. It is the pure embodiment of the laws of nature: its geometric order and organic growth. Nature's creative process of crystallisation is seen as a paradigm for human creative achievement. Representing the emergence of order out of chaos, the crystal is a paradigm of creativity generally. In Symbolism and Surrealism, with their emphasis on the transformation of reality, the crystal, and especially the diamond, takes on the connotations of the philosopher's stone, the ultimate goal of the alchemical Opus, and the saviour of the world. The crystal, together with glass and gold, is also the material of the Heavenly Jerusalem of St John's vision. These themes are examined in D. Motycka Weston, 'The Problem of Space in Early Twentieth-Century Art and Architecture', Ph.D. dissertation, University of Cambridge, 1994, Chapter 7. Le Corbusier was perhaps influenced in this area by Peter Behrens, in whose practice he had received some of his architectural initiation. Drawing on Nietzschean mysticism and the alchemical correspondence between the crystal and the philosopher's stone, Behrens had

chosen the crystal as an emblem of the *Gesamtkunstwerk* for the artists' colony at Darmstadt. See R. H. Bletter, 'The Interpretation of the Glass Dream – Expressionist Architecture and the History of the Crystal Metaphor', *Journal of Architectural Historians*, March 1981, pp. 20–43.

17 Le Corbusier, *The Radiant City*, p. 14. This painting is an illustration to Petrarch's 'The Triumph of Death'.

18 Le Corbusier, *The Radiant City*, p. 152. The sculpture in question is a small figure of Abraham with three of the elect, from a voussoir of the central, Last Judgement portal of the south transept. Le Corbusier's caption below the photograph reads 'Chartres: Eternally permissible product: the work of art, final end of human nature', suggesting the possibility of the ultimate redemption of humanity through art.

19 Whitewash is zealously urged as an instrument of moral order in Le Corbusier, 'A Coat of Whitewash, the Law of Ripolin', in *The Decorative Art of Today* (orig. 1925), London, The Architectural Press, 1987, pp. 186–92.

20 Indeed, further in his caption, Le Corbusier acknowledges an affinity between them.

21 The hand features prominently in Le Corbusier's imagery throughout his life. The late *Poème de l'angle droit*, Paris, FLC/Editions Connivances, 1989. is punctuated by a series of cryptic hand gestures, inspired perhaps by his study of mystical Indian hand signals. The different manifestations include the hand that gives and receives, the creative hand reconciling opposites (through the making of the right angle, or inter-clasping, as in the Ascoral diagram). There is also the metaphorically masturbatory, creative hand (see plate C2 of the *Poème*, where Le Corbusier's hand, poised over his menhir-like penis, is juxtaposed with the crouching nude figure of Yvonne), apparently deriving from Egyptian creation myth, where Amun's hand is represented as the wife of the god, which stimulates him to create the universe. See H. Frankfort, *Kingship and the Gods*, Chicago, University of Chicago Press, 1948, p. 153. The hand/dove reading of the Chandigarh monument (in addition to its allusion to peace) can also, in my view, be seen as an evocation to the reciprocity of the body (hand) and soul or spirit (bird/dove), the marriage of earth and heaven (cosmic renewal). It is another expression of the perennial Corbusian theme of the 'fusion of matter and spirit', seen in the *Hand and Flint* painting.

22 The pose of the hand in this painting, with open fingers and palm turned towards the viewer, is the same as that of the interlocking hands of the Engineer and the Architect in the Ascoral diagram (which later reappears as plate A5 of the *Poème*), suggesting thus the conciliation of supposed opposites.

23 'Tenderness . . . Hand kneading hand caressing/hand brushing. The hand and the seashell love each other.' Le Corbusier, section C3 Flesh, *Poème de l'angle droit*.

24 'To make architecture is/to make a creature', Le Corbusier, section E4, *Poème de l'angle droit*.

25 The term is used in the sense of Heidegger's notion of familiar things being 'ready-to-hand'.

26 The key mediating role and lyrical significance attributed by Le Corbusier to tools is evident in his dedication of the concluding section G3 of his *Poème* to the *outil* (the French word itself celebrating usefulness).

27 Le Corbusier's emphasis on personal creativity, rooted in the Romantic ethos of the artist, is already evident in his earliest writings. See, for example, Le Corbusier, *The Decorative Art of Today*, p. 192.

28 Building on the Arts and Crafts aim of replacing dehumanising toil with creative work, Le Corbusier elevates creative action further, to the highest kind of ethical endeavour, emulating the creativity of nature. This requirement places, one would imagine, considerable demands on the inhabitants of this Utopia.

29 For example, see Le Corbusier's tribute to Louis XIV at the end of *The City of Tomorrow*.

30 Traditionally (in Classical or Gothic architecture, for example), ornament was an inseparable part of the meaning of architecture. That meaning, particularly in sacred buildings, referred

to the order of the whole: cosmos. Our word for facial ornamentation, cosmetics, retains something of this ancient meaning. This idea is implicit in Owen Jones's emphasis on facial tattoo as the earliest form of ornament among 'savage tribes'. *The Grammar of Ornament*, London, Day and Son, 1856, p. 13. Le Corbusier recalled how during his training in La Chaux-de-Fonds, his mentor Charles L'Eplattenier, saw ornament in this microcosmic way:

> My master had said: 'Only nature can give us inspiration . . . Study its causes, forms and vital development, and synthesize them in the creation of *ornaments.*' He had an exalted conception of ornament, which he saw as a kind of microcosm.'
>
> (Le Corbusier, *The Decorative Art of Today*, p. 194, original emphasis)

The young Jeanneret's understanding of ornament is evident in his numerous travel drawings, museum studies and in his early houses. See especially P. Saddy and C. Malécot (eds) *Le Corbusier: Le Passé à réaction poétique.*

31 This is perhaps best exemplified by the Villa Fallet and the Cernier-Fontainmelon Chapel interior. See Mary Sekler's discussion of their ornamental schemes in 'Ruskin, the Tree and the Open Hand', in R. Walden (ed.) *The Open Hand Essays on Le Corbusier*, Cambridge, MA, MIT Press, 1982, p. 61. There are striking affinities between Purist theory and the position put forward by Owen Jones in *The Grammar of Ornament*. Jones's insistence on beauty resulting from appropriateness and truth, on the regulating laws of nature, on the significance in ornamental art of geometry and proportion, and his admiration for the power of the primitive, all have echoes in Purist texts. Interestingly, Jones associates ornament with primal creativity (which expressed itself originally in facial ornament).

32 Le Corbusier, *The Radiant City*, p. 67. This private meditation is to be offset by the civic activities of the city. The model for this vision of private contemplation and communal participation appears, again, to be the Carthusian monastery.

33 Le Corbusier, *New World of Space*, New York, Reynal & Hitchcock, 1948, p. 8.

34 The original photograph of Raoul La Roche's bedroom is reproduced in T. Benton, *The Villas of Le Corbusier* New Haven, Yale University Press, 1987, p. 74.

35 Le Corbusier, *The Modulor*, London, Faber, 1954, p. 74.

36 This is evident from their art, which was indebted to Cubist preoccupations with different aspects of embodied experience (a detailed discussion is contained in Motycka Weston, 'The Problem of Space', especially Chapters 2 and 6). In his writings, Le Corbusier, for example, sometimes refers more or less explicitly to the wonder of lived vision, belonging to the primary dimension of experience which modern man needs to rediscover.

37 Colin Rowe was among the first commentators on the structure of Purist space, beginning with his influential 'transparency' studies (with R. Slutzky and B. Hoesli) in the 1950s and 1960s. The phrase is owed to Peter Carl.

38 Le Corbusier, *Precisions on the State of Architecture and City Planning* (originally 1930), English translation, Cambridge, MA, MIT Press, 1991, pp. 8–9.

39 The phrase belongs to Dalibor Vesely. See his 'Architecture and the Ambiguity of the Fragment', in Robin Middleton (ed.) *The Idea of the City*, London, Architectural Association, 1996.

40 This notion is implicit in Colin Rowe's essay 'The Provocative Façade: Frontality and Contraposto', in M. Raeburn and V. Wilson (eds) *Le Corbusier: Architect of the Century*, Exhibition Catalogue, London, Arts Council of Great Britain, 1987, pp. 24–8. Recently, Daniel Neagele has highlighted a similar projection/niche ambivalence in certain Le Corbusier photographs in his 'Photographic Illusionism in the "New World of Space"', in *Le Corbusier: Painter and Architect*, exhibition catalogue, Aalborg, Nordjyllands Kunstmuseum and FLC, 1995, pp. 83–117.

41 This work is reproduced in W. Rubin, *Picasso and Braque: Pioneering Cubism*, Exhibition Catalogue, New York, MOMA, 1989, p. 322.

42 It is this dimension of Cubist assemblage which proved such a fertile inspiration for the Russian Constructivists, who honed the process of architectural making (through the notion of the *faktura*) into a metaphor and model for the construction of the envisioned new egalitarian society. Le Corbusier felt an affinity with the Russian avant-garde, especially around the issues of social justice. The idea of constructing art using real, everyday materials and objects (as a critique of the traditional art materials of oil paint, marble and bronze), and thus producing highly heterogeneous objects, was gaining currency among a wide spectrum of artists. Ready-mades were used by both Picasso and Duchamp in 1914. All of this reflects the new iconic significance accorded to the humble daily object, which also animated Purism.

43 This was the cardboard guitar (illustrated in Rubin, *Picasso and Braque: Pioneering Cubism* p. 251), which was the model for the famous sheet metal version. This assemblability is suggestive of the notion, dear to Le Corbusier, of the mass-production of typical objects, of the kit-of-parts standard house which would be used to make up the new city. For Le Corbusier the idea of construction/assembly from a set of purified, constant elements (the *objets* in his paintings, the *type* elements in his houses etc.) would eventually take on a complex meaning allied with the regeneration of society and, most importantly, with the democratic vision of individual creativity which was the ethical motor of the new city.

44 This work is reproduced in C. Green, *Léger and Purist Paris*, London, Tate Gallery, 1970, p. 37.

45 Le Corbusier et Pierre Jeanneret, *Œuvre Complète, 1910–1929*, 14th edn, Zurich, Éditions d'Architecture, 1995, p. 55.

46 The reference here is to what Merleau-Ponty calls the phenomenon of 'constancy' – the curious fact, explored by the Cubists, that the forms which we know are not subject to the limited viewpoint of perspectival representation. Rather, familiar things retain their memorable form and stable essence regardless of the momentary position of the observer. This notion acknowledges the role played by memory and the imagination in perception. M. Merleau-Ponty, *The Phenomenology of Perception*, London, Routledge, 1962, pp. 8, 46, 313.

47 Although Le Corbusier denied a direct influence of Surrealism, he was immersed in the same Parisian culture. His thinking in many areas (such as the primary role of perception and the imagination, the power of the erotic, alchemy and the occultation of geometry) bears a strong affinity with that of the Surrealists. When on occasion he referred explicitly to their work, it was generally to praise their achievement in unlocking a fresh and exciting domain of figurative meaning in art, drawing on dream and the imagination. See, for example, Le Corbusier's text in J. Petit (ed.) *Le Corbusier: Suite de dessins*, Paris, Editions Forces Vives, 1964, n.p.

48 Some of Le Corbusier's preparatory sketches for this painting indicate his explorations of the book as both a convex object and a concave niche within the painting. See Raeburn and Wilson (eds) *Le Corbusier: Architect of the Century*, pl. 48. The table top was similarly ambiguous. See Le Corbusier sketches in G. Baker, *Le Corbusier: The Creative Search*, New York, Van Nostrand Reinhold, 1996, p. 253.

49 His later wood sculptures, carried out in collaboration with Joseph Savina, illustrate the paintings' plastic potential. See also C. Green in Raeburn and Wilson (eds) *Le Corbusier: Architect of the Century,* p. 119.

50 Le Corbusier, *New World of Space*, New York, Reynal & Hitchcock, 1948, p. 16.

51 The art of the Surrealists, for example, has shown the primordial kinship of phenomena as they are given to our perception. Reality is experienced as a world of latent, mysterious connections and affinities. This is in contrast to the supposed sum of unrelated facts characteristic of an objectified understanding. Metaphoricity arises spontaneously, helping us make sense of the world.

52 This is memorably discussed in J. Rykwert, *On Adam's House in Paradise,* New York, MOMA,

1972. See also his 'One Way of Thinking about a House', in *The Necessity of Artifice*, London, Academy, 1982, pp. 85–7, and John Summerson, 'Heavenly Mansions: An Interpretation of Gothic', in *Heavenly Mansions and Other Essays on Architecture*, New York, Norton & Co., 1963.

53 Rykwert, *On Adam's House*, pp. 191–2.

54 In traditional iconography, the temple, the house of the gods on earth and an imitation of divine order and perfection, remained distinct from the house until the Renaissance. It was chiefly due to the efforts of Andrea Palladio that pedimented temple fronts, previously the preserve of religious structures, became a dominant motif of domestic architecture. Palladio's justification for his apparent violation of Vitruvian *decorum* was the argument that the house preceded the temple and gave it its form. J. Ackerman, *Palladio*, Harmondsworth, Penguin, 1966, pp. 61–5. By the twentieth century, through the thematics of the 'secular sacred', Le Corbusier was able to use these paradigms interchangeably.

55 *L'Esprit Nouveau* 5, 1921, reprinted in *Towards a New Architecture*, London, John Rodker, 1927, pp. 65–79.

56 Summerson, *Heavenly Mansions*, p. 18. Summerson stops short, however, of seeing this as symbolising the Heavenly City.

57 See J. P. Vernant, *Myth and Thought Among the Greeks*, London, Routledge & Kegan Paul, 1983, pp. 127–33, and J. Rykwert, *The Idea of a Town: the anthropology of urban form in Rome, Italy and the Ancient World*, Cambridge, MA, MIT Press, 1976, pp. 99–109.

58 Le Corbusier, *Mise au Point*, Geneva, Editions Archigraphie, 1987, p. 34, excerpted in 'Nothing is Transmissible but Thought', in Le Corbusier, *The Last Works*, London, Thames & Hudson, 1970, p. 176.

59 I am indebted to Peter Carl for the notion of the 'secular sacred'. See his 'Natura Morta', *Modulus* 20, 1991, pp. 27–70.

60 Le Corbusier, *Creation is a Patient Search*, pp. 54–5.

61 P. Carl, 'Le Corbusier's Penthouse in Paris, 24 Rue Nungesser-et-Coli', *Daidalos*, 1988, p. 67.

62 Le Corbusier, *Œuvre Complète* I, p. 23.

63 Le Corbusier endowed his reinforced concrete frame with the iconography of an ideal, universal order (represented by the purity of its modern materials and form, its *'droiture'*, and bearing a resemblance to the ideal grids of his cities). Motycka Weston, 'The Problem of Space', Chapter 7.

64 1914, The Tate Gallery, London.

65 A detailed discussion of this theme is contained in Motycka Weston, 'The Window: Some Reflections on its Meaning', *Scroope Architecture Journal* 3, 1991.

66 The interchangeability of the laid table and a woman (or marital bed) as the twin symbols of marriage was noted in his patients' dreams by Freud. W. Spies, *Max Ernst: Loplop: The Artist's Other Self*, London, Thames & Hudson, 1983, p. 99.

67 Ozenfant and C. E. Jeanneret, 'Purism', reprinted in R. Herbert (ed.) *Modern Artists on Art: Ten Unabridged Essays*, Englewood Cliffs, NJ, Prentice Hall, 1964, p. 64.

68 Beside the Cubist examples, this metaphoric affinity was made explicit by Man Ray, when he superimposed f-holes on a photograph of the nude back of a female model in *Ingre's Violin* (1924). Also, musical instruments, through music, partake of cosmic harmonic proportions, in a similar way as traditionally does the human body.

69 Other related works are illustrated in Mogens Krustrup, 'Le Soir', in *Le Corbusier: Painter and Architect*, pp. 158–65.

70 Peter Carl provides an illuminating interpretation of this Corbusian sign, which he aligns, among other meanings, with the thematics of typicality, tool, and of the horizon. 'Standard: "Tout devient étrange et se transforme"', unpublished draft 1993. Krustrup draws attention to this sign as being swastika-like (*Le Corbusier: Painter and Architect*, p. 163), presumably representing nature's eternal fecundity.

71 The idea of the making of the right angle as a kind of marriage is encapsulated in the G3
    plate of the *Poème de l'angle droit*, which shows the artist's hand drawing a cross with a piece
    of charcoal in a kind of uterine enclosure (Carl has aptly dubbed this form 'the cranial womb
    in which architecture is conceived'. 'Ornament and Time: A Prolegomena', *AA Files* 23, 1992,
    p. 56). The gesture of the clasped hand, with thumb and index finger making a circle, is a
    vernacular sign for sexual intercourse. One must also note the regenerative connotations of
    the cross.

72 On the cosmic renewal inherent in hierogamy, see, for example, M. Eliade, *The Myth of the
    Eternal Return*, London, Arcana, 1989, pp. 23–5.

73 The somewhat facile way in which Le Corbusier is ready to equate an ethical with a
    mathematical order is a striking feature of his polemics.

74 For a summary of the traditional iconography of light, see O. von Simson, *The Gothic
    Cathedral*, Princeton, NJ, Princeton University Press, 1988, pp. 50–5. Le Corbusier's attitude
    to light, especially at this early stage, clearly echoed many of these traditional meanings,
    having a distinctly ethical content. Keeping in mind his soteriological programme, there are,
    for example, interesting hints that a significant aim in flooding the dwelling with sunlight
    (with which Le Corbusier credits the reinforced concrete frame and strip windows (see
    'L'Architecture d'époque machiniste', pp. 30–2) was the liberation (through a kind of
    resurrection) of corporeal man to a higher spiritual plane and 'eternal life'. Similarly, the
    theme of creation and creativity, which was to play the chief regenerative role in the
    envisioned new city, seems to be linked back to its symbolic antecedents as a function of
    illumination. This rich thematic content makes light an essential element in the programme
    of ethical transformation and renewal to be accomplished by Purist art and architecture.

75 See note 1.

76 Here one needs to recall Paul Turner's argument in *The Education of Le Corbusier*, New York,
    Garland Publishing, 1977, about the influence on the young Jeanneret of the style of thought
    presented by Eduard Schuré in *Les Grands Initiés,* to the point where he was able to identify
    himself with Christ. Mogens Krustrup, writing about the numerous hidden self-portraits in Le
    Corbusier's work and coming from a different direction, has interestingly interpreted the lamp,
    especially as it appears in its linear, luminous crystal form in works such as *La Lanterne et le
    petit haricot* (1930), as Le Corbusier's self-portrait (allied to the stone head/philosopher's stone
    portrait in the *Poème*). He saw the sign of the lantern and glass in the *Poème* as one of a series
    of double self-portraits, with Yvonne represented by the uterine glass, and Le Corbusier by the
    lamp. M. Krustrup, 'Persona', in *Le Corbusier: Painter and Architect*, especially pp. 134–40.

77 See Le Corbusier, *Une Maison – un palais*, Paris, Crès et Cié, 1928, p. 6.

78 This analogy is manifest, for example, in Etruscan burial hut urns. The house is here
    identified with the body or soul of the dead, but also with the womb of the earth, to which
    the deceased returns.

79 The motif of the subdivided rectangle formed by the face of the lantern in the *Pale Still Life* is
    one which can be found in other Le Corbusier compositions (for example, in the plans of the
    Villa Stein). However, Le Corbusier was aware of the possible significance of similar
    rectangles in sacred architecture (see Rykwert's *On Adam's House*). Interestingly, an
    examination of the underlying geometrical structure of this painting reveals a series of at
    least three proportionally similar rectangles in ascending size. If one accepts the lantern as a
    sign for an inhabited dwelling, one may then suggest that these repeating rectangles are a
    further elaboration of the theme of enclosure.

80 In furnishing the *casiers* of the Pavillon d'Esprit Nouveau, Le Corbusier used real laboratory
    crucibles as examples of machine-made practical ware. Yet these also make an implicit
    reference to the work of the alchemist. See Le Corbusier, *Almanach de l'architecture moderne*,
    Paris, Crès et Cié, 1926, pp. 159, 168, 169.

81 See Richard Moore, 'Alchemical and Mythical Themes in the Poem of the Right Angle 1947–1955', *Oppositions* 19/20, Winter Spring 1980, pp. 111–39.

82 In elevation these were linked by the Golden Section ratio, as Le Corbusier emphasised in the published elevation drawings (*Œuvre Complète 1910–29*, p. 144). The volumes of the house/cube and of the large terrace were also proportionally related as successive elements of the Golden Mean spiral.

83 As a further manifestation of the persistence of the theme of the fruitful ambiguity of inside and outside, see Le Corbusier's revealing series of sketches entitled 'The Outside is always an Inside', in *Precisions on the Present State of Architecture and City Planning*, Cambridge, Mass, MIT Press, 1991, pp. 78–9.

84 Le Corbusier, *Œuvre Complète I*, p. 145.

85 Construction photos show that this oculus was actually built, but was later filled in, leaving only the glass block panel.

Part III

Faith

Omnipresent in the discussion on the city and on the architecture appropriate to it in the twentieth century is the image of the New Jerusalem. Beyond the obvious benefits of improved health, higher productivity, and social accord, the reform of the city and of the conditions of urban existence, it was argued, would bring moral and ethical improvement. The three chapters in this section critique this proposal.

Chapter 7

'Cities more fair to become the dwelling place of Thy children'

Transcendent modernity in British urban reconstruction

Rhodri Windsor Liscombe

The quotation in the title of this chapter was printed on the title page of the 1941 Bourneville Village Trust Research Publication *When We Build Again: A Study Based on Research into Conditions of Living and Working in Birmingham*.[1] The phrase is taken from the prayer recited by the Bishop of Birmingham at the Civic Service organised in the Anglican Cathedral on 7 September 1941 during the worst air raids on the city – a site of both the consequences as well as the generation of mechanistic modernity: 'That Thou wilt guide all those who plan the rebuilding of our cities, so that from this midst of destruction there may rise cities more fair to become the dwelling-place of Thy children.' The full sentence manifests the theological structuration and religious representation which, this chapter will argue, remained embedded and embodied in Modern Movement planning theory and practice in late imperial Britain, 1924–51. The following is thus a discussion of the enfolding of Judaeo-Christian ontology in the British Modernist planning project. Modernism's theological, religious and mental/visual templates will be mapped first through broader discussion of planning discourse, then in the theological impetus for social housing and town planning, and, finally, in the religious framing of social and urban reconstruction. The problematisation draws upon the revelatory analyses of memory and psyche most associated with Pierre Nora and Gaëtan de Clérambault, together with the rhetorical hermeneutics of Steven Mailloux.[2]

The prayer was intoned by the Bishop of Birmingham at a cataclysmic moment in the civic and national history, a moment at which current events seemed to many only explicable in the traditional epistemology of evil and good. It duplicated the eschatological language evoked by the First World War, which had provided a stimulus for the wider acceptance of Modernist design as well as for a techno-secular reconceptualisation of progress. The latter response had been uncompromisingly articulated by the student authors of the Architectural Association journal *Focus* in 1938, 'We were born into a civilization whose leaders, whose ideals, whose culture had failed.'[3] Nevertheless the Modernist theory they espoused appropriated the prophetic and catechetical, and elevated the advocacy of abstract values and universalised properties into a belief system further justified by the sublime scale of events during the Second World War. In that sense the Birmingham Prayer coincided with a widespread belief in the efficacy of theoretical modelling in societal re-formation: The Word become not Flesh but social reconstruction, albeit predominantly scientific and deriving from the transcendent empowering of ideology.[4] The full sentence on the title page of *When We Build Again* can thus be read as the surrogate prayer of British planners in the first phase of Modernism. Its phraseology seems to integrate Old Testament scripture from the Books of Isaiah (61:4), Ezekiel (36:10), Amos (9:14), with Psalm (43:4) and inadvertently to voice the displacement rather than rupture of traditional tropes within its construing.

The persistence of theological ideation and of Judaeo-Christian spiritual imagery in the legitimation and implementation of Modernist planning in post-First and -Second World War Britain is best charted in the areas of professional and popular discourse. Beneath all those processes of framing, declaration and adoption are the specific mental structurations – literary/visual descriptors and metaphors – of the agents and recipients: that is to say, theory is inescapably modified by and implicated in the realm of personal biography and the happenstance of events.[5] This discursive critical method also addresses the manner in which all modalities of knowledge ultimately operate anecdotally. Ideas are not infrequently reconfigured nor even partially resisted through their communication, as well as in their comprehension no less than their contestation, let alone their consolidation. The complex genealogy of thought entering upon action penetrates through the synthetic fabric of theoretical allegiance in figures of speech or analogous definition and text-image formation in professional-to-popular publication.[6] These range from official reports to promotional literature and guide books. They reflect the multi-faceted connectivities, consensual and conflicting, formed within and between subjects engaged in effecting objects of endeavour. Urban design is particularly representative of such intersection between the conceptual and visceral. It involves the manifestation of the perceived plus the remembered and thereby carries the potential for the infiltration of even negated schema.

These factors lie at the opposite remove from the overtly sacramental Birmingham Prayer for Reconstruction. The prayer reiterated a conviction intensified by traumatic events which, although challenging the grounds of conventional religious belief, contributed to performing its transformation into the discourse of Modernist planning. Two incidents in the life of one of Modernism's leading progenitors illustrate an earlier manifestation of this process of transformation. Charles Edouard Jeanneret's earliest written record was a letter to his mother briefly recounting attendance at the Independent Protestant Church in La Chaux-de-Fonds.[7] Subsequently Le Corbusier would regularly refer to the imminent divine order as the essential inspiration of harmonious design, and ascribe his sense of the communal, 'the indissoluble binomial-individual collectivity', to a visit in 1907 to the Carthusian monastery at Ema in Tuscany.[8]

The inclusion of Le Corbusier in this exploration of the transcendent dimension of British planning 1924–51 corresponds with the problematisation of theory as ultimately anecdotal in operation. Le Corbusier was influenced by the British Picturesque and Garden City/Suburb movements, and was aware of their sociological recasting by Patrick Geddes, if also critical of their decentralising anti-urban tendencies. In turn, his reinterpretation of those influences affected the Liverpool School of Planning, revised the thinking of Patrick Abercrombie and energised the urban renewal envisaged by the Modern Architecture Research Society. MARS was founded in 1933 by Le Corbusier's close friend, Wells Coates, as the British branch of the Congrès Internationaux de l'Architecture Moderne (CIAM). Son of a missionary in Japan and engineering graduate of the University of British Columbia, Coates had joined a group of young designers from the Dominions as well as escapees from totalitarian Europe in promoting Modernism in Britain. In 1938 Coates invited Le Corbusier to open the MARS exhibition of Modern architecture and planning at the New Burlington Galleries in London.[9] This invitation reflected the extent of Le Corbusier's reputation in Britain, one initiated by Frederic Etchell's translation

in 1927 of his *Vers une Architecture* (1923) as *Towards a New Architecture*.
This rapidly became the main English text of Modernism in architectural
schools. Le Corbusier's prestige was sustained by Etchell's translation *The
City of Tomorrow and its Planning*, 1929, precursor of *La Ville Radieuse*
(1933) – the eventual English version of which was entitled *The Radiant
City* (1967). *La Ville Radieuse* clarified the latent references to the Book of
Revelation (especially 21:1–12) and to St Augustine's City of God. Le Cor-
busier's example would continue to be significant into the mid-1950s due to
British professional interest in his St Dié reconstruction scheme and Unité
d'habitation in Marseilles, 1946–52, only receding before the critique of
Peter and Alison Smithson and their Team Ten allies within CIAM[10] Le Cor-
busier's principles of zoning, graduated circulation and densification were
moderated by landscaping in the 1937–8 MARS plan for redeveloping the
London region. However, also illustrating the anecdotal facet of theory, the
MARS plan had a more complex and conservative lineage.[11]

Beyond those predominantly Corbusian principles are ideas
derived from Modernist Dutch and German as well as later Garden Suburb
practice, including the derivative Neighbourhood Unit model. A further
level of more nebulous and pervasive frames of reference can be unpacked
from the plan for Greater London. Cobbled together under the chairman-
ship of Arthur Korn, the members of the MARS planning committee shared
a privileged socialisation process. Their education included biblically based
pedagogy and not infrequently conventionalised daily religious regimen, the
pattern of which was still imprinted on the ordering of social affairs. Their
secularly defined righteous condemnation of the decrepitude of late capitalist London and envisioning of both a more just and a more efficient urban
organism betrays tacit knowledge of a fundamental type in the Old and the
New Testament. That type can be identified as a redemptive reconstruction
following upon retributive destruction. It is a dialectic, surprisingly predic-
tive of Marxian theory, metaphorically focused on the fall of Babylon and
subsequent rise of the New Jerusalem that reaches an apogee in the final
chapters of the biblical Book of Revelation. This is not to claim the Holy
City imagined in Revelation as the paradigm for the MARS plan. Its verte-
brate arrangement of landscaped Neighbourhood Units separated from
industrial zones cannot, any more than Le Corbusier's more regulated Ville
Contemporaine, be aligned directly to the verbal schema of St John the
Divine. Nevertheless, the revelatory vision of unpolluted and harmonious
community does resonate into the Modernist envisioning of rational and
democratic urbanism. The residual memory of the 'river of the water of life
bright as crystal flowing from the throne of God and of the Lamb through
the middle of the street of the city' also resonates in the MARS plan's

7.1
Scheme for a
district unit of
6,000 people from
the MARS Plan
1937–8, from
Arthur Korn,
*History Builds the
Town*, London,
Lund Humphries,
1953, plate 82

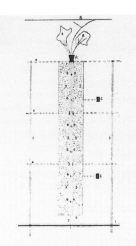

Transport grid of a district unit of
600,000, showing the main reception point for all goods and the two
sub-distribution points.

Diagrammatic transport grid with
the main artery along the work area,
the local arteries serving the district units of 600,000 and the ring
line serving distribution centres on
the outside of the town.

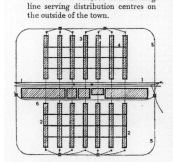

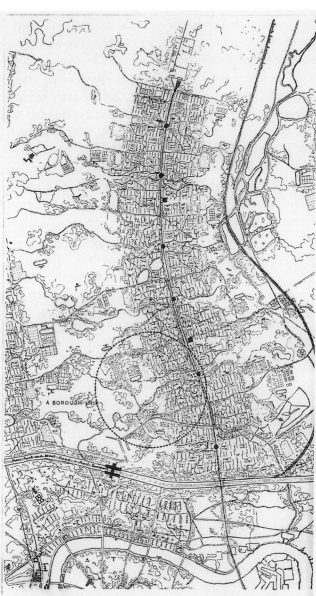

A district unit of 600,000 people, composed of three sub-units of 200,000
which again are subdivided into four borough units of 50,000. One of these units
is indicated by the circle.

Plate 82

preoccupation with the rehabilitation of the Thames. This objective compounded in the 1943 County of London and 1944 Greater London Plans, chiefly devised by Abercrombie, the 1951 Festival of Britain and post-war redevelopment of the South Bank.[12] Abercrombie stated the obverse side of the enduring biblical paradigm in his book *Town and Country Planning* (1933), revamping both Francis Bacon and William Cowper in writing, 'it was the Fall that set men planting, revising and refining upon nature and thus inventing the art of landscape design and town planning'.[13]

Before interrogating the moral aspect of the modern urban project, the presence in the MARS plan of two other religiously inspired co-ordinates merits attention. First is the Neighbourhood Unit that Abercrombie would also recommend as the basic component for renewing the existing metropolitan area of London. The concept had been codified by the US planner Clarence Perry under the inspiration of the Garden City Movement.[14] An intriguing factor in the Neighbourhood Unit is the choice of a population of between six and ten thousand people. Primarily determined according to the script of the County of London Plan by relation 'to the

7.2
Proposed redevelopment of the Thames, from *The County of London Plan explained by E. J. Carter and Ernö Goldfinger*, West Drayton, Penguin, 1945, p. 61. Copyright E. J. Carter and Ernö Goldfinger 1945. Reproduced by permission of Penguin Books Ltd

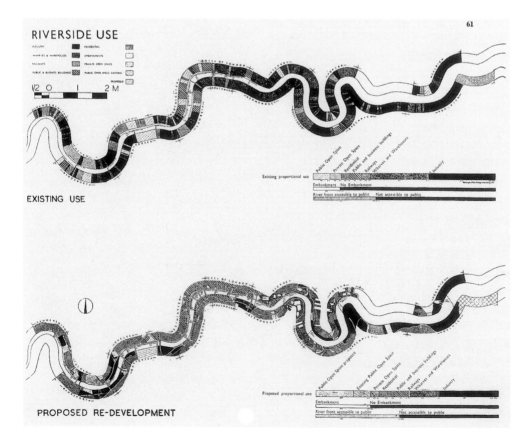

elementary school area it serves', the optimum population corresponds with
the ideal urban units allegorised by Thomas More in his religious allegory
Utopia: 'Each town consists of six thousand households.'[15] The towns were
to have central markets or, in contemporary terminology, shopping centres,
a feature of particular importance in the planning of the Lansbury Reconstruction Area in Poplar, London. Begun in 1949, the Lansbury neighbourhood functioned as the Exhibition of Architecture Town Planning and
Building Research at the 1951 Festival of Britain and as the material
demonstration of 'one corporate reaffirmation of facts in the nation's
future'.[16] An economically practical as well as communal centre had also
been a primary requisite for Ebenezer Howard, whose *Tomorrow: A Peaceful
Path to Real Reform*, 1889, and more so *Garden Cities of Tomorrow*, 1902,
defined the second co-ordinate for the MARS planners. Howard's vision of
the Garden City was intended to resolve the problems of congested cities
and depressed countryside consequent upon industrialisation by reducing
inflated land values while resuscitating husbandry in the Green Belts sep-
arating central and garden cities.[17] Those productive Green Belts certainly
retain a paradisal connotation and recall the 24-mile sylvan cordon between
the 'splendid towns [that] look exactly alike' described by More's interlocu-
tor Raphael.[18] Their uniformity was policed (*avant* Foucault) by the scopic
District Controller. This official presaged both Frank Lloyd Wright's regional
architect in the 1934 Broadacre City project and the collaborative architect-
planner given distinguished reality in the post-1945 decades by two
designers later closely associated with the University of Edinburgh. Sir
Robert Matthew and Percy Johnson-Marshall exercised an enlightened
authority in the London County Council's Architect-Planning office and
realised More's idea of state control: a control that, emerging from an imag-
inary 'no-place [*Utopia*]', could be implemented anywhere.

Central control and universal standards in design, even including
an aesthetic of iteration, were reified in Modernism, especially as it became
conventionalised in the post-1945 decades. The reductionist notions then
answered a deep anxiety about difference, whether national, racial, social
or economic, and an equally profound urge to mobilise in material terms
the communitarian millennial imagery rooted in the western Humanist
tradition. The 1940 Barlow Report on the Distribution of the Industrial
Population and the 1941 Scott Report on Land Utilization in Rural Areas
recommended comprehensive, centralised planning and the public acquisition and control of land envisaged in 1516 by Thomas More: 'in *Utopia*
where everything's under state control'.[19] By 1941, the cumulative impact of
two intercontinental conflicts wrought a socio-political disjunction in which
the transcendent could be translated into the technical. Similarly, one

phrase from the report of the 1942 Uthwatt Expert Committee on Compensation and Betterment in advocating 'national planning with a high degree of initiative and control by the Central Planning Authority' bespeaks the attainable despite invoking scientific bureaucracy and religious hierarchy.[20] The phrase clearly defines the attitudinal divide underlying the ineffectual or limited between-the-wars and the thoroughgoing post-1945 planning legislation and activity. That divide is respectively typified by the 1932 Towns and Country Planning Act or Wythenshawe housing development by the Manchester City Council, as against the 1947 Town and Country Planning Act or New Towns enacted from 1946.[21] The rhetoric inscribes a realism absent from Ebenezer Howard's address to the National Town Planning Conference arranged by the Garden Cities and Town Planning Association in London on 10 December 1909:

> We must uprear – no less an aim is worthy of our powers – the most beautiful and harmonious City the world has yet seen – a City of Industry and Commerce, indeed, but also a City of Homes for the people, without one slum or festering sore in all its wide expanse.[22]

Howard was romantic where Uthwatt is instrumental in articulating the modern urban mission. The caesura can, however, be exaggerated. Those social democratic Reports were preceded by the Royal Warrant which intoned an older social ordering, 'George the Sixth by the Grace of God, of Great Britain, Ireland and the British Dominions beyond the Seas, King, Defender of the Faith . . .' The incorporation of older with newer vision is evident on the cover of a compendium of the Barlow and Scott Reports together with the Beveridge Report on Social Insurance and Allied Services (1942). Published as *Maps for the National Plan*, the cover illustration shows the British Isles seemingly surrounded by a mandorla (see 7.6).[23] More mundane, but comparable in its evocation of traditional values, is the advertisement for the Triumph Renown sedan in the official Guide to the Lansbury Exhibition. The motor, costly version of the Modernist icon of affordable technocracy and social mobility, is parked in a Cotswold village, the mythic arena of conservative British reform from before the Arts and Crafts and Garden City movements.[24] Car ownership is here visualised as permitting the return to civil society, a blend of still potent nostalgic conventions including the village church, vernacular buildings and humanly tended countryside: 'God's in His [Her] Heaven. Wo/Men are in their rightful place; All's well with the world.'

The power of the village community as the natural urban form further illustrates the complex genealogy of twentieth-century British town

Robert Whitten, Architect, assisted by Gordon Culham, Landscape Architect

A 160-ACRE NEIGHBORHOOD UNIT SUBDIVISION

Liberal recreation spaces gained through comprehensive planning

7.3
A 160-acre neighbourhood unit subdivision, with two churches in the central area, from Clarence Perry, *Housing for the Machine Age*, New York, Russell Sage Foundation, 1939, p. 58

planning and modern social reform. Ultimately the idea of benign renewal of the person through contact with nature – one embracing the monastic tradition of spirituality and fundamental to Le Corbusier's urban design – can be traced in Western thought to the paradigmatic Mosaic and Christian contemplative withdrawal from society: a liminal physical and mental-spiritual place between the human and the divine that prepared the participant for active social intervention. This vein of practical cosmology became embedded in the Roman Catholic and more so evangelical Protestant doctrine. It is especially apparent in the litany of confession and absolution, but equally important to the establishment of church-related institutional charity. Such willing or shamed altruism on the part of the church and privileged individuals was held out as the preferred method of social enlightenment by A. W. N. Pugin in *Contrasts* 1836 (1841 illustrated edition).[25] Pugin romanticised the medieval Christian tradition and exaggerated the divorce between revived Catholicism and rational-cum-utilitarian thought. A substantial quotient of Enlightenment formulation and policy modified theological proposition, and coincided with a remarkable range and dynamic of

189

[226]

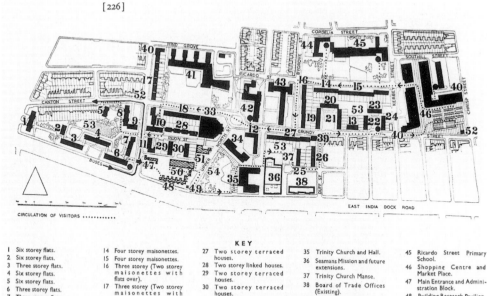

CIRCULATION OF VISITORS ···········

KEY

1	Six storey flats.	14	Four storey maisonettes.	27	Two storey terraced houses.
2	Six storey flats.	15	Four storey maisonettes.	28	Two storey linked houses.
3	Three storey flats.	16	Three storey (Two storey maisonettes with flats over).	29	Two storey terraced houses.
4	Six storey flats.	17	Three storey (Two storey maisonettes with flats over).	30	Two storey terraced houses.
5	Six storey flats.			31	(Not shown). Future Health Centre on the site of 47-50.
6	Three storey flats.	18	Two storey terraced houses.	32	(Not shown). Future R.C. Presbytery on the site of 51.
7	Three storey flats.	19-24	Three storey terraced houses with a few single room flats for old people.	33	R.C. Church.
8	Six storey flats.	25	Two storey terraced houses.	34	Upper North Street School (Existing) will be used for future Community Centre.
9	Three storey flats.	26	Two storey terraced houses.		
10	Three storey flats.				
11	Three storey flats.				
12	Two storey flats for old people.				
13	Three storey flats (Existing).				

35	Trinity Church and Hall.	45	Ricardo Street Primary School.
36	Seamans Mission and future extensions.	46	Shopping Centre and Market Place.
37	Trinity Church Manse.	47	Main Entrance and Administration Block.
38	Board of Trade Offices (Existing).	48	Building Research Pavilion.
39	Public House (Existing).	49	Vertical Feature.
40	New Public Houses.	50	Town Planning Pavilion.
41	R.C. Secondary School.	51	Cafeteria.
42	Old Peoples Home.	52	Lavatories.
43	R.C. Primary School (Existing school and future extensions).	53	Childrens playgrounds.
44	Ricardo Street Nursery School.	54	Amenity Park.
		●	Show flats, show houses and show classrooms.

47

socially conscious religious reform. An epitome is the forging of an association between theology and empiricism at Cambridge deriving from the philosophy of John Locke.[26] Equally important is the generally non-conformist background of those Edinburgh and Glasgow thinkers and early professionals who forged the matrix of reasoned yet inspired exploitation of natural resource for societal benefit. Without denying the concurrent development of agnosticism or atheist rationality and functionalism, the linking of improvement with atonement (as individual spiritual regeneration) is apparent in all the major debates about social change through the nineteenth and early twentieth centuries. These debates are epitomised by the abolition of slavery and gradual provision of social welfare infrastructure, including public housing, in which the religious conscience was effectively mobilised to counter sectional interest.[27] Religion, be it escapist opiate or communitarian inspiration, revived through industrialisation as both justification of the heightened social disparity it engendered and mystical or socialist antidote. Among the socially engaged religionists were the Cadburys, who founded Bourneville in 1895 as a model landscaped urban community, and the supporters of the Garden City Association, who

7.4
Plan of Stage One of the Lansbury Redevelopment Neighbourhoods showing the proposed route for viewing during the Festival of Britain exhibition, from Percy Johnson-Marshall, *Rebuilding Cities*, Edinburgh, Edinburgh University Press, 1966, fig. 47, p. 226

7.5
Models of Stage
One of the Lansbury
Redevelopment
Neighbourhood,
from *Rebuilding
Cities*, figs 48 and
49, p. 227, showing
the Market (lower
left) and (bottom)
the Roman Catholic
Church

promoted Letchworth as the first Garden City in 1903 (followed by Welwyn in 1919) to realise Ebenezer Howard's Damascus-like epiphany to build a 'new civilization based on service to the community and not self-interest'.[28]

191

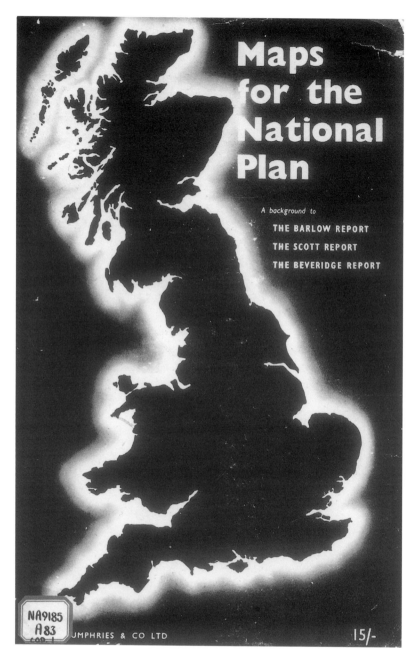

7.6
*Maps for the
National Plan,*
London, Lund
Humphries, 1945,
cover

The 'social gospel' became a potent focus for late Victorian and
Edwardian Christianity and was recognised as a powerful political force in
such phrases as 'Exeter Hall' or 'Non-conformist conscience'. Diverse in con-
stitution and specific goals, this moral force, energised by the cataclysmic

events of the euphemistically denominated Great War, rendered low-income housing a primary objective of public policy from 1918. The attainment of that objective, aphorised by George Cadbury junior as 'the general movement Towards Social Betterment', was achieved by a dense weft and weave of ideological and material factors. The anecdotal realm of individual persons and events, and their intersection and impact, can be proven by reference to the lives of just three figures variously involved in British housing and town planning policy during 1924–51. One is George Lansbury (1859–1940). A devout Anglican socialist, Lansbury was a member of the 1905–9 Royal Commission on the Poor Laws and elected Labour Member of Parliament for the Bow and Bromley Division of Poplar in 1910 (resigned 1912), and again from 1922 until his death in 1940. In his honour the model Reconstruction Neighbourhood exhibited at the Festival of Britain was named Lansbury.[29] The second is John Walsham, 1st Baron Reith (1889–1971), son of a Minister of the Free Church in Glasgow whose last public post was Lord High Commissioner of the General Assembly of the Church of Scotland.[30] As Minister of Works and Planning (1941–3) and Chairman of the New Towns Committee (1946–7), Reith constructed the legislative foundations of the seminal 1946 New Towns Act and the 1947 Town and Country Planning Act. The 1947 Act was especially remarkable for its legislation of a central Land Bank, comprehensive regional planning and expropriation of privately owned land. The Labour government minister who successfully steered both Acts through Parliament was the third figure, Lewis Silkin (1889–1972), eldest child of a teacher of Hebrew in the Jewish community of East End London. Silkin also oversaw the promulgation of the National Parks and Access to the Countryside Act in 1949 as another legacy of the English Picturesque and Garden City movements.[31]

The achievement of particular individuals should not, however, be privileged to the exclusion of either group dynamic or the thought-collective active during specific eras.[32] One example is British socialism, which in promoting the cause of social housing and welfare coalesced trade unionism with the idealist socialism of William Morris and the intellectual socialism of the Fabian Society. Another fundamental thought-collective spanning the two post-war periods was, in biblical language, the redemptive opportunity opened up by the retributive outcome of conflict. This idea, justifying the tremendous destruction of people and property in each war, is encapsulated in the frontispiece of Sir Gwilym Gibbon's *Reconstruction and Town and Country Planning*, 1942. It shows St Paul's Cathedral amidst bombed-out buildings with the aphoristic caption: 'A Disaster – and an Opportunity'.[33] Those external events empowered the performance of the

7.7
Frontispiece from
Gwilym Gibbon,
*Reconstruction and
Town and Country
Planning*, London,
Architect and
Building News,
1942

formerly marginalised rhetoric of communal rebuilding voiced by Raymond Unwin at the 1909 National Town Planning Conference:

> We have to begin to see our towns as a whole, to realise that the individual's place is a part of a whole, and though we must struggle to maintain a true scope for individual effort and for new individual ideas, still we must see the growth of our towns in its true perspective – we must see the whole first, and the parts as contributing to the whole.[34]

The trauma of warfare conflated the relationship between the worldly and heavenly cities defined by St Augustine in Book XV of *The City of God* (written amidst the decline of an earlier empire): 'one set in the present affairs of their world, the other in the hope of God'.[35] Hence this sentence from Abercrombie's 1943 *A Plan for Plymouth*:

> The opportunity is now before Plymouth [the personified urban entity or embodied civic identity] to initiate a great scheme of civic rebuilding and development: out of the disasters of war to snatch a victory for the city of the future.[36]

The theorisation of town planning as a redemptive process of social renewal consequent upon political chaos had emerged from Lloyd George's post-1918 rhetoric, with its promise of 'Homes fit for Heroes'. Resisted by establishment economic interests, it did result in partial insurance and health coverage, the Tudor Walters Committee on Housing 1918, Addison Housing and Town Planning Act 1919 and 1932 Town and Country Planning Act. In addition some 5.5 million low-income or lower-income houses were constructed by the building industry and local authorities: notably the Becontree, London, 1919–24; Wythenshawe, Manchester, 1926–33; Speke, Liverpool, 1928–36 and Quarry Hill, Leeds, 1936–7, housing estates.[37] And at the reconstituted 1925 British Empire Exhibition (inaugurated 1924) the erstwhile Palace of Engineering – designed by the Modernist engineer-architect, Sir Owen Williams, then the largest clear-span reinforced concrete structure in the British Empire – was converted into the Palace of Housing and Transport primarily directed towards 'showing the efforts that are being made to put an end to the housing shortage'.[38] At the opening ceremony on 9 May 1925 the Bishop of London delivered 'An Empire Collect'. This prayer introduced urban renewal as part of the divinely ordained civilizing mission of the war-tested imperialism:

> Purge the cities of our Empire from those sources of corruption which have so often made sin profitable and made hard the way of uprightness . . . Give our leaders a fresh vision for the future of this Empire and set all their hearts on fire with great ideals. Raise up generations of public men who will have the faith and daring of the Kingdom of God in them, who will enlist for life in a holy warfare for the freedom and rights of all Thy Children.

As a finale the massed military bands, personnel and civilian audience sang the hymn 'Fight the Good Fight', nicely representing the confluence of spiritual with secular power in popular ideation of national progress. This progress was, however, increasingly measured by improved societal conditions exemplified by the formation in 1926 of the Pioneer Health Clinic in

Peckham, South London, and completion of a new building in 1935 designed in the Modernist idiom by Owen Williams.[39]

Social welfare and housing provisions attained compounding importance in the official depiction of national achievement in British state pavilions at ensuing international exhibitions.[40] Most notable were the displays arranged by the Modernist designer Misha Black at the Glasgow Empire Exhibition of 1938 and New York World's Fair of 1939. At the New York Fair the socio-aesthetic propaganda war between republican and imperial democracy and fascist and communist dictatorship was intense. The Pavilion of the United Kingdom, Australia, New Zealand and the British Colonial Empire was organised sequentially around constitutional monarchy as a sacred institution of benign secular power. It was succeeded by the more typical manufacturing Maritime and Metals Halls (including photographs of Modernist architecture and a model of Lincoln Cathedral) culminating by way of a section on English gardens in the Magna Carta and Public Welfare Halls. Thus the seat of modern democracy and enlightened imperialism was simultaneously represented as the site of societal regeneration.[41] The text for the display, 'The Town of To-day', in the official *Guide* declared:

> The slums are being steadily pulled down, and in their place a garden suburb is springing up on the outskirts with all the facilities for healthy recreation. Most significant of all are the numerous buildings scattered over the town which are devoted to public welfare services unknown a hundred years ago.

The 'New Homes for Old' policy was appropriated to claim British international pre-eminence in the construction of low-cost housing due to a veritable crusade of rebuilding: 'a determined attack has been made on the slums. They are now being swept away at a rate of over 200 houses a day, and replaced by modern low-cost houses'.[42]

The transformative capability of redemptive theology in the transformative agency of Modernism is most evident in C. B. Purdom's book *How Should We Rebuild London?* Written in 1943 at Welwyn Garden City, but not published until 1945, and illustrated with satirical illustrations by Batt, the text extended William Blake's prophetic moral critique of early nineteenth-century London into the Blitz. If the 'explosions and flames' were caused by Nazi megalomaniacs rather than 'the wrath of God', they nonetheless 'compelled [citizens] to face the necessity of making a new London'.[43] The theology is admittedly wayward, seeming to endorse the heresy of 'evil be my good'. But throughout, the language of Purdom's argument is couched in religious convention and literary tradition, even with the reification of the River Thames as the 'natural cause of London', commercial surrogate of the River of Life in the Holy City.[44] Purdom longed 'to see London the noblest of cities, and the most beautiful, brought more into relation with its inner spirit and more in harmony with the soul of its people than it has been'.[45] The ensuing chapters, and Batt's prefatory visual satires, cast the history and future of London as a contest between creative/collective and corrupting/sectional forces; quite literally transposing the liturgical dialectic of the 'bondage of sin and death' versus the 'freedom of everlasting life' in the *Book of Common Prayer*. Echoes of sacramental practice recur in

7.8
Frontispiece to Chapter 4, 'Supreme Functions', drawn by Batt, from C. B. Purdom, *How Should We Rebuild London?*, London, J. M. Dent, 1945

197

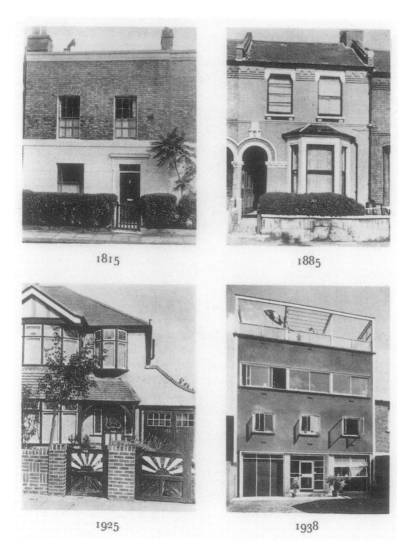

1815

1885

1925

1938

7.9
'The Return of the Prodigal Son', from Lionel Brett, *The Things We See: Houses*, West Drayton, Penguin, 1947, p. 5

the chapter titles, notably 'Supreme Functions' – including churches, hospitals, schools, libraries, museums and art galleries. The seventh chapter was more straightforwardly entitled 'Architecture and Building'. In it Purdom enjoined 'a new architecture, native to our national genesis' neither transatlantic nor continental and divested of the 'building speculators' and other purveyors of 'individual rapaciousness'.[46] Architects were charged to intervene in modest emulation of the Great Architect Divine and with proper humility, 'giving up mere drawing-board cleverness and the copying of continental propagandists of modernity with their hard and blatant exaggeration of anti-individualism', adding with yet a further displaced religious figure, 'which is a sort of sheepishness not characteristic of us'.[47] In his final chapter, 'London Rebuilt' (remarkable for its comprehensive review of the limitations of transatlantic housing reform), Purdom urged the creation of a civic organism enabled by public ownership and central planning in order to expurgate the vice of greed and support the virtues of

> the civic solidarity of a free people … This means that London has to be redeemed and given a worthy interpretation of the experience of its citizens during the war … it must henceforth exist for the good of all and represent the most elevated aims of national life.[48]

The representation of national idealism was obviously still mediated by perhaps half-remembered religious practice. That sense of almost unconscious transposition, even in so technical a field as architecture or planning, assumes colloquial guise in a popular book by the Eton- and Oxford-educated architect Lionel Brett, 4th Viscount Esher. The first plate in his *The Things We See: Houses*, published in 1947, traces the demise and recovery of true domestic design from 1815 to 1883, 1925 and 1938 (this last a house by Taylor and Greene in Highgate, London).[49] The aesthetic-functional resurrection is, not altogether reasonably, summarised in the caption 'The Return of the Prodigal Son'. The residual allegiance to theological socialisation and uncritical transference of identity into religious form explains the profound resentment for the so-called Baedeker air-raids by the Luftwaffe on the cathedral cities. The destruction of Coventry Cathedral and churches in the City of London or Bristol alike elicited particular public anger, followed by the determination to reconstruct and, ultimately, especially in the case of Coventry, for reconciliation. Those responses are apparent in Thomas Sharp's *Exeter Phoenix: A Plan for Rebuilding*, 1946.[50] On several occasions, even when proposing the introduction of 'an entirely modern' commercial-institutional 'Civic Centre' modelled on a US example, Sharp emphasised the religious dimension.[51] His rebuilding scheme was predicated on opening views to the cathedral, 'Exeter's heart', and deeper understanding of civic life: 'It promotes spiritual as well as material good. It is a *whole* city'.[52] The reinstatement of the visual dominance of St Paul's Cathedral was a major issue for the Royal Academy Planning Committee who published *London Replanned* in October 1942 (via the magazine *Country Life*) as well as for Abercrombie and Forshaw in their 1943 *County of London Plan*, and Abercrombie's 1944 *Greater London Plan*; it was an overriding concern for Charles Holden and William Holford in their 1947 report subsequently published in 1951 as *The City of London: A Record of Destruction and Survival*.[53] Holden and Holford also incorporated the proposals of the

text and the exhibition. The new Britain of the New Towns and inner city renewal Lansbury pioneered would direct its resources in desanctified emulation of the New Testament Beatitudes to the children and the old and infirm. The reconstitution of religion into secular reconstruction bears out a remarkably lengthy section on 'Religious Organizations' from the Interim Report of the New Towns Committee chaired by Lord Reith:[57]

> [Although] those who are active in church work and in atten-
> dance are a minority ... Religion has a status and influence
> which extend far beyond the immediate circle who attend places
> of worship. The population in general still has associations with
> religion and takes from it the traditional sanctions of family and
> community life. Moreover, the Christian Churches are, by their
> very tenets, concerned with man's duty to his neighbour; ... The
> Churches therefore hold high place among the community
> builders ... They are of vital importance in a new town and
> should be enabled to play their full part. Adequate facilities must
> be made available for their places of worship and the ancillary
> buildings their manifold activities need.[58]

7.12
Photomontage showing the model of the proposed St Anne's Neighbourhood Redevelopment superimposed on an aerial photograph with Nicholas Hawksmoor's St Anne's Church, Limehouse (1730), in the foreground, c.1955, from *Rebuilding Cities*, fig. 66, p. 239

The churches built in the fifteen New Towns completed during the two post-1945 decades probably did contribute as signifiers of rooted social practice to the realisation of the visions for 'self-contained and balanced communities for work and living'.[59] By contrast, the absence of religious and even more so secular community facilities from British public housing, particularly in inner city areas from the 1960s, would produce the condition inadvertently presaged in the name of one typically reductionist scheme, 'Starkleigh Way'.[60] British cities became more stark than fair as the social gospel receded before consumerist and materialist tenets in parallel with the decline of Modernism into orthodoxy.

Acknowledgements

This chapter was prepared with research funding from the Social Sciences and Humanities Research Council of Canada and the John Simon Guggenheim Memorial Foundation.

Notes

1   Published in London by George Allen & Unwin, the book had a Foreword by the Prime Minister Lord Balfour, acknowledging the failure of post-1918 policy, 'above all because the key to good planning was absent; that is the national control of the use of land'.

2   In particular see P. Nora, trans. A. Goldhammer, *Realms of Memory: Rethinking the French Past*, New York, Columbia University Press, 1996, 3rd edn, and for Clérambault, J. Copjec, *Read My Desire: Lacan against the Historicists*, Cambridge, MA, MIT Press, 1994. The modalities of knowledge are examined astutely by P.-F. Guattari, for which see *The Guattari Reader*, ed. G. Genosko, Oxford, Blackwell, 1996 especially Chapter 8, 'Regimes, Pathways, Subjects', trans. B. Massumi. Steven Mailloux's most relevant books are *Reception Histories: Rhetoric Pragmatism and American Cultural Politics*, Ithaca, NY, Cornell University Press, 1998 and *Rhetorical Power*, Ithaca, NY, Cornell University Press, 1989.

3   *Focus 2* (1938) and also quoted in C. McKean, *The Scottish Thirties: An Architectural Introduction*, Edinburgh, Scotland Associated Press, 1987, p. 40. However, church architecture became a site of modernising in Britain, exemplified by articles in the *Journal of the Royal Institute of British Architects*, notably those by N. F. Cachemille-Day, 14 October 1933, and Edward Maufe, 12 January 1935; in the former, Cachemille-Day avers with reference to F. X. Velarde's St Gabriel Blackburn:

> Unless there is a strong spiritual conviction which is shared at least to a considerable extent by all men, there is a danger that modern architecture will become more subjective and unusual without expressing any deep and fundamental impulse belonging to humanity as a whole, as it did in the past.
>
> (October 1933, 40: 14, p. 837)

4 H. McG. Dunnett, *Guide to the Exhibition of Architecture Town-Planning and Building Research*, London, Her Majesty's Stationery Office, 1951, p. 8, commented on the work of the Building Research Pavilion at the Lansbury Exhibition, 'All can be solved through scientific research.' The broader assumption of the improving power of theoretical system, especially planning, during this period is unproblematically summarised in J. F. Coughlin, *New Housing in Canada and Other British Nations*, Toronto, privately printed, 1937:

> It is inspiring to observe the results already obtained of careful zoning and town-planning, whether the objects of that care be a Garden City in England, or a Native Township in South Africa. The ultimate benefits are ennobling and perform a lifting up of humanity, for all Nations to follow.
>
> (p. 21)

The interconnections between war and progress, but with an Augustinian interpretation of the transcendent heavenly city, is the subject of conversation between Naphta and Settembrini in Thomas Mann, *The Magic Mountain*, trans. H. T. Lowe, New York, Alfred & Knopf, 1977 edn, pp. 382–3. The two world wars were identified as a major stimulus to the creation of a 'Housing Conscience', and therefore to the public acceptance of housing as a 'social service' in *Homes for the People*, London, Association of Building Technicians, 1946, ed. A. Boyd and C. Penn, Foreword by Aneurin Bevan, Minister of Health.

5 This problematisation relates to actor-network theory, which, though devised by John Law, is most associated with Bruno Latour whose work includes *We Have Never Been Modern*, Cambridge, MA, MIT Press [1991] 1993, trans. C. Porter.

6 This corresponds with the interrelation of text and fabric in Anthony Vidler's study of French architectural theory and design in *The Writing of the Walls: Architectural Theory in the Late Enlightenment*, Princeton, NJ, Princeton University Press, 1987.

7 Reproduced in H. Allen Brooks, *Le Corbusier's Formative Years: Charles Edouard Jeanneret at La Chaux-de Fonds*, Chicago, University of Chicago Press, 1997, p. 13.

8 For example, in *Urbanisme* (1924) translated by F. Etchells and published as *The City of To-morrow* by the Architectural Press in 1929 (London, 1949 reprint), Le Corbusier declared that architecture should 'recognise the God we seek'. One of his British admirers, the architect Lionel Brett, in his book *Architecture in a Crowded World* [London, 1970], New York, Schoeken Books, 1971, p. 19, quoted Le Corbusier's assertion that 'Harmony, reigning over all things, regulating all the things of our lives, is the spontaneous, indefatigable and tenacious quest of man animated by a single force: the sense of the divine.' Le Corbusier ascribed the inspiration for the Unité d'Habitation at Marseilles to his 1907 visit to the Monastery of Ema in *Œuvre Complète, 1952–1957* [Zurich, 1957] New York, George Wittenborn, 1964, p. 174, cited in N. Evenson, *Le Corbusier: The Machine and the Grand Design*, New York, George Braziller, 1969, p. 32.

9 *New Architecture: An Exhibition of the Elements of Modern Architecture Organised by the MARS Society*, London, 1938. The exhibition catalogue had a Foreword by George Bernard Shaw, pp. 2–3, commending Ely and Chartres Cathedral as well as the Parthenon in defining 'Martian [MARS] architecture' as 'a violent reaction against impressive architecture' as epitomised by Baalbek, even if 'It has no religion to impose.' Nonetheless, the Group chose to problematise modern design around Sir Henry Wotton's 1624 paraphrase of Vitruvius, 'Commoditie, firmnes [sic] and delight.'

10 In *Town and Country Planning* [1933], London, Oxford University Press, 2nd edn, 1944, Patrick Abercrombie described Le Corbusier as a 'brilliant practitioner', p. 131. St Dié was praised in, for example, L. Brett, 'The New City Centres of Europe,' *Journal of the Royal Institute of British Architects*, June 1950, and F. Gibberd, *Town Design*, London, Architectural Press, 1953, p. 56. In 1953 Le Corbusier was awarded the RIBA Gold Medal.

11 The MARS plan for London is defined and contextualised in E. S. Morris, *British Town Planning and Urban Design: Principles and Policies*, London, Longmans, 1997, see especially pp. 68–70; this plan is also discussed briefly by A. Korn in his *History Builds the Town*, London, Lund Humphries, 1953, pp. 83 and 89.

12 Revelation 22:1–4. The monumental refurbishment of the Thames from Putney to Tower Bridge was a major element in the Royal Academy of Arts Planning Committee reports, chaired by Sir Edwin Lutyens, see especially *London Replanned* published by *Country Life* in October 1942.

13 *Town and Country Planning*, 1944 2nd edn, p. 9. In *Rebuilding Cities*, Edinburgh, Edinburgh University Press, 1966, Percy Johnson-Marshall, Professor of Urban Design and Regional Planning at Edinburgh, stressed the spiritual dimension, 'In the creation of a civilised environment the vital spark of vision is of critical importance, yet it is liable to be extinguished in the complex technical and administrative process of planning,' p. 109. For the conflation of the 'fall' with the classical myth of the Golden Age, see R. Waswo, *The Founding Legend of Western Civilisation: From Virgil to Vietnam*, Hanover, NH, University Press of New England, 1997.

14 C. Perry, *The Neighbourhood Unit*, New York, New York Regional Planning Association, 1929; see also his *The Rebuilding of Blighted Areas*, New York, NYRPA, 1933.

15 The County of London text was quoted by the more secular socialist Modernist architect Richard Sheppard in *Building for the People*, London, George Allen & Unwin, 1948, p. 109. Nonetheless, Sheppard quoted the New Testament in his Introduction when commenting on the social purpose of architecture, 'By their works ye shall know them,' p. 7. Thomas More's description is from Book I, p. 79 in *Utopia* [1516], trans. P. Turner, Harmondsworth, Penguin, 1965; this edition includes an excellent Introduction by Turner on the genre including William Morris' *News from Nowhere*, 1890. See also J. L. Machor, *Pastoral Cities: Urban Ideals and the Symbolic Landscape of America*, Madison, WI, University of Wisconsin Press, 1987, especially Chapter 1.

16 *Utopia*, p. 80 and Dunnett, *Guide*, p. 2. The Lansbury market shopping precinct was designed by Frederick Gibberd, reviewed pp. 144–5 in his *Town Design*, London, Architectural Press, 1953; see also P. Johnson-Marshall, *Rebuilding Cities*.

17 R. Fishman, *Urban Utopias in the Twentieth-Century: Ebenezer Howard, Frank Lloyd Wright, and Le Corbusie*r, New York, Basic Books, 1977. The biblical origins were argued in L. Ginsberg, 'Green Belts in the Bible', *Journal of the Town Planning Institute*, 1955, vol. 1, p. 165; another intersection of biblical reference and secular planning theory is J. Punter, 'The Ten Commandments of Architecture and Urban Design', *The Planner*, 1990, vol. 76, pp. 10–14.

18 *Utopia*, p. 70. It should be noted, however, that Percy Johnson-Marshall, in *Rebuilding Cities*, p. 104, described *Utopia* as 'a not very inspiring urban vision'.

19 *Utopia*, p. 78, earlier Raphael speaks of 'communal ownership instead of private property', p. 64, and states 'But there's no hope of a one, so long as private property continues', p. 66.

20 *Uthwatt Report*, London, House of Commons, Cmd. 6386, Sept. 1942, p. 12.

21 Besides Morris, *British Town Planning* (note 11 above), see also M. Glendinning and S. Muthesius, *Tower Block: Modern Public Housing in England, Scotland, Wales and Northern Ireland*, London and New Haven, CT, Yale University Press, 1994.

22 *The Practical Application of Town Planning Powers*, London, Garden City Association, 1909; the proceedings of the conference with contribution by Thomas Adams, Patrick Geddes and Raymond Unwin.

23 Published in London by Lund Humphries in 1945.

24 The Arts and Crafts Guild was relocated, unsuccessfully, to Chipping Camden; P. Davey, *Arts and Crafts Architecture: The Search for an Earthly Paradise*, London, Architectural Press, 1980.

J. Paxman, *The English*, Harmondsworth, Penguin, 1998, quotes C. Henry Warren, *England is a Village*, 1940, 'The best of England is a village', p. 149. The embedding of the village paradigm in the Garden City Movement is exemplified by the title of the Tract (no. 109) that Raymond Unwin wrote for the Fabian Trust in 1902, *Cottage Plans and Common Sense*. For the wider issue of natural values in social thought see K. Thomas, *Man and the Natural World: Changing Attitudes in England 1500–1800*, London, Allen Lane, 1983.

25 P. Stanton, *Pugin*, London, Thames & Hudson, 1971; N. Pevsner, *Some Architectural Writers of the Nineteenth Century*, Oxford, Oxford University Press, 1972, and M. Belcher, *A. W. N. Pugin: An Annotated Critical Bibliography*, London, Mansell, 1987.

26 B. Young, *Religion and Enlightenment in Eighteenth Century England: Theological Debate from Locke to Burke*, Oxford, Oxford University Press, 1998; and B. Hilton, *The Age of Atonement: The Influence of Evangelicism on Social and Economic Thought 1795–1865*, Oxford, Oxford University Press, 1988.

27 The provision of low-income housing is usefully reviewed in the British context by J. S. Curl, *The Life and Work of Henry Roberts 1803–1876: The Evangelical Conscience and the Campaign for Model Housing and Healthy Nations*, Chichester, Phillimore, 1983.

28 Howard's account of his revelatory experience from *Tomorrow: A Peaceful Path to Real Reform* (1898) is quoted in G. E. Cherry (ed.) *Pioneers in British Planning*, London, Architectural Press, 1981, p. 79; from H. Miller's chapter on 'Patrick Geddes'. The chapter by M. Miller on 'Raymond Unwin' records Lewis Mumford's retrospective characterisation of him as 'a bit of a Quaker', (ibid., p. 96); George Pepler, the subject of a chapter by Cherry, was a Quaker. In a wider perspective, Unwin's plan for Hampstead Garden Suburb, 1907, was influenced by Bruno Taut's idea of the 'Stadtkrone', for which see I. B. Whyte, *Bruno Taut and the Architecture of Activism*, Cambridge, Cambridge University Press, 1983. Conversely in his article, 'The Formal and Technical Problems of Modern Architecture and Planning', *Journal of the Royal Institute of British Architects*, May 1934, vol. 41, pp. 679–94, Walter Gropius acknowledged the influence of Unwin on the European housing movement, p. 686. On the general issue of religious thought and Modernism, H. S. Goodhart-Rendel in 1932 described functionalist design as 'a close analogue of puritanism', cited Brett, *Architecture in a Crowded World*, p. 75.

29 *Dictionary of National Biography 1931–1940*, ed. L. G. Wickham Legg, Oxford, Oxford University Press, 1949, pp. 524–6.

30 *Dictionary of National Biography 1971–1980*, ed. Lord Blake and C. S. Nicholls Oxford, Oxford University Press, 1986, pp. 713–15.

31 *Dictionary of National Biography 1971–1980*, pp. 774–5. Silkin was the first Minister of Town and Country Planning 1945–50; his second wife Frieda was a daughter of the Reverend Canon Pilling of Norwich.

32 The term thought-collective was originated by L. Fleck in *Genesis and Development of a Scientific Fact*, ed. T. J. Trenn and R. K. Merton, Chicago, University of Chicago Press, 1979 edn. The intent of the argument of this chapter is also captured in Kant's phrase 'empirically ideal and transcendentally real', quoted in S. Cavell, *Must We Mean What We Say*, Cambridge, Cambridge University Press, 1998, p. xix.

33 The book, originally printed in articles in the *Architectural Building News*, which published it, included an 'Examination of the Uthwatt and Scott Reports'. A less dramatic link between warfare and reconstruction was drawn by Geddes in *Cities in Evolution: An Introduction to the Town Planning Movement and to the Study of Civics* [1915], New York, Howard Fertig, 1968 (with an Introduction by Percy Johnson-Marshall), p. 82:

> as we rebuild our cities as well as our fleets, as we modernise our universities and colleges, our culture-institutes and schools, as we have sought to do to our

Dreadnoughts, there will be far less fear of war and far more assurance in whatever issue.

34 *Practical Application of Town Planning Powers*, p. 39.

35 *City of God*, trans. J. W. L. Ward, London, Oxford University Press, 1965, p. 256. An earlier example of such conflation can be found in early British settlement in North America, for which see M. Vessey, 'The Citie of God (1610) and the London Virginia Company', *Augustinian Studies*, 1999, vol. 2, pp. 257–81, and, more generally, M. Vessey (ed.) *Introduction to History, Apocalypse, and the Secular Imagination: New Essays on Augustine's City of God*, Bowling Green, OH, Bowling Green State University, 1999, pp. 1–17.

36 *Plan for Plymouth*, Plymouth, Underhill, 1943, p. 11, written in conjunction with J. Paton Watson, the City Engineer and Surveyor. In the following sentences, however, Abercrombie provided a more materialist definition of planning:

> The fundamental essence of planning is first, the knowledge of life and the understanding of human beings and their difficulties: and, secondly, to secure a well-balanced distribution and relationship in the use of land to ensure that the places where people live, work and play and their means of movement are arranged and shaped to obtain a maximum of health, safety, convenience, prosperity and enjoyment for everyone.
>
> (ibid.)

A somewhat less positive interpretation of the Blitz appeared in *The County of London Plan Explained by E. J. Carter and Ernö Goldfinger*, West Drayton, Middlesex, Penguin, 1945:

> Has the Blitz cleared our vision too and made it possible to see what London might be? And, if we can see this, have we the imagination and power to realise our hopes, or shall we just return to the old unplanned city blocks, to the same old wild activity of private speculation, to recreate the same old jumble of courtyards and streets and competing facades?
>
> (ibid., pp. 12–13)

37 The statistics of housing units 1918–1942, 1.5 million with state assistance, appears in Abercrombie, *Town and Country Planning*, 1944 edn, p. 157. See also Sheppard, *Building for the People*; Gibbon, *Reconstruction*; and Morris, *British Town Planning*. The Garden City at Welwyn established in 1919 experienced such slow growth that it was reorganised in 1934.

38 *British Empire Exhibition 1925 Official Guide*, London, Fleetway Press, p. 45. The links between post-war Imperial propaganda and Modernist design are examined in the author's 'Refabricating the Imperial image', in J. MacKenzie (ed.) *Exhibiting the Empire*, Manchester, Manchester University Press, forthcoming.

39 Anthony Jackson, *The Politics of Architecture: A History of Architecture in Britain*, Toronto, University of Toronto Press, 1970.

40 Liscombe, 'Refabricating the Imperial Image' and Paul Greenhalgh, *Ephemeral Vistas: The Expositions Universelles, Great Exhibitions and World's Fairs 1851–1939*, Manchester, Manchester University Press, 1988. The light-industrial/agricultural village valorised in the 'Democracity' Exhibition in the Trylon-Perisphere complex at the New York Fair organised by Henry Dreyfuss was influenced by Ebenezer Howard, as noted by Dell Upton, *Architecture in the United States,* New York, Oxford University Press, 1998, pp. 183–4.

41 *The British Pavilion Guide*, London, Her Majesty's Stationery Office, 1939: the quotes in the succeeding sentences are from pp. 23 and 30.

42 The 'garden suburb' was probably closer to the Modern Garden City designed by Marcel Breuer and F. R. S. Yorke in 1936, praised by Johnson-Marshall, *Rebuilding Cities*, p. 115.

43 *Rebuild London*, London, J. M. Dent, 1945, p. 4; Purdom, Manager of Welwyn Garden City

company, also published *The Garden City*, 1913; *The Building of Satellite Towns*, 1925; *A Plan of Life*, 1939; *The New Order*, 1941; and *Britain's Cities To-Morrow*, 1942.

44 *Rebuild London*, p. 7.

45 *Rebuild London*, p. 12.

46 *Rebuild London*, pp. 125–41, including on p. 131, 'The business of the architect is not to make hell tolerable, but to see that it is not created. We must admit that the architect has had precious little to do with London', and on p. 133, 'All future building should be in architectural hands, and every part of London should be under architectural expression.'

47 *Rebuild London*, p. 134; although Walter Gropius, for one, endorsed Purdom's rejection of the idiosyncratic and repetitive. Later on p. 208, Purdom rejected American high rise architecture and complex traffic systems together with Le Corbusier's 'City of To-Morrow', as a 'heady glory of steel and glass, a city of skyscrapers for business and tenements for houses'.

48 *Rebuild London*, pp. 237–8. A comparable zeal informs in Frank Pick, *Britain Must Rebuild*, London, Kegan Paul, 1943.

49 *Houses*, Harmondsworth, Penguin, 1947, p. 4. A comparable slippage into religious language acquired through socialisation (social church attendance and schooling) is evident in Gwilym Gibbon's choice of title for the fifth chapter of Part I of *Reconstruction* (1942), 'The Parable of the Open Space'.

50 *Exeter Phoenix*, London, Architectural Press, quoting a German propaganda broadcast of 4 May 1942 regarded as typifying the evil regime of Hitler, 'We have chosen as targets the most beautiful places in England. Exeter was a jewel. We have destroyed it', p. 28. At the end of the book Sharp reiterated the opportunity-of-war argument, 'And the positive and comprehensive rebuilding and renewal of the centre of the city has been made possible by German bombs and a British Bill – the Town and Country Planning Act of 1944', p. 130.

51 Ibid., p. 97.

52 Ibid., respectively pp. 116 and 51.

53 *City of London*, London, Architectural Press, 1951, p. 46, stating that the cathedral 'should remain its chief building'.

54 The Merriman Committee is cited in Purdom, *Rebuild London*, pp. 140–1; the illustrations of these ruinscape gardens in *The City of London* were drawn by Gordon Cullen, author of *Townscape*, London, Architectural Press, 1961.

55 Illustrated in model form in Dunnett, *Guide*, pp. 10–11 and 20–1.

56 The importance of the church designed by Nicholas Hawksmoor, 1714–20, is evident in the aerial photographs printed by Johnson-Marshall in *Rebuilding Cities*, pp. 238–45; pp. 215–37 shows the Lansbury Reconstruction Area.

57 *Interim Report on Choice of Agency*, 21 January 1946; incidentally the fourteen-member committee included a member of the Cadbury family.

58 *Interim Report*, section 10, pp. 54–5.

59 *Interim Report*, p. 3, this vision was in deliberate contrast to the satellite principle harboured with the original Garden City concept.

60 *Tower Block*, plate 1. Starkleigh Way formed part of the Bonamy-Delaford Development in the Metropolitan Borough of Camberwell designed by a team led by F. O. Hayes in 1964. Brett in *Architecture in a Crowded World*, p. 2, expressed the failure of good intentions thus, 'Conversely, the garden cities and other model communities appeared to be the negation of art, and it seemed inconceivable that any Dickens or Baudelaire would see the light of day in a New Town.' Brett also wrote *Landscape in Distress*, London, Architectural Press, 1965, mapping the steady erosion of the countryside by poorly planned urban expansion and private development which was to be exacerbated during the Thatcher era.

Chapter 8

Privet

Theologies of privacy in some modernist urbanism

Rob Stone

> And there in my garden, upon a bench covered with green
> turves, we sat down talking together.
>
> (Thomas More)[1]

> We see row upon row of unwashed clothes in the gardens,
> waving in the wind as if joyously antagonistic. Would it not be
> possible to erect some kind of high screen to hide this eyesore?
>
> (Lindsay Grant)[2]

As a major figure in the literature of heroically Modernist architectural
innovation, Serge Chermayeff is perhaps best known for his overt architectural gestures towards a decidedly public kind of living. Such communalism
may be described in such an iconically Modernist work as the De La Warr
Pavilion, at Bexhill-on-Sea, which Chermayeff designed in collaboration
with Erich Mendelsohn, and which was completed in 1935. As a theorist of
architectural practice, however, Chermayeff is just as well known for his
rather later interests in the notion of privacy: what it means, and how it
may be spatially accomplished.

     The role of this public/private dichotomy at work in the charac-
terisation of Chermayeff's *œuvre* deserves consideration. The drawing out of
this dichotomy would be helped, in part, by placing it in a context of the

character of privacy in some particular examples of public housing ventured during the period 1930–70, and I shall address this here. It is important, I think, to note that while it is a striking feature of it, the significance of Chermayeff's career should not be seen entirely in terms of a gradual shift of attention from public responsibilities in the 1930s, to the achievement and preservation of privacy in the 1960s. Clearly the difference between the Bexhill project and his highly influential book *Privacy and Community*, co-authored with Christopher Alexander in 1963, marks such a shift.

Chermayeff's interests may be seen in terms of an intensifying and increasingly nuanced repudiation of distinctions between the public and private spheres, though. This second perspective, while richer and more allusive, is more difficult to dignify in the simple terms of a close reading of Chermayeff's works alone. A context of Modernist historiographical prejudices concerning the aesthetics of privacy, and the further context of illuminating anecdotes regarding the use and expectations of specific types of public and private space during these two periods in Chermayeff's career, will help cast this rather mysterious facet of the modernist spatial-cultural objectile into a new and hopefully revealing light. This is a discussion that will need to make reference to back gardens and railway carriages, as well as near-mystical experiences of modernist urban space – among other things.

Cultivating an acquaintance

This is not quite as narcissistic as it may at first appear. I live in a small, low-rise, gardened, ex-council maisonette in the Elephant and Castle area of London. It is a rather beautiful example of one of those buildings, designed by the London County Council's architecture department, which was emancipated from municipal interference by those unhinged statutory attacks on public housing which were made in Britain during the early 1980s.[3] As products of the imagination of the British working class, we share a birthday, my house and I. We were both eighteen years old when that legislation was passed. Thatcherism hit us both at the same age, and we suffered accordingly. New landmark changes were heralded. In April 2000 a set of tentative governmental proposals were published by the Department of the Environment, Transport and the Regions in a green paper. Called *Quality and Choice: A Decent Home for All*, it aims to outline a housing strategy for the next century.

Happiness or discomfiture at what has passed, or what may come, is not quite the subject of this chapter. Clearly much has changed in the course of twenty years, and more is scheduled to change. But few of those changes are detailed in the housing legislation. Recently, while leafing through Miles Glendinning's and Stefan Muthesius's monumental history of public housing in Britain, *Tower Block*, I was struck by the idea of my own place in such an architectural history, a history which itself tracks changes in statutory responses to political attitudes to mass-housing provision.[4] I was struck at the same time with a question concerning the extent to which it is possible to personalise an augmentation of this history, while still maintaining some pertinent relationship to statutory instruments. What would this pertinence require?

If you cut through the elegantly 'Georgian' West Square at the end of my road, you will eventually end up in a mixed area of small, private and municipal estates which were developed in the period from the late 1950s to the very early 1980s. One of these estates is composed mainly of attached, single-storeyed, two- and three-bedroomed courtyard houses that were built by the council in 1964/5.

They are fascinating. Not necessarily for the fact that, during this most recent inflation of house prices in central London, one of them will set you back by a little fortune, and not even because they are referred to in the most diffident, approximate and unglossed manner by Pevsner as 'Scandinavian-looking'. Though all of these things of course figure, the buildings fascinate perhaps because of the peculiarly enclosed lifestyle option that they depict as buildings; introverted seclusion in the densest of urban residential enclaves.

These courtyard houses also offer some intractable subjective challenges. What is recognised in the literature concerning this kind of courtyard building, is the fact that, where overlooked from the towers nearby, they present a rather obdurate prospect of large expanses of flat, bitumenised roof. It seems that in some regards they lack urban decorum, and it is a comfort to know that this architectural metonym of the overseen party roof is nestled away there in the literature on modernist public housing.

Despite their propinquity and partial contiguity, these buildings seem to be adrift. They present few windows facing onto public areas. They seem blithely to ignore their surrounding thoroughfares; though there doesn't seem to be any surliness or *hauteur* in the buildings' attitudes. Pristine, they are also open to desecration. Apart from one striking and locally reviled instance of applied rustication, there are no demotic additions to the semantics of defensible space here. There is no broken glass or razor wire on the walls. But the areas around the houses do feel surreal. Not hostile, but disturbingly 'empty-yet-populated'. And, if it sounds like I am shaping this response to urban space according to the visual theories of haunted desertion forwarded photographically by people like Eugene Atget, or even Paul Nash, for instance, that's not so bad. The area is odd. I would say it was uncanny, but that is both too precise and here inaccurate a term.

Invariably, I feel an uncomfortably paradoxical sense of being caught between a starkly vulnerable nudity and the curious licence to be prurient, which seems to be precipitated by the shy comportment of the buildings. It would be tempting to escape that sense by vaulting one of these spatial demarcations, these baldly polite and mutely exclusive walls. Were it not for the certain knowledge that this would cause such an existential catastrophe for the privacy of any witness to that sanctuary-seeking intrusion (something akin to crashing through the roof of an occupied glasshouse), I wouldn't hesitate to do it.

There are two kinds of space dreamed with these houses. One is the surrounding, public one, though that is completely the wrong word – 'public'. It is an ambiguous space, a street-space, one which seems, paradoxically, to behave in too inappropriately an operational manner. That is to say, that by foregrounding itself annunciatively as a thoroughfare, and letting the conventional modes of urban deportment flow unpreparedly past, the vicinity of these buildings makes for some kind of crisis for everyday promenading or idling or perambulating or commuting or going on errands. That crisis might be a surreal one, but there are probably better terms and you might need a poet, someone like Robert Creely, for example, to supply the right images for the workings of this precise propinquity to privacy and to articulate the deceiving sense of sudden cultural novelty or uniqueness involved in it.

Equally problematic, the other kind of space could be described as a private one. But, it is perhaps more than private, more like a temporally suspended and even silent space, a refuge; that of the garden and interiors on the other side of the un-dressed, un-graffitoed walls.

These buildings seem both to depict and to be performative of a set of emergent social relations that bear on a notion of everyday, vernacular architectural *flânerie*. The kinds of privacy and the kinds of public space suggested by these buildings and the mutually defining relationships between these two terms 'public' and 'private' are new. They are informed by, but are not dependent upon, their 1930s' precedents, their 1960s' context, and their place in a contemporary and subjective form of overlain, pluralised urbanism. An urbanism which is both popular and philosophical.

There is another, and for me, a larger reason for my interest here. This is to do with my long-standing attempts to find a way of making my grandfather an object of interest for architectural history. My paternal grandfather's brother, my great-uncle, was a cabinet-maker. He lived in Poplar, in east London, all his life. In that regard, he is implicitly of interest to aspects of architectural history and design history. He already is an archival element in the recounting of the history of the East End furniture trade.[5] So, my relationship to his memory is similar to these houses that I have mentioned. For a particular architectural historian, they are caught up in, and probably describe the gaps between, both public historical and private historical figurations.

In 1938, my grandfather – a painfully polite and private man – left Poplar and London from Liverpool Street Station.[6] He moved, with his first son and his ebullient, gregariously matriarchal wife, my grandmother, to a semi-detached house on a recently built estate on the edge of the old market town of Rochford. Rochford is towards the end of the suburbanised drift that was then developing along the Essex coast from Tilbury to Southend.

My grandparents' house was built in 1932, and what I have become interested in is its very un-Modernist, gardened, semi-detached value by the early 1960s. This is not simply a question of shifting fiscal realty values. Or rather it is, but the question of realty values requires some sense of cultural modulation. A period of thirty years, here, embraces a series of shifts in the nature of architectural Modernism's encounter with the working and lower middle classes in Britain. Architectural history, as a discipline, is well used to apprehending this relationship as the sometimes heroic and sometimes damnable implementation over time of a series of diktats concerning minimal housing requirements, for instance, handed down from the various meetings of CIAM. This view certainly has some virtues in terms of evaluating the cultural significance of particular canonical Modernist architectural paradigms. However, an attention to the spaces of this other kind of domestic, vernacular architecture, and the ambiguously shifting cultural ambitions of some of those who inhabited it, will cast some of the conventional understandings of the emergence of Modernist architectural types in a different light.

My grandfather was called up almost as soon as he arrived in Rochford: Royal Air Force groundcrew. When he came back from the war, he resumed a job with Wiggins Teape, the paper manufacturers, with whom he had started work as a stable-boy in the 1920s. This meant him commuting everyday back between Rochford and Liverpool Street Station in order to get to the factory at Aldwych. This placed him, theologically, in a curious kind of temporal paradox. He had access to a private domain, the rear garden of his suburban semi, with its complex organisation of space, its trellises, sheds, fences, hedges and drifts of fallow and planted soil. He also had a public domain, with its different modes of association, its shifting temporalities, its habits of daily migration and its ritualised kinds of reading and contemplation.

There seems to be a kind of isotopic relationship between his garden and the courtyard gardens of the houses in Southwark mentioned above. My grandparents were good gardeners. That is to say, that they conformed to a standardised approach. It might be said that people like my grandparents practised a particular kind of almost patriotic gardening that revelled in its provincialism and its curious integrity. It was a type of domestic horticulture that made a metonymic representation of the morality of national agriculture. Something that was shot through with allusions to the Digging for Victory rhetoric of national self-sufficiency, but which, falling carefully between meagreness and thriftless excess, managed also to articulate a kind of buttoned-up, responsible and modest domestic prosperity. Few enough potatoes to avoid signifying poverty; just enough tomatoes to signify prudence. But always, plenty of fish, blood and bone. Described and characterised by the magazine *Amateur Gardener* and its related publications, it was a kind of gardening that might be said to have had its conventions. Moreover, at the time, to develop those conventions would have been, in fact, to disappoint them. Also, it can be seen that in journals like the *Amateur Gardener*, despite a courting of industrial modernity, suggested in allusions to modern pesticides and fumigating and spraying techniques, that there was a sense of timelessness articulated in its ongoing conversations about the restrained practicability of the English, suburban, working-class garden between the 1930s and the 1960s.

It is important to recognise that, closer to home, the civic side of Rochford and the day-to-day running of the garden was largely my grandmother's affair. My grandfather hardly saw the place in daylight, except at the weekend, when it was transformed by his reticent presence. Otherwise, he had his public life; his unobtrusive commuting, with his head politely buried in the *Daily Herald*.[7] This commuting had, as I've suggested, a different temporality to it. He was one of that commuting generation of working-class people who, for the large part, were the first to have mortgages. That is to say, that he and my grandmother had, for their class, a new, temporal relationship to property and to propriety. Reading the newspaper, watching international crises develop and pass and his own anxieties for his mortgage with them, my grandfather told me that he could feel the temporal unfolding of the mortgage, its value increasing, his personal 'place' changing.

This is already a theological conception, simultaneously metonymic and metaphoric. The paradox of the public life occasioning the contemplation of moving, material time and the private life of timeless time, all time in a garden's instant, is a metonymically Augustinian conception, one which became interesting again to all sorts of people in the 1930s through all sorts of media, including crime fiction, popular architectural history, the radio as well as papal encyclicals. It is, for instance, something that T. S. Eliot rested on when he described the timeless and pervasive English Catholic greeneries in 'Little Gidding' and the other poems of the *Four Quartets*.

> Here, the intersection of the timeless moment
> Is England and nowhere. Never and always.[8]

Some things represent obvious hiatuses in even attempting to secure a happy, linear and uncomplicated route between the 1930s and the 1960s. Changes in the physicalities of 'public' space of cities, TV and tourism, suburbanisation, new construction techniques, the rhetoric of 'Reconstruction', the war, all have this effect of discontinuation. All these, and more, intervene historically between the dates. But interpretatively too, there is the invention and promulgation of new forms of art and architectural history, the apparent materialism of the pronouncements leading up to the Vatican II, interests in Aquarianism and numerologies, changes of heart by major architectural polemicists, the availability of new, episodic literatures, such as the thrillers that supplanted the philosophical rigours of the 1930s' detective novel. It is a highly various array of available morphologies.

And, it is as a function of this change and inconsistency that I would like to think about Serge Chermayeff in the 1930s *and* in the 1960s.

Privet

The early writings of Nikolaus Pevsner embrace complex theological intrigues: a native but lightly worn Judaism, a purposefully adopted Lutheranism and a fascinating, unadvertised intellectual dalliance with Catholicism. In these latter Catholic interests, he seemed to unpick almost everything that constitutes his reputation; that of an ascetic, teleologically minded, rather insensitive, integrationist and rudely Modernist cultural commentator. Sometimes he did this unpicking pseudonymously, taking the Baroque-inspired *nom de plume* of Peter F. R. Donner to write of his interests in suburban domestic design.[9] Sometimes he simply did not bother with such feints. His writings of the late 1920s and 1930s are particularly marked with a desire to suggest the architectural articulation or externalisation of different kinds of spiritual inner life.[10] These things are related.

It is possible that he may have been talking more sympathetically to a suburban audience than we generally care to think. Such issues as the organisational role of popular fiction in his arguments, the temporal structure of mortgages, the relative sophistication of broadcast radio technology (there are important musical implications here both for his writing and for his audience's reading skills) and the state of the anglophone debate on the nature of the Baroque at the time may all be seen to figure in this unexpected suburban sympathy. We need to be aware of politically and aesthetically allegorical sophistication when reading Pevsner, especially when he writes of different sites and forms and deposits of urban cultural modernity. We should pay attention to his theologies.

Pevsner had some interesting things to say about privacy. Though, as you might expect from someone so keen to allegorise architectural honesty, frankness in the expression of structure and so on, he did so allusively. In 1968, he published a paper in the *Journal of the Warburg and Courtauld Institutes*, entitled 'The Architectural Setting of Jane Austen's Novels'. Pevsner's discussion of privacy, here, was largely implied, and he did it by directing to some suggestive narrative moments of Austen's spatial and emotional privacy, while choosing to maintain himself in the guise of the learned, but perhaps slightly perplexed, 'Herr Doktor Professor'. My guess is that he thought to address those arch-consumers of both Austen and dreams of privacy, then and now: a suburban audience. More, it seems likely that he was supplying yet more dissidence for his own reputation as an insistent and poetically naïve historian.

I mention Pevsner and his playfully delinquent toying with notions of privacy, because the more recent literature of architectural history is, by and large, weak on the issue. The word is used often, but its meanings are taken too frequently to be singularly self-evident, when really the term is profoundly multifarious and far-reaching.

To be fair, there has been some important structuring of the question in recognition of this. In a pungently polemical article in the *Architect's Journal* in 1983, Ian Davison took issue with the tropological meaning of 70 feet (the more familiar 21 metres) that is statutorily required in Britain as the distance between the frontages and the backs of houses.[11] In the course of wondering why planners in the 1980s, as he thought, were so disablingly affected by the demands of privacy, he alluded to some migration of the meaning of the figure of 70 feet between the early 1920s (the period of the Tudor Walters Report) and the early 1960s (the period of the Parker Morris Report).

Davison highlighted a significant moment in 1952, in an HMSO pamphlet entitled 'The Density of Residential Areas', and argued that here was a decisive moment when 70 feet ceased to be sponsored by Raymond

Unwin's entrancement by the modern access of light to buildings as way of exorcising the image of dark and dripping congeries from the urban imagination, only to be replaced by a suburban and perhaps slightly paranoid and prudish desire not to be overlooked either indoors or in the back garden, to have direct and unshared access to a rear garden, not to hear or to be overheard, not to be unceremoniously bothered by the neighbours or any suspicious callers. All of these things were to be secured by a refiguring in terms of privacy of the significance of the already legislated 70 feet. This was a set of decorums which Davison felt could only hinder the ambitions of urban residential planning in the mid-1980s. It is a highly emotive piece. Davison tried to say that privacy was a state of mind in the observer and observed, not a denumerably spatial concern.

Architectural history also has at its disposal Beatriz Colomina's astonishing essay on the intruding relationship of Le Corbusier to Eileen Gray in the design of Gray's private residence, E1027, in the late 1920s.[12] By focusing on the symbolic significance of a bit of lesbian pornography, uninvitedly muralled onto the definingly 'Modernist' interior walls of the house, and by making some historical observations about the panoptical function of Modernism as represented by Le Corbusier's decision to build a small, almost Laugian hut on the site that overlooked E1027, Colomina, like Davison, has isolated an important moment in the transition of the figural structure of privacy. For all its apparent overtness, Corbusian Modernism was riddled with secrets, codes and small mythologies on how to live and found ways of reaching in from the public arena of architectural discourse right to the most intimate moments of a particular private life.

Colomina's essay is important in showing the way that the 'civic' or the 'social' sphere holds the public and the private in mutual relation. By showing both to be constituent parts of the social, she demonstrates that the private is not synonymous with the unpoliced, unobserved, unnameable and unrecognisable personal, physical and psychological activities of people. Rather, she implies that for one dominating, 'social' understanding, the public and the private may not be pulled apart from each other. Except, that is, when the nature of long-established conceptions of the relationships between them have actually already dehisced into touchily isolated seclusion, on the one hand, and anonymous urbanity on the other.

Which leads me to a third variety of architectural discussion of privacy. This is the much more instrumentally minded research into the roles of privacy in open-plan office design, put forward by Virginia Kupritz. In the early 1990s, Kupritz produced extensive work on bull-pen style, stock-trading offices and the need for some kind of demarcation of private office space (by low immovable screens, for instance) that could be easily transgressed by the traders.[13] No more than a mere signifier of defensible space. A form of sociability is functionally vital in these places. And, paradoxically, this sociability decreases when there is no architectural suggestion of the possibility of privacy, and of the alleviation of the spectre of unbroken mutual surveillance. The traders' habit of hugging phones to their ears is probably meaningful itself in this particular territorialisation.

Her findings are based on interview. She has provided some important insights into such familiar corporate layouts, but what is more important is perhaps the way that she developed these insights into functional privacy.

Kupritz has devised an analytical technique: Heuristic Elicitation Methodology. This is a schema which, through a series of informed estimations, interpretations, leading questions and other structuring of interview material, attempts to ascertain information that the subject might not either be willing to divulge or even have the appropriate conceptual skills and vocabulary to articulate.[14]

That habit of interpolating the 'actual' nature of spatial symbolic meaning by critically revising the stated emotional relationships of individuals to their environment is a profoundly established architectural-historical one. A desire to give externalised visual and verbal form to interior, private, perhaps even unformed mental conditions and conceptions is precisely the line devised by Erwin Panofsky in his theorisation of iconology as a conceptual mode for the pursuit of architectural history in the late 1930s. Panofsky was at his most explicit about describing this desire for figural, public exteriorisation of psychological experience and understanding in 1951 in his iconological essay on Aquinas's *Summa Theologiae* and Gothic Architecture.[15] Many architectural commentators, including Pevsner, have taken his lead.[16]

This kind of profound cognitive relationship between architectural history and theology as mediated by understandings of the relationship between public and private – as seen in Panofsky – while nothing new and very likely uncontentious, is nevertheless important. The theological framing of the aspects of discourse on urban space in the 1930s is familiar.

Some examples: in 1929 W. H. Brindley published a collection of essays on urban culture under the title *The Soul of Manchester*.[17] One of these was Lord Crawford's 1924 essay, given as the Roscoe lecture of that year, and published in the *Town Planning Review* at the time. It was called 'The Soul of Cities', and, as an important Mancunian civic politician, he wished to speak about Manchester. Now, this was not an overtly Thomist excursion into the theological poetics of images of the city of the kind written at the time by the likes of Charles Williams or T. S. Eliot or

G. K. Chesterton, for instance, but it was theologically structured. In a paper inventing an ancient, European urban history, Crawford exercised the familiar conceit of the purview, and imagined himself atop the Gothic pile of Alfred Waterhouse's Manchester Town Hall.[18] From there he surveyed the development of Manchester to the south and south-west and took umbrage at the encroachment of the city's new suburbs onto the campus of the university. His point was quite clear: the university should be regarded as part of the discrete integrity of the urban civic body and the suburbs should be further exurbanised. A green belt should stave off the dormitories' corruption of the integrity of the civic centre. He cited John Evelyn and the rebuilding of London and, perhaps, in doing so, intended some unpleasant reference to a view of the desirable exurbanisation of undesirable religious minorities. He spoke of the corporal condition of ancient cities. The metaphors he used for the physical and conceptual integrity of the body were directly theological, and, as a piece of philology, the impact of the essay was remarkable. It continued to be quoted in the town planning literature of the 1930s.

When, in 1934, C. H. Reilly – then Head of the School of Civic Design at Liverpool University – was asked to give the Roscoe lecture, he returned to Crawford's theological metaphorics though the use of the visceral images of a healthily functioning city.[19] He insisted that it was the observable interaction of the various components of the body of the city that constituted its soul. It is a neat example of the exercise of urban taxonomy to establish the typological *mysterium* of the city.

Reilly had odd ideas about models for public life. In his biography, *Scaffolding in the Sky*, he suggested the offices and political dimensions of Liverpool University as a paragon.[20] Like others, he saw the model of the university as one shaped by understandings of the Greek *polis*. A public system of senate meetings, boards of study and other forums which were transparent in, and accountable for, their actions. What he saw this enabling, however, was the effective activity of private, actually secret, caucuses. In fact, he wrote that he was very proud of the way that such a caucus, 'The New Testament Group', went surreptitiously about securing its apparently decent but in any event unquestionable political and pedagogic programme.

These ideas of the civic function of secretly formulated and enacted private interests were reflected in his urban design proposals. Reilly was unusually convinced of his own town planning proposals. He suggested cloistered living. The idea was for communities of 250 households surrounding very large greens which were themselves surrounded by an outward-facing wall of houses.[21] It was intended that people would live

8.1
Serge Chermayeff
and Erich
Mendelsohn, Cohen
House, 64 Old
Church Street,
Chelsea, London,
1936, street front,
from F. R. S. Yorke,
*The Modern House
in England*, London,
Architectural Press,
1937, reprint 1947,
p. 32

either in family houses or in small, unkitchened, bridal suites. District heating, obviously. Cooking and cleaning provided communally for those entitled: meals were to be delivered in insulated containers. A privacy was allowed, but so comprehensively rationalised was the suggested establishment for intimacy, that it is difficult to see how privacy could come to signify anything here. This privacy certainly did not represent a constituent of the kind of social realm synthesised by the interaction of public and private life suggested by J. M. Richards and by Thomas Sharp.

Nevertheless, in people marrying and having children early, and living on such a site for the rest of their lives, Reilly saw the end to crime, prostitution, slatternliness, nervousness, venereal disease, child abuse, abortion, hysteria, alcoholism, adultery, bad heredity (everyone would know the bad families) and petty savagery. Anyone not wishing to live in his communities, whom he defined as 'deliberately' childless couples, would not get access to a house. Simple as that. Though it may be said that each town plan has in mind its ideal private and public subjects, very few town planners of this time in Britain located their proposals so overtly in a moral framework of the policed and policing family unit. This all has Distributist overtones, that is to say, it shares elements of the form of economics proposed by those at the time who invented and pursued a model of social reform derived from various readings of the papal encyclicals on such issues that were promulgated and referred to in the 1930s.[22]

This is not all that is extrapolable from and connected to this pattern of theological references in the 1930s. Note needs to be taken of the way that Crawford and Reilly's references to the theologically flavoured

8.2
Maxwell Fry and
Walter Gropius,
Levy House, 66 Old
Church Street,
Chelsea, London,
1936, view from
balcony showing
Georgian houses on
Old Church Street
in background,
from F. R. S. Yorke,
*The Modern House
in England*, London,
Architectural Press,
1937, reprint 1947,
Frontispiece. The
view in the reverse
direction would
show the prospect
from the Cohen
House across the
shared garden and
onto the rear
gardens of the
houses in Chelsea
Square.

overview of the city describe some familiar parallels with the panoptical purview of architects and architectural critics at the time. The image of the rationalised discreteness of the Corbusian city was articulated and promoted in a view from above (one incidentally championed by the then converting Evelyn Waugh).[23] It evinced too in the taxonomical accounts of London provided by Steen Eiler Rasmussen, especially those famous aerial photographs in *London: The Unique City*.[24]

It is important, though, that both of these examples gesture their overviews with reference to aerial images, rather than the view supplied by the 'authentic' tradition of 'English-Catholic' architecture proposed by Crawford and Reilly. That is to say, that the discreteness of somewhere like Manchester could be poetically enjoyed from the city's own architectural substance, whereas London and the *Plan Voisin* required a suitable, extra-architectural mediation.

The extension of Reilly's poetics of the visibility of the social soul of the urban fabric seems to provide some kind of analogue to the then developing writings of another figure, Thomas Sharp. His views on the integrity of civic life and the demand for a return to the Georgian street as

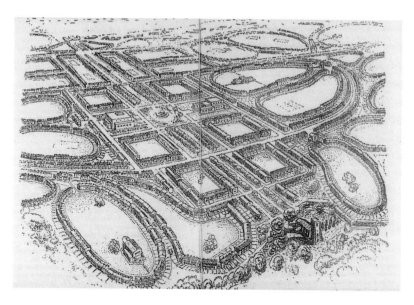

8.3
C. H. Reilly,
Housing Proposal,
bird's eye, from
Lawrence Wolfe,
*The Reilly Plan: A
New Way of Living*,
London, Nicholson
and Watson, 1945,
p. 144

the place where civic society would play itself out and, importantly, see its own social processes were taken by some to be of fundamental value.[25]

Just one instance of this partial identification with Sharp was in the way that in the Introduction to F. R. S. Yorke's *The Modern House in England*, J. M. Richards made sure that he staged the significance of two adjacent houses built on Old Church Street in Chelsea in 1936 by Mendelsohn and Chermayeff (No. 64, the 'Cohen House') and Gropius and Fry (No. 66, the 'Levy House'), by drawing attention to the coordinate harmony between them and the Georgian houses in the background of the supplied photographs.[26] This was no idly speculative aestheticism on Richard's part, but the employment of Richard Payne Knight's repopularised theories of connoisseurial association in the invention of a gentlemanly notion of English modernism.[27] It seems that there was a concerted attempt on Richards' part metaphorically to locate emergent modernist design in the dreamed character of the vigorous, renewing bourgeois democracy of the eighteenth and early nineteenth century, by alluding to the politics of the street.

It should be noted with regard both to this and to what I mentioned earlier about the walls surrounding the gardens of those courtyard houses in Elephant and Castle, that Reilly's plans for settlements included the ringing of any group of houses with an unbroken belt of outward-facing houses that would demarcate the area of the settlement, give it place. That is an interestingly ambiguous relationship in Reilly where front walls of houses also take on a defensive, almost military and parochially demarcatory role along with decorative and other possible roles.[28]

If we go back to that image of the space I suggested surrounded the courtyard houses in Elephant and Castle in my earlier remarks, it seems that though driven by a desire for unimpeded public interaction, Reilly's ideological outlawing of unpoliced privacy leads to a public space no less surreal than that produced by the ideologically insisted-upon unpoliced privacy.

Interestingly, although they are there in the drawings, Reilly does not talk about back gardens. As I suggested, there existed in the 1930s a mature discourse on the meaning of the back garden. It became an important cultural trope. Not just in terms perhaps of the everyday gossipings and cooperations that passed over fences and hedges, but in broader terms, the rear garden became a site for publicly playing out the image of private England.

The following is from an episodic little book, *The Heart of London*, by the travel writer and chronicler of the British historical landscape, H. V. Morton. Morton wrote regular columns for the press, and was read by my grandfather a lot while commuting. In general, his articles sat alongside the muscular Christian socialism of those by George Lansbury in my grandfather's favoured daily paper, the *Daily Herald*. Morton wrote:

> For fourpence ha'penny you can have an exciting peep into roughly ten thousand lives by buying a ticket at Fenchurch Station and sitting in a train drawn by a keen little elder brother to Stephenson's Rocket. I know few things more provoking than the back gardens of London. It seems that the front of a house must be as glum as the face of a poker player. You must never be able to tell from the front of a house what is going on inside. But the back of the house casts off all restraint.[29]

Morton went on to describe mad collectors of scrap metal, Hogarthian women, 'dreary dumps littered with past enthusiasms', examples of unadulterated gallantry, hearty exchanges, physiognomies suggesting thoughts of immortal loyalty, great hate or just the expense of sausages for breakfast; all as the features of the suburban back garden. Is this the externalisation of hidden social domain?

Maybe. It is difficult to know if anything can be externalised or successfully mimed in this kind of episodic parabling. Morton's is, after all, a very recognisable urban typology. What is evinced, though, is an attempt to animate the timeless sociability of Merrie England. This kind of writing is very reminiscent of Chesterton's Chaucerian arguments about what lies beneath the façades of modern England.[30] It is also related to the invention and reinvention of local feudal tradition – May Queens, morris dancing, yeomen, historical tableaux and horticultural shows – popular at the time as

a means of inventing foundations for new suburban cultures. That Augustinian, metonymic temporal metaphor is revisited time and again.

Modern liturgies

What is further interesting in Morton's commentary is the nature of the space from which he observed all of this hidden civic activity. This mobile observational platform, the train carriage, regularly inhabited by my grand-

8.4
C. H. Reilly,
Housing Proposal,
perspective, from
Lawrence Wolfe,
*The Reilly Plan: A
New Way of Living*,
London, Nicholson
and Watson, 1945,
p. 112

father, could easily equate to the hut that Le Corbusier built to overlook Eileen Gray's domestic arrangements – panoptical, like Le Corbusier and like Reilly. Morton's train carriage could also be conceived of as eminently a modern, if not a Modernist, space, as a functional space, that is to say, as itself, a thoroughfare – apparently deprived of a truly meaningful public social virtue.

This is an old and well-established argument. It has been defended and relied on by cultural commentators as diverse as Hannah Arendt, Richard Sennett, Marc Augé and Henri Lefebvre.[31] It runs thus: the utter imbrication and mutual definition of the public and private spheres as they are articulated by the idea of social space have been largely destroyed during the past fifty years. This is because, in great part, the physical arenas of civic association have themselves been destroyed in the post-war period – by all sorts of things, but chiefly by something called architectural Modernism. They have been replaced by thoroughfares. Operationally conceived spaces. Functional spaces.

This is where the articulation of common urban space takes on its theologically defined characteristics very well. It is well known that one of the things that Nikolaus Pevsner was accused of in the 1960s was a kind of astylist rhetoric of functionalism. That is to say that he contributed to a widespread notion, with roots in a number of traditions, that 'Beauty Will Look After Herself'. If a certain rigorous honesty is applied to the resolution of practical concerns, rather than what were regarded as sheerly superfluous aesthetic concerns, then a new and epochally appropriate aesthetic would emerge.

'Nonsense!', replied Reyner Banham, a little later. Pevsner was talking about a style as florid as any other, and he should own up. At the time, even semi-sympathetic commentators in the 1930s, like Geoffrey Boumphrey and Martin Shaw Briggs, could see the value of understanding the socially, semantically 'functional' nature of the decorated façade. Yet the functionalist's conceit was widely agreed upon. As a result the 'successful' Modernist architecture, design and urban planning of the 1930s has been thought successful precisely because, miraculously, it did not signify anything other than itself as described by its identity with its function. Form does not allude to function, it *is* function. An agreement with this idea of the miraculous and at the same time everyday suspension of signification demands a profound fideism. A parallel for it, perhaps unsurprisingly in the general context of this chapter, might be found in the moment of Transubstantiation in the Eucharist. The moment where the wafer in an everyday miracle, for those in faith, stops signifying 'potential' or 'latency' and actually becomes the Body of Christ, with all the integrity implied by that. It does not signify anything; it merely, annunciatively, is.

This is just an interpretative morphology which, in a secularised form, could have been recognisable to some, perhaps privately. It could be seen as precisely the thinking that lies behind the acceptance of functionalism and it can be seen to represent a variety of small, Catholic, often socially dissident traditions which converse in order to constitute the Modernist debate in Britain at the time.

No convincing shape

I said I would return to Serge Chermayeff and the meaning of a garden. In Britain, the design of the De La Warr Pavilion, at Bexhill, with Erich Mendelsohn, is the work for which Chermayeff is best known. This building may give the impression that he was overly concerned, like Reilly, with indiscriminately inflicting a public and healthful life through 'the New Leisure' exercised by the population.[32] That really should apply only if one insists on seeing the Bexhill project through a view of English Modernism that takes Owen Williams' contemporary Pioneer Health Centre, in Peckham, as its paradigmatic example. This is especially so if the Pioneer Health Centre is taken literally by its overtly stated intentions to supply a kind of communal spa for newly suburbanised working-class families, at which the anthropologically minded medics of the area could study their object of interest in comfort, in private and at close quarters, while that object of interest learned new and complicated skills of municipal public association.[33]

On the other hand, one 1935 review of the Pavilion has already been cited by Stevens and Willis as saying that it was 'by far the most civilised thing that has been done on the south coast since the Regency'.[34] It is because of that Regency context again, and the implication for a view of a gentlemanly Modernism of the civic street of Sharp and Richards, that I'd like to look a little more closely at Chermayeff and Mendelsohn's 'Cohen House' at 64 Old Church Street in Chelsea, mentioned at the start of this chapter. Its street façade is uncompromising; even though Pevsner suggests the term 'unconvincing'. As in many of the most contentious buildings of the period, those by Connell, Ward and Lucas at Ruislip, for example, the services are exposed. Stairways, kitchens and cloakrooms all face onto the street. Their fenestrations comprise the façade. The long, white wall enclosing the gardens of this site and that of the adjacent building by Fry and Gropius is constituted in part by the street façade (the fenestrations) of the Chermayeff and Mendelsohn house.[35] The wall lends integrity. I mentioned that ambiguous defensive/decorative nature of the wall around the Reilly settlements. And, despite Richards's hopes for its civic virtue, the house has its back turned to the street as much as the courtyard houses in Elephant and Castle that I have described.

Henri Lefebvre has argued that the key conditions of an understanding of the end of the defining relationship and consequent change in the separate meanings of private and public space are that functional space appears to be transparent and non-signifying and that, also, this kind of space effects a kind of social sorting. By their nature, thoroughfares are

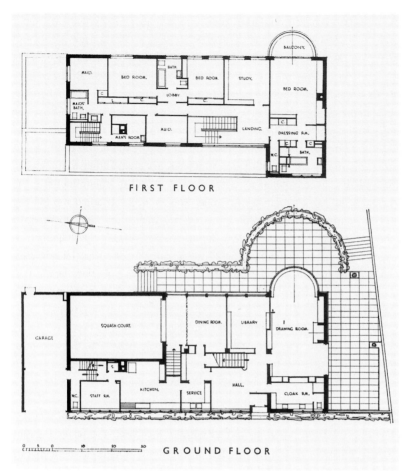

FIRST FLOOR

GROUND FLOOR

8.5
Serge Chermayeff and Erich Mendelsohn, Cohen House, 64 Old Church Street, Chelsea, London, 1936, ground and first floor plans, from F. R. S. Yorke, *The Modern House in England*, London, Architectural Press, 1937, reprint 1947, p. 32

used by particular people at particular times. That social sorting cuts across any number of potential taxonomies of class, cultural difference, gender, sexuality, and so on. If it can be sustained that certain kinds of functional space manufacture and occupy certain kinds of people, then the snubbing of the street by the Chermayeff/Mendelsohn house is simultaneously supported and undermined by its interior arrangements. The services, the 'functional' parts of the house are part of the façade, part of the enclosing wall and thus of the street. In that regard, there is a paradox. The façade's signification of a private realm beyond it is achieved through the articulation of the public, functional components of the building. Yet the servants' quarters on the first floor are in the rooms directly adjacent to those of the owners and look out onto the enclosed garden. This was actually a quite unremarkable form of propinquity in the 1930s.

The view from the garden into the house is as with any other courtyard-type of house, generous, open, mainly glazed. Clearly the design of the building envisaged no problems of intrusiveness from other members of the household. It is worth recalling, too, that the availability of F. R. Yerbury's photographs of the building secured a rhetorically public image of that private view. The building's apparent disavowal of the sorting capacity of domestic functional space has been defied by the way that the owners of the house and some of their employees so freely rubbed shoulders with each other.

Here is a notion of the bourgeois, isolated, rather than private, world, living out, in microcosm, a deceased aspect of public life with the bourgeois family and its employees as its actors. All cuddled around the private, unobservable, rear garden. As an objectile, as a field upon which relations may be brought together, Chermayeff's house may perhaps best be seen as a rite, a fetishising memory of a pre-modern set of social relations, one isolated from what was described at the time, in Yorke's book, as a modern functional, 'busy thoroughfare' and which renders Chermayeff's modernist wall ambiguous – enclosing of space and revealing of function – precisely at the very point of its functionalism.

Dwelling in booths

The meaning of the rear garden is certainly a troubling one here. There is potential for a delicious ambiguity, where the garden falls between different civic-theological suggestions, realising something that might be described as an extra-diegetic space. That is to say, something precipitated by, but never reducible to, the relationships between differing conceptions of garden space, as they rub against each other. The fact that the Cohen House itself lies within spitting distance of the last remaining fragment of the wall of St Thomas More's large formal garden – a metonymic reminder of a dissident, pre-modern, Catholic political time and space – is, in itself, interesting enough. So, too, in another way, is the fact that since its construction in the 1930s the frontage of the house has acquired for itself a stretch of privet, tucked up tight against the wall. In ways it appears incongruous, this terse nod to a distinctly suburban signifier of defensible space. It is so close to the wall that it seems to comprise a part of the frontage of the building as much as the fenestrations of the stairways and kitchens mentioned earlier. It is forced to announce its function strictly as a signifier only. It screens nothing. In other ways, though, this privet is less incongruous; rhyming with the usage of shrubbery in other parts of this area of the eighteenth-century Chelsea village.[36]

The prospect from the rear garden itself is one of further private realms. It only overlooks other rear gardens, those of the houses backing on to it from Chelsea Square, dating from 1812. These are precisely the type of Georgian houses that Richards made figure so significantly in the Introduction to Yorke's book. It is this propinquity of Regency and Modern that starts to suggest some kind of sense for the way that the frontage of the Cohen House turns its back on the street and towards the private demesnes of its neighbours, even as those very neighbours maintain their elegant and democratic comportment towards the civic arena of Chelsea Square.

The garden to the Cohen House is not something that either H. V. Morton or my grandfather could have seen from any train journey. It is not overlooked by public spaces, only other private ones. Yet it may have been available to my grandfather in other ways. Erich Mendelsohn, the co-author of the Cohen House with Chermayeff, was someone who was at the time soon to assume the position as the leading designer of modernist synagogues. He was just starting to make the social and political connections that were to secure that position for him. There may have been a form of unlikely isotopism between my grandfather's garden and the garden of the Cohen House. If this isotopy existed at all it would have been only a transient and irregular similarity, but similarity nevertheless. I have mentioned that my grandparents' gardening was of a type, and that this type was concerned with the schematic signification of agriculture and self-sustenance,

8.6
Serge Chermayeff and Erich Mendelsohn, Cohen House, 64 Old Church Street, Chelsea, London, 1936, garden front, from F. R. S. Yorke, *The Modern House in England*, London, Architectural Press, 1937, reprint 1947, p. 33

before anything else. I even suggested that the very practice of gardening somehow signalled their own sense of having moved as well. I should have added that there was a curiously pagan sense to the local cultural landscape in Rochford at the time.[37] My grandmother took her sick children to the local doctor. Her neighbours took theirs to the white witches in nearby Hawkwell, Pagglesham and Canewdon. Perhaps, then, in light of this, I should also have added that, in my grandmother's hands at least, the garden was decidedly Church of England; this was less the case for my grandfather.

The possible relationship between her garden and what may happen in a Jewish garden is something that, through friendships made in Poplar, my grandmother knew about. The notion of the 'goodly trees' as a representation of an agriculture in 'the land of Egypt' and as laid down in the sections of Leviticus detailing the Jewish feasts (23:40) is something that chimes with the representative nature of her own gardening practice. Moreover, the practice at Sukkot of building tabernacles (temporary, lightly covered booths) in the garden, as a reminder of the years wandering in the wilderness, is something that may well precipitate a sense of public space for the Cohen garden. The ritual occupation of this archetypal, though certainly not Laugian hut during Sukkot may be regarded as intellectually private, even isolated, but equally, metonymically, public; known to be the shared preoccupation of others, something concerned with the performative contemplation of shared identity and history.[38]

This is without doubt a scavenging and speculative form of archivalism. How else could these and other meanings be secured historically for the Cohen garden, except conversationally, through recourse to half-started, half-finished stories? It does, however, throw more light on the possible functionalism of Chermayeff and Mendelsohn's wall. And, this becomes interesting where these meanings for functional privacy in Chermayeff's architecture are allowed to migrate into the context of the 1960s. Working at Harvard, Chermayeff published his influential book *Community and Privacy* with Christopher Alexander in 1963. As the title suggests, an intuitive architectural issue dominates the book – the search for the form of a domestic sanctum. The heaping of rhetorical gestures (the non-street, for instance) and statistics and interpretations all lead quietly to the illustration of a series of studies and examples of courtyard houses at the back of the book. All of these offer one thing: a bit of courtyarded, timeless nature unique to each room of the house.[39]

The rest of the text in the book is made up of suggestions explaining why people might want to live out this elegant, civic comedy of isolation within the community of the household. There are some interesting

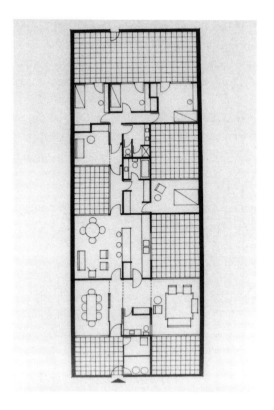

8.7
Serge Chermayeff
and Robert Gordon,
proposal for a
courtyard house,
from Serge
Chermayeff and
Christopher
Alexander,
*Community and
Privacy*, Doubleday,
Garden City, NY,
1963, p. 225

discussions of locks; small *antecameras*, with the dominating function of acting as buffer spaces. This is phrased with some hint of embarrassment at the idea of their transgression of Modernism's insistent poetics of open-handed honesty, social and architectural frankness.

In the 1930s, it seems that Chermayeff may have responded to the enormously complex public articulation of desires for isolation in residential buildings by the use of quite fascinatingly ambiguous frontages. In the 1960s, he offered the enclosed sanctum as the option for timeless, natural stability in overpowering modern urban diversity. He broke utterly with the traditions of the civic rear garden.

When these solutions were represented to a new public in the 1960s, the justification was largely a computational one; it is what describes the book's notoriety. Christopher Alexander supplied the novel statistical modelling that served to ratify Chermayeff's intuitive designs for courtyard living. When, in 1964, Christopher Alexander took the opportunity to speak for himself, he was more than happy to describe, if at a poetic remove, the Thomist basis of his conceptions of statistically led design form.[40]

If there was some form of urban-redemptive, theological context for Chermayeff's work in the 1930s, was there in Alexander's 1960s' supplement to it a pragmatic mathematics of privacy, or, perhaps rather more charmingly, was it some wildly romantic, personal and hermetic urban numerology? This would be interesting, because it is something that my granddad, as a practised water-diviner and someone with an interest in some of the mystical 'radio' groups that emerged in Britain in the mid- and later 1930s, happened to know something about.

Notes

1 T. More, *Utopia* (1516), London, Dent, 1991, p. 16.

2 Letter from Lindsay Grant complaining to Shena Simon (then Chair of the Housing Committee of Manchester Council) about the apparent decrease in the value of his new house on Ford Lane, Wythenshawe (19 June 1932). This started a long and important episode of correspondence for Simon in her role in implementing the Council's decision to build Wythenshawe, as part of a massive programme of modernisation for the city in the 1930s. The process of modernisation included proposals for a new airport, underground system, as well as the building of E. Vincent Harris's new town hall and library, a number of smaller libraries, and the substantial development of Wythenshawe and other suburban areas. This particular episode of correspondence relates to attempts to establish an acceptable means of screening for suburban gardens and new bye-laws preventing washing being hung out. See the archive of Simon's official correspondence, held at Manchester City Library.

3 The 'Right to Buy' scheme, enabling the tenants of municipally owned housing to buy, at enormous discount, the houses that they occupied, was introduced under the Housing Act of 1980. It was one of the first Acts passed by the new Conservative government.

4 M. Glendinning and S. Muthesius (eds) *Tower Block: Modern Public Housing in England, Scotland, Wales, and Northern Ireland*, New Haven, CT, Paul Mellon Centre for Studies in British Art and Yale University Press, 1994.

5 See, for instance, P. Kirkham, *Furnishing the World: The East End Furniture Trade, 1830–1980*, London, Journeyman Press, 1987.

6 For an interesting autobiographical parallel to this, see Pevsner's description of his own departure from Liverpool Street Station as the opening conceit in his volume on Essex for the Buildings of England series, published by Penguin in 1954.

7 For a discussion of the character of the *Daily Herald*, and its place in Labour politics in Britain until the mid-1960s, see H. Richards, *Bloody Circus: The Daily Herald and the Left*, London, Pluto, 1997.

8 T. S. Eliot, *Collected Poems*, London, Faber & Faber, 1964, p. 215.

9 See the series of suburban-minded articles Pevsner produced for the *Architectural Review*, as Donner, during the early 1940s under the title Treasure Hunts. The name comes from Georg Donner, his most favoured sculptor (see his comments in N. Pevsner and S. Sitwell, *German Baroque Sculpture*, London, Duckworth, 1938.). Note Henry-Russell Hitchcock's all-too-knowing celebration of 'Mr. Donner's little exercises in the London suburbs' (H.-R. Hitchcock, 'Some Problems in the Interpretation of Modern Architecture', *Journal of the American Association of Architectural Historians*, 1942, p. 29). Note, too, Reyner Banham's outrage at the perceived wartime betrayal of the Modernist project both by Pevsner and by

J. M. Richards, author of the Betjemanesque elegy to nineteenth-century suburbia, *Castles on the Ground*, London, Architectural Press, 1942 (in R. Banham, *Brutalism: Ethic or Esthetic*, London, Architectural Press, 1966).

10 See, for example, his essay 'Early and High Baroque', published first in *Reportorium für Kunstwissenschaft* in 1928, and later in volume 1 of his selected writings, *Studies in Art, Architecture and Design*, London, Thames & Hudson, 1968.

11 Davison, 'In the Privacy of One's Own Home', *Architect's Journal*, vol. 177, no. 6, 1983, pp. 75–6.

12 B. Colomina, 'Battlelines', in F. Hughes, (ed.) *The Architect: Reconstructing Her Practice*, Cambridge, MA, MIT Press, 1997.

13 See, for example, 'Privacy Regulation in Work Organisations', *Building Research and Information*, vol. 23, no. 1, 1995, pp. 17–23; and 'HEM: Directed Means for Improving the Current Means of Privacy Research', *Journal of Architectural and Planning Research*, vol. 13, no. 4, 1996, pp. 310–28.

14 It is in no way an architecture-focused text, however. In this brief discussion of the extant literature on privacy and architecture, mention should be made of Martin Pawley's early book, *Private Future: Causes and Consequences of Community Collapse in the West*, London, Thames & Hudson, 1973.

15 E. Panofsky, *Gothic Architecture and Scholasticism* (1951), London, Meridian Books, 1957.

16 It might be that there are some *Zeitgeist*-style relationships between, on the one hand, Panofsky's essay of the 1950s, on the other, the earlier mentioned moment in the 1950s, cited by Ian Davison, when privacy stopped being about light and started to be about shyness and, on a further array of hands, a host of other, differently intentioned essays produced during those years and which reduce to a line or two about the invasion of privacy and the danger of gossip leading residents of certain estates to exclude or limit the possibility of visiting, to reject the possibility of friendship with immediate neighbours and to reject too the street as a locus of civic activity, let alone public civic virtue. Those possible relationships *could* be articulated in terms of spirit of the age sentiments.

17 W. H. Brindley (ed.) *The Soul of Manchester*, Manchester, Manchester University Press, 1929.

18 It is worth drawing a contemporary comparison here with Michel de Certeau's Catholic-inspired exercise of a similar gambit in his enormously popular essay 'Walking in the City' (1974). See M. de Certeau, *The Practice of Everyday Life*, Berkeley, CA, University of California Press, 1984, pp. 91–111.

19 See C. H. Reilly, 'The Body of the Town', *Town Planning Review*, vol. 16, no. 2, 1934, pp. 89–93.

20 C. H. Reilly, *Scaffolding in the Sky*, London, Routledge, 1938.

21 See L. Wolfe, *The Reilly Plan: A New Way of Living*, London, Nicholson & Watson, 1945.

22 In a series of encyclia promulgated between 1923–30, Pius XI insisted on a return to the philosophical principles of Loyola, Augustine and Aquinas. These texts came to inform much of the cultural production of the period in Britain, in various ways. At the same time, much was made of Leo XIII's earlier call (1879) to a similar order of Christian philosophy coupled with a re-popularisation of the tenets of the *Rerum Novarum* of 1891. This latter document, the founding theological and socio-economic text of Chesterton-style Distributism, provides a justification for a system of syndicalism based on the private ownership of land and the ability to 'trade-up'. There are notable similarities between it and the image of the provisions for self-improvement of an individual within a particularly conceived meritocracy presented at the time by both Le Corbusier and Frank Lloyd Wright.

23 Note Waugh's enthusiasm for a Catholic-minded appreciation of Le Corbusier. See E. Waugh, 'Cities of the Future', *Observer*, 11 August 1929, p. 13. It is worth remembering too, that much has been made of Le Corbusier's interests in the near-mystical writings of aviator Antoine de Saint-Exupéry.

24 S. E. Rasmussen, *London: The Unique City*, London, Faber & Faber, 1934.

25 See, for instance, his arguments in *English Panorama*, London, Dent, 1936, and *Town Planning,* London, Penguin, 1940.

26 F. R. S. Yorke, *The Modern House in England*, London, Architectural Press, 1937.

27 For a discussion of this, see S. Lang, 'Richard Payne Knight and the Idea of Modernity', in J. Summerson (ed.) *Concerning Architecture: Papers Presented to Nikolaus Pevsner,* London, Penguin, 1968.

28 Reilly was influential in a number of ways and in a number of different spheres. It seems that his influence went as far as informing the views of, if not Barry Parker, then certainly Ernest Simon in the political moments that led up to Manchester Corporation's eventual decision to build Wythenshawe.

29 H. V. Morton, *The Heart of London*, London, Methuen, 1925.

30 For just one example of this in Chesterton's work, see his *Chaucer*, London, Faber & Faber, 1932.

31 For arguments concerning the 'true' meaning of public space, in this context, see H. Arendt, *The Human Condition*, Chicago, University of Chicago Press, 1958; R. Sennett, *The Fall of Public Man*, Cambridge, Cambridge University Press, 1977; M. Augé, *Non-Places: Introduction to the Anthropology of Supermodernity*, London, Verso, 1995; H. Lefebvre, *The Production of Space*, Oxford, Blackwell, 1991; R. Deutsche, *Evictions*, Cambridge, MA, MIT Press, 1996.

32 For the term 'the New Leisure', see Harry Roberts's cultural commentary in 'Leisure at the Seaside', *Architectural Review*, vol. 80, July, 1936, p. 16.

33 See, for example, M. Bowing, 'Incentives to Parenthood: Some Data from the Pioneer Health Centre, Peckham', *Eugenics Review*, vol. 35, 1943–4. See, too, the documentation of the centre and the staging of the preferred mode of the use of the Pioneer Centre in *The Architectural Review*, 1936.

34 See R. Stevens and P. Willis, 'Earl De La Warr and the Competition for the Bexhill Pavilion, 1933–4', *Architectural History*, vol. 33, 1990, pp. 135–66.

35 Note that the recent renovations of the building by Norman Foster's practice in 1992 have included the decision to paint the walls of the Cohen House a modishly blue, ash-white. This gesture achieves at least two things. It states a kind of revision of the 'Modern' architectural precepts thought to sustain the reputation of Foster's practice. It also breaks the contiguity of the two buildings, conclusively describing their distinction. This decision may have gone some way in resolving what Pevsner described as the 'unconvincing' shape of the dyadic façade.

36 This applied scrub is visible in the early models for the building, but is not seen in the early photographs of the completed structure.

37 For a rather more popular and hysterical view of the white witches in Essex, see Dennis Wheatley's series of novels, first published during the early to mid-1930s.

38 It is worth mentioning in this discussion of the *sukkah*, the second and the sixth songs of Solomon; Old Testament texts frequently referred to the celebration of Jewish weddings, often occurring in gardens, and ordinarily under the cover of a *chuppah*. In these texts, love is conjured in the poetics of the flora of a walled garden.

39 Gordon started to work with Chermayeff *c.*1957, after Chermayeff secured a grant to study low-rise welfare housing options in the USA.

40 C. Alexander, *Notes on the Synthesis of Form*, Cambridge, MA, Harvard University Press, 1964. It is worth pointing to the ways that these arguments then developed: in A. Tzonis and S. Chermayeff, *The Form of Community*, London, Penguin, 1971; and Tzonis's solo-authored complaints about notions of privacy and the mathematical divination of approaches to urbanism in *Towards a Non-Oppressive Environment*, Boston, MA, I. Press, 1972.

Chapter 9

Rudolf Schwarz, the *Hochstadt,* and the reconstruction of Cologne

Rudolf Stegers

To look through the encyclopedia for other German architects of around the same age as Rudolf Schwarz would lead to the rather sad realisation that his is an under-represented generation. While the first generation of modernists were born in the 1860s with Peter Behrens and Hans Poelzig, and the second generation followed in the 1880s with Bruno Taut and Erich Mendelsohn, very few leading names were born in the years 1890–1904. Fritz Schupp, Richard Döcker, Hans Scharoun, Karl Schneider, Hans Döllgast and Otto Ernst Schweitzer form a group born within seven years before Schwarz; and Ferdinand Kramer, Hans Schwippert, Paul Baumgarten, Konrad Wachsmann, Bernhard Hermkes and Egon Eiermann all took their first breaths within seven years of Schwarz's birth. Those who had built something before 1930, generally the older ones, enjoyed regional reputations, but none of them – with the exception of Scharoun – could be counted among the great names.

A native of the Rhineland, Rudolf Schwarz was a builder, a writer and a believer: an open-minded polymath. He was born on 15 May 1897 in Strasbourg and died on 3 April 1961 in Cologne. In his youth

Schwarz thought radically and dialectically, in old age poetically and con-centrically. In his early essays one hears the voice of youthful criticism addressed towards the old guard. He responded to their buildings, which might be understood as simply expressionist, or simply constructivist, or simply functionalist, with an architecture that is entirely rational. Yet as a young man it was virtually impossible for him to use the term 'rational'. On the one hand, his spiritual milieu – the Catholic 'Lebensbewegung' (move-ment for life) – was never reconciled to the spirit of modernism and associ-ated rationality only with atheism. On the other hand, rationality was paraphrased in architecture as the dogma of functionalism and efficiency on the model of the mature Bauhaus, whose leadership – according to Schwarz – cultivated sympathies with communism. Another word was needed, there-fore, to describe his own project. Speaking of geometry, he could not have appealed to rationalism, but to *Die belehrte Unwissenheit* of Nikolaus von Kues, to assert that mathematics offers the greatest contribution to the understanding of the divine.

Schwarz located his own buildings in an area beyond tradition and modernity. His models were Hans Poelzig and Ludwig Mies van der Rohe. Poelzig became a father figure in May 1923, when he accepted Schwarz as a pupil into his master-class at the Akademie der Künste in Berlin. Previously, between 1914 and 1918, Schwarz had studied archi-tecture at the Technische Hochschule Charlottenburg, and had spent a year in the Philosophy Department at the University of Bonn, studying Catholic theology, history and philosophy. The influence of Poelzig remained power-ful. As Schwarz wrote in 1947 in the journal *Baukunst und Werkform*, 'We learned from him to risk our hearts on the great goal and not to waste it on the unworthy.'

Shared roots in the Catholic Rhineland, whence Schwarz came from an old Cologne family, bound him to his other great influence, Ludwig Mies van der Rohe, who was born in Aachen in 1886. They were also united in their commitment to an architecture grounded on geometry, in steel and glass in the case of the older man, in brick and stone with the younger. Yet in both cases geometry was understood not as the expression of a utilitarian or technocratic new society, but as the embodiment of nobler spiritual essences and goals.

Although he had been taken on by Poelzig as a master-student for three years, Schwarz left Berlin in February 1924 after only nine months and returned to the Catholic west of Germany. Here he was engaged as the resident architect of Burg Rothenfels am Main, a conference centre for the Catholic youth movement 'Quickborn'. After a short intermezzo as a teacher at the Technische Lehranstalten Offenbach (1925–7), Schwarz was

9.1
Castle at Rothenfels
am Main, Knights'
Hall, 1928, from
Rudolf Stegers,
*Räume der
Wandlung: Wände
und Wege: Studien
zum Werk von
Rudolf Schwarz*,
Wiesbaden, Vieweg,
p. 23

appointed Head of the Handwerkeren- und Kunstgewerbeschule (Handwork
and Applied Art School) at Aachen in 1927.

The year 1933 was a caesura for Schwarz. Neither a member of
the National Socialist Party nor its political opponent, his subsequent intellectual and architectural engagement with the new regime oscillated
between accommodation and resistance. Yet, as his cultural identity as
essayist and editor was determined by his association with the right-wing
journal *Die Schildgenossen* (Comrades in Arms), it is quite obvious that his
position was closer to coalition than opposition. None of his circle of friends

rejected the National Socialists unequivocally. On the contrary, they obeyed – some with more reluctance than others.

Meanwhile, the Kunstgewerbeschule (School of Applied Arts) in Aachen was running into difficulty. Empty coffers in Prussia had already led to the closure of art academies in 1932. To save the academy located in the Südviertel of Aachen, Schwarz and two colleagues privately published a pamphlet entitled *Werkschulung und Staat: Organischer Aufbau der Werkschulung in der Rheinprovinz* (Craft Training and the State: The Organic Structure of Craft Training in the Rhine-Province). This polemical text, sent to numerous public figures after August 1933, proposed the integration of all the schools of design in a hierarchy of local, regional and national centres, modelled on the lodges of the medieval masons. With the vision of the religious order and of the cathedral workshops in mind, the authors pleaded for a 'völkische Gemeinschaft', a 'community of the people', as a vehicle for the divine law that every educational system and syllabus should serve. This community would also explicitly resist the influence of capitalism and liberalism. First, said the authors, the material needs of the German people should be satisfied; second, the cultural needs. Third, the cities should be dissolved and their inhabitants resettled on the land. On cultivated fenland and moorland around the borders of the state, 'racially valuable families' should build a human 'rampart'. A perverse fantasy, but one that brought little response from the new regime. Similarly, the attempt to reach an arrangement with the Kampfbund für Deutsche Kultur (Fighting League for German Culture) also failed. Director Schwarz was sacked in February 1934, his school was closed down in April that year. At 37, and older than other colleagues forced to take the same step, Schwarz set himself up as an independent architect.

He was far too agile intellectually to be satisfied simply with the design and construction of houses. He also wrote. *Vom Bau der Kirche* (*The Church Incarnate*) was his main work. On both occasions when it was published, first in 1938 and then in 1947, it came at the wrong time and sold badly, as immediately before and after the war, the Germans had other, more pressing concerns.

Schwarz characterised the state of man with words like 'doom' and 'depravity', 'denial' and 'despair'. With words like 'emptiness' and 'void' he described the task of the church builder – a task which, in contrast to the swaggeringly positive mood of his contemporaries, he saw as ultimately insoluble. Anyone who says that the admission of impossibility is the presupposition of church-building has no faith in the healing powers of history. Yet the occupation of history by the Nazis made this claim rather precarious. Whereas Wilhelm Pinder in his 1933 lecture *Die bildende Kunst im*

neuen deutschen Staat (The visual arts in the new German state) anticipated, thanks to Adolf Hitler, the rebirth of a neo-medieval sense of unity,
and while Dominikus Böhm and Albert Boßlet paid homage to a defiant
Romanesque in their respective designs for St Engelbert in Essen (1936)
and St Salvator in Münsterschwarzach (1938), Schwarz vigorously rejected
the reprise of historical models. Copies like this were merely 'mock-ups', he
said, only suggestions of the sacral, which, rather than looking for the
modern equivalent, were content to assume the identity of an earlier, albeit
magnificent epoch.

Manuals of church-building follow convention. They pass on the
received knowledge from the old to the young. Not so Schwarz's book. The
challenge is already to be found in the Introduction. First, when the author
speaks of active hands and seeing eyes as the alpha and omega of true perception, he is aligning himself with the *tabula rasa* of architectural modernism; architecture is building out of pure form, which although it has a
past and a future, has no causality. Second, in those areas where society has
no aesthetic positions that are uncontaminated by ideology, not only the literary but also the architectural discourse presses towards nature and myth.
Both unify and give meaning to form. For this reason, their tenets offer a
particularly appropriate basis for church-building. Abstract schemes give
spatial expression to the relationship between man and God. It is a matter
of architecture *in potentialis*, an architecture of circular forms, axial forms,
and finally of ascending forms. Circle/semi-circle/straight line/semi-circle/
circle; or, rest/exit/journey/entrance/rest; or, seed/stem/flower. With
sequences like this, Schwarz portrayed architecture as analogous to onto-
genesis and biogenesis, which he called 'natural' processes of creation. Only
towards the end of the book do we find the recurrence of the language that
Schwarz had favoured during his years in Aachen. One must develop a
church like a motor out of its intrinsic laws. This is 'sakrale Sachlichkeit'.

The words come round again, but with shifted meanings.
Whereas in the late 1920s Sachlichkeit was understood as objectivity and
the building as stereometric composition, by the late 1930s the former had
taken on the meaning of authenticity, the latter of choreographed form.
Schwarz was so fascinated by the 'Cathedrals of Light', installed at the Party
rallies in Berlin and Nuremberg by Albert Speer, that he wanted to link
these ephemeral architectures to the liturgy.

While the book resembles texts from distant worlds, and Schwarz
– perhaps to strengthen this impression – is stingy with names, it is also a
product of the Germany of the brown hordes. The language of the slave,
which opponents must adopt when they wish to pen their thoughts, shimmers through Schwarz's critique of the bad taste that accompanies power.

9.2
Rudolf Schwarz,
Sankt-
Fronleichnam-
Kirche (Corpus
Christi Church),
Cologne, 1930, view
from Düppelstrasse,
from Rudolf
Stegers, *Räume der
Wandlung: Wände
und Wege: Studien
zum Werk von
Rudolf Schwarz*,
Wiesbaden, Vieweg,
p. 60

Isolated from the social context, religion becomes a refuge. Suddenly house-building mutates into church-building, and every house becomes a 'monument to marriage', where daily life is transformed into revelation.

With the invasion of Poland and France by German troops, military aggression created a positive swing towards the state from which Schwarz, too, was not immune. The journal *Die Schildgenossen* speaks the language of the fellow-traveller. In its final volume, which reached subscribers in May 1941, Schwarz as editor reviewed a book by Werner Picht, the advocate of mass education in the years of the Weimar Republic, entitled *Der soldatische Mensch* (The Soldierly Man). All Germans, said Picht, must henceforth take on the character of soldiers. According to Schwarz, no-one has the right to a gentle life; duty will decide. 'And this duty will be tough, even after the victory.' In June 1941, the architect began a new career. First in Thionville, then in Metz, and then in Saarbrücken, Schwarz directed the building and reconstruction programme in Lorraine, which had been annexed by Germany.

The city surrounding the cathedral

In later life Rudolf Schwarz presumably regarded the period as one of luck in misfortune. After nine months in the Pioneer Corps and a further nine months in French captivity, he was released early in February 1946. Commuting between Cologne and Frankfurt, new paths opened up for him. Professional prospects were to be found not only on the Rhine and Main. He was also offered positions in Hamburg and Lübeck, in Karlsruhe and Munich. When, in October 1946, he turned down an offer from the city authorities in Ulm, he had long since decided to work in Cologne. For the cathedral city in which his mother lived had become his home. And only here, in the shadow of the Romanesque Middle Ages – in the semi-circle encompassing St Kunibert in the north and St Severin in the south – could Schwarz realise his vision: the utopia of Catholic urbanity.

Schwarz – as chief planner and Director of the Wiederaufbau GmbH (Reconstruction Corporation) – worked on the realisation of this idea from the end of 1946 until the beginning of 1952. As church builder and regional planner, Schwarz considered himself equipped for this enormous task not least through the positions established in the course of writing his book *Von der Bebauung der Erde* (On the Building of the Earth, 1949). The main body of this text offers a résumé of the Lorraine planning project, which had already been produced during the second half of the war. With an additional chapter at both beginning and end, the book appeared in 1949. It is a long book. And the sentences, too, are long. On page 100, for example, one endless tapeworm of a sentence writhes along for over twenty lines. Thanks to words like 'Gegangenheit' (the concluded past) and 'Zergangenheit' (the faded past), besides the more familiar 'Vergangenheit' (the past), the vocabulary sounds as pretentious as the language of Martin Heidegger. Spiritual ecstasy and the smell of incense shroud much of the text; the homiletic and the tautological jostle side by side. Although adorned with beautiful drawings, the book found hardly any buyers, as the publisher, Lambert Schneider, repeatedly bemoaned. Uniquely, Martin Wagner – the former chief city architect of Berlin in the Weimar period – wrote to the author on 4 March 1950 from the USA, saying that he had been 'gripped by the book from the first page to the last'.

Perhaps Wagner's praise referred to the Introduction. What Schwarz noted under the title 'Raumplanung' (spatial planning) could be described – shunning 'scholarly' – as both green and right-wing. Schwarz understood the world as *Oikos*, which we should treat as householders who understand how to sustain its resources. Society, according to Schwarz, follows neither Rousseau's social contract nor the Hegelian dialectic. Rather, it needs both a 'völkisch' (populist) and 'ständisch' (hierarchical) structure. Within this structure the planner must function as both master and servant in one person. His realm extends in all directions and reaches from the deepest roots to the highest treetops. With reference to Lorraine, the author veers towards another theme: the nature of the Germans. Whereas Schwarz had made every effort in his book *Vom Bau der Kirche* to avoid any proximity to the jargon of the Nazis, one senses in the post-war text how strongly the years in the 'Westmark' (German-occupied Alsace-Lorraine) had dulled his thinking. Suddenly we find Schwarz using arguments both commonplace and barbaric to explain German aggression and expansionism. There is talk of Germany as a great nation trapped in a small land, a double demand for both harmony and destruction, even a lusting after kitsch and death, and sentences like 'supported by the sword stands the German Reich'. All this leaves today's reader, who has grown out of hasty condemnation, with a certain problem of comprehension. What are we reading? The views of a bewildered soul, compelled by his confrontation with the reality of the Holocaust, towards defensiveness rather than mourning?

A more sensitive editor would have advised Schwarz to dispense with political instruction, and to sing instead, at the beginning of *Von der Bebauung der Erde*, the hymn of praise to the earth that follows the perplexing chapter on order in space. This polyphonous *jubilate* to geology – a wonderful text on basins and bays, lichens and layers, crests and coasts, caves and canyons – has an analogy as its *continuo* voice. The history of walls and the history of man is one and the same. And just as if the author senses that every fern and every cabbage from smallest to largest are morphologically related, he sees the forms of nature as derived everywhere from the eternal prototype, growing from the 'Stufenturm als Weltgestalt' (lit. Ziggurat as world-form). Modifying his earlier position, however, Schwarz linked an assumed social hierarchy with an assumed hierarchy in the natural world simply by equating them. Work is carried out on the land, learning is pursued on the hilltop, sovereignty in the mountains, prayer on the mountain peaks. Man stands before God on narrow heights in rarified air, like 'the wanderer above the sea of mist' in the painting by Caspar David Friedrich.

And the city? This, says Schwarz is the place where the landscape becomes more and more dense, the place where work and learning, sovereignty and prayer encounter each other every day. Thanks to the accelerating pace of economic and technological development, town and country have lost their rigid boundaries. Yet the dismal mixture of the urban and the rural also has advantages. For the periphery relieves the metropolis from the dirt of industry and from the lowly masses – as Hugo von Hofmannsthal sighed from on high: 'Some down below, of course, must die.' Into the calm thus created, the old city centre can return, forming in the heart of the city the *Hochstadt* – the noble or sublime city. As it did in the past, the historic and religious core should serve the exceptional and precious needs of the society. Freedom here, according to Schwarz, would not mean the sense of detachment and unconcern so often mentioned in the essays of the *flâneurs*. On the contrary, the *Hochstadt* demands the community of ennobled spirits to become the reserve of the élite.

Schwarz's book *Von der Bebauung der Erde* must have struck the reader in 1949 in much the same way as the reader today. The book is somehow distant. And the reaction to the first chapter is as negative as the reaction to its final chapter is positive. Already published in 1947 in the new journal *Baukunst und Werkform* under the title 'Das Unplanbare' (The Unplannable), this closing chapter stood in absolute opposition to the brisk, forward-looking position of the planners of this period. The whole world is not the universe of the planner, insisted Schwarz, and city planning should be reversible. Confronted by the choice between crystal and chaos, Schwarz voted for the charm of disorder. His advocacy of planning as a piecemeal activity, his plea for the coexistence of the irreconcilable, negated the command to re-establish discipline, which until then had been the dominant voice. It was as if Schwarz had studied Karl Popper's *The Open Society and its Enemies* (1945), in order to criticise the chiliastic expectations of the utopians. Only on the penultimate page does Schwarz finally lapse from British pragmatism into German pessimism. 'Creation means sinking', he says. And goes silent.

Sentences like this had little in common with the daily life of Cologne. Ideas and plans for the redevelopment of the great city on the Rhine had existed long before the last bombs fell. In the summer of 1945 two memoranda by local Cologne architects, one by Karl Band and one by Wilhelm Riphahn, were presented to the Mayor, Konrad Adenauer. Band tended towards traditionalism, Riphahn towards modernism. Band was thinking primarily of the sense of home and locality, Riphahn about traffic. In questions of architecture, Band was inclined towards reconstruction, while Riphahn was concerned with typology. Further-reaching than the concise proposals of these architects were two books that had been written during the war but were first published in 1946. One, by the publicist Carl

Oskar Jatho, was entitled *Urbanität: Über die Wiederkehr einer Stadt* (Urbanity: On the Return of a City); the other, *Der Neuaufbau der Stadt Köln* (The Rebuilding of the City of Cologne), was by the journalist Hans Schmitt. Jatho gathers a group of melancholic intellectuals on a summer afternoon to argue about the future. The setting is a beehive converted into a primitive cottage in a vineyard in the Rhine Valley. Urs and Ursula, Severin and Sibylle, together with a stranger, dream of Cologne as an 'urban work of art', which needs neither specific cultural or political institutions, nor tourist attractions, since human society in Cologne lives under the mandate of God. For this reason, the entire central area around the Romanesque sanctuary should, argued Jatho, become an 'Immunität' – an area solely under the legislation and jurisdiction of the Catholic Church and protected from the pressures of the modern city. Schmitt, too, proposed to ban all traffic from the semi-circular old town, which he wanted to dedicate to high culture and high commerce. Arcades, passages and terraces, as well as houses with flat roofs and roof gardens would, in the future, give the city its character.

9.3
Rudolf Schwarz,
Redevelopment
Plan for Cologne,
1948, from Rudolf
Stegers, *Räume der
Wandlung: Wände
und Wege: Studien
zum Werk von
Rudolf Schwarz*,
Wiesbaden, Vieweg,
p. 94

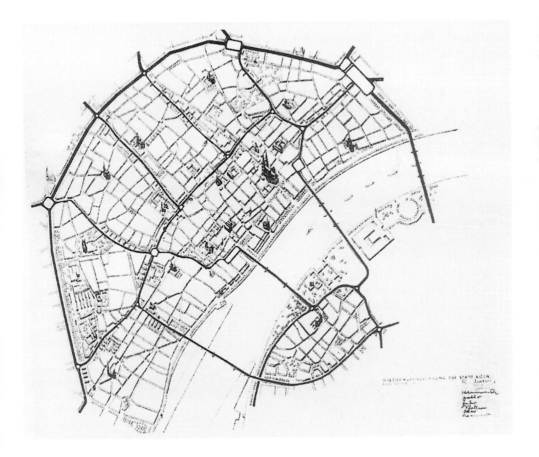

Without question, Schwarz found in the spectrum of proposals from Band to Schmitt much with which to agree and disagree. Many of the ideas and details of his own planning were based on these precursors. Were one to compare the respective positions of Schwarz and Jathro, the former would tend towards pragmatism, the latter strongly towards idealism. Yet for Schwarz, too, utopia illuminated the horizon. His proposals for the reconstruction and rebuilding of Cologne, first outlined hardly six months after taking on the task, contained almost all the main features of the project that first became known to the wider, non-professional public in 1950 in his book *Das neue Köln: ein Vorentwurf* (The New Cologne: A Preliminary Design).

First, the political union of larger and smaller municipalities on both banks of the Rhine into a city federation. Second, the *Hochstadt* as the site of spiritual elevation linked to the parishes structuring the old town. Third, the idea of a twofold daily existence, determined partly by the muses and partly by the machine, and given physical expression by the strict separation of traffic, which would distinguish between life on foot and on wheels. Fourth, the conception of an architecture that renounces reconstruction and develops a 'franconian attitude', as displayed by the three-window house typical of Cologne. Fifth, the establishment of a northern, industrially driven extension for over 300,000 inhabitants, based on the 40,000-strong municipality of Fühlingen. Sixth, the proposition to build organic housing colonies comparable to Bourneville, the model housing estate near Birmingham of the English chocolate company Cadbury; everyone should live in their own house with their own garden. Seventh,

9.4
Rudolf Schwarz, St Christophorus-Kirche (St Christopher's Church), Cologne-Niehl, 1954–9, from *Wolfgang Pehnt, Bewohnte Bilder: Rudolf Schwarz 1897–1961: Architekt einer anderen Moderne*, Ostfildern, Hatje, 1997, p. 195. Rheinisches Bildarchiv Köln

landscaping of the hills of rubble located around the greenbelt, and of the banks of the Rhine.

A progression of landscape and land use runs through Cologne, beginning with the villas of Koblenz and ending with the factories in Duisburg. In a lecture given in 1947, Schwarz named the changing functions simply 'causes', and listed them as commerce/education/ sovereignty/prayer. His proposals for replanning Cologne followed this logic. Commerce is located in the north around Chorweiler; education in the south in Lindenthal; sovereignty is located around the Alter Markt; and prayer focused on the cathedral. Schwarz wanted to embrace the left and right halves of the city within curved arterial roads that would have formed a reversed S and freed the urban nucleus from through traffic. These main North–South and West–East Streets and their feeder roads would border the new church lands, but would never penetrate them. The area around the churches should be dedicated to the human and not the technical side of man.

Suddenly we find ourselves in the centre of the *Hochstadt*. Unfortunately, notes Schwarz, the old Cologne families have moved out to the green suburbs, to be replaced in the old houses by people 'without roots'. The *Hochstadt*, however, must be populated by those who pursue the most noble and sublime goals on behalf of the community, and for this reason Schwarz had no scruples about arguing for social segregation. The highest of the high is the cathedral, the epicentre of the bishop's see. For the planner Schwarz, it was already vexing that the cathedral hill had disappeared under steps and streets during the Wilhelmine period. In order to restore the area to the spiritual ownership of the Catholic community, Schwarz worked up strategies in 1947 to revalorise the site. His ideas included the siting to the north-west of the cathedral of an academy combining university and monastery, which in the church of St Andreas would proclaim and protect the heritage of the scholar Albertus Magnus, whose remains rest in the crypt. On the south-east side of the cathedral Schwarz envisaged a repository for cult objects, which would be kept as if in a sacristy and not a museum, so that their true essence, their religious rather than their aesthetic qualities, would once again become paramount. Although never implemented, Schwarz still held to this vision in his monograph *Kirchenbau: Welt vor der Schwelle* (Church-building: The World in Front of the Threshold, 1960), in which he proclaimed: 'The metropolis is dead, long live the *Hochstadt*!'

To return to the beginnings of the post-war planning: when the Americans entered Cologne in March 1945, a little over 100,000 people were still living on the left and right side of the river. Nine-tenths of the old city lay in ruins; 32 million tons of rubble filled the streets and public squares. Three years later the streets were clean again. In August 1948, Cologne celebrated the seven-hundredth anniversary of the laying of the foundation stone of the cathedral. As if it were a funeral rite for the thousands of dead and missing beneath the rubble, the relics of the saint were placed on a bier beside the ruins of the St Maria Lyskirchen. The populace looked out from the piles of rubble and through empty window frames onto the purple-clad procession. Women bowed their heads, men doffed their hats, children fell to their knees as the priests passed across the Heumarkt and the Alter Markt to the cathedral.

Meanwhile the banking quarter around the station in the northern part of the Old Town had already regenerated itself vigorously; where money flows and people throng, everything moves more quickly. But the provisional nature of the individual buildings, the streets and the railway tracks hindered the implementation of any proposals for further development. Schwarz and his team made public their plans for the rebuilding of the Old Town in the autumn of 1948 at the Deutz Exhibition Hall. The audience was amazed that the west side of the Cathedral Bridge would no longer lead axially towards the polygonal chapel, but would be shifted slightly northwards. Even more amazing was the proposal to move the Main Station out of the centre to a new site on the Hansaring. Freed from the impact of its clamorous neighbours, the cathedral – the greatest church building in Cologne – would stand alone once more. Nothing except its Gothic magnificence would determine the meaning of the historic city core.

The project to move the Cathedral Bridge and relocate the Central Station failed. Equally unsuccessful was the plan to lead the new North–South Street on a serpentine course through the city centre, to stop drivers using the invitingly direct street to rush through the precious Altstadt. The reasons for these failures are different in each case; what they have in common, however, is the precedence given to the private over the public interest, and to the fetishised motor car, whose lobby ensured ever longer and broader streets in the major West German cities.

Following Joseph Stübben in the last quarter of the nineteenth century and Fritz Schumacher in the first quarter of the twentieth, Schwarz was the third great planner of Cologne. The legacy of Stübben is particularly visible in the Neustädte (city extensions) and the ring roads; the legacy of Schumacher's green belts is less visible. And Schwarz? On a first look it would seem that he has left no threads or knots at all in the fabric of the city – astonishing, given the vast possibilities that followed the monstrous destruction of the war. In volume 11 (1960) of the London journal *Town and Country Planning*, Thomas Greene – a lecturer at MIT – wrote that,

9.5
H. Waltenberg,
O. Schmitt and
H. Brunner, Central
Station, Cologne,
1957, from Rudolf
Stegers, *Räume der
Wandlung: Wände
und Wege: Studien
zum Werk von
Rudolf Schwarz*,
Wiesbaden, Vieweg,
p. 105

having already admired the cathedral through the glazed façade of the Central Station, he strolled full of expectancy through the Hohe Straße and the Schildergasse to the Neumarkt. But when he got there, the provisional, almost accidental urban solution that greeted his view was very disappointing. Was Greene looking, perhaps, for a stronger gesture, something of the quality shared – in spite of all their differences – by the Prinzipalmarkt in Münster and the Hansaviertel in Berlin?

Schwarz would have responded to the visitor from Cambridge, Massachusetts, with all his customary verve. First, the unique identity of Cologne is derived from the all-powerful presence, both institutional and architectural, of the cathedral. Second, this very presence precludes useful comparison either with traditionalist reconstruction as practised in Nuremberg and Freiburg, or with the more modernist approach to rebuilding pursued in cities like Braunschweig and Kassel. Third, Schwarz would have pointed to an essay by Carl Oskar Jatho, *Das neue Köln* (The New Cologne), where Jatho speaks of 'dignity' and demands that the area embracing the twelve great Cologne churches should be declared an *Immunität*. The nonplussed American planner might then have asked if the centre of Cologne was somehow exempt from the constitutional laws of West Germany. Schwarz would have noticed this slightly impertinent response immediately, assuring his guest that while he was sympathetic to Jatho's pious hopes, he found them rather unrealistic. Changing the topic, Schwarz might have shown his American visitor some buildings by Karl Band, which exemplified the typology of the Cologne business house: a narrow rectangular site with three or four storeys above the ground floor; half-timbered construction, low-set but tall windows with parapets, a hip-roof, pulling back sharply above the eaves to form a high pitch. On this tour of Cologne, the only part of the city better left unmentioned would be the area around the churches. Maybe the guest would have noted with some pleasure the high proportion of apartments housed in the buildings grouped around St Maria im Kapitol. But of Schwarz's idea to create an island of peace and calm amid the turmoil of the city there would have been no trace. Schwarz's post-war vision of a *Hochstadt* as the essential focus of the city, both physically and spiritually, had proved a chimera. On the West–East Street, the traffic thundered in the direction of the Deutz Bridge.

Bibliography

Introduction

Wassily Kandinsky, *Über das Geistige in der Kunst*, Munich, Piper, 1912; English edition as Wassily Kandinsky, *Concerning the Spiritual in Art*, trans. M. T. H. Sadler, reprint of 1914 edition, London, Constable, 1977.

Bruno Taut, *Die Stadtkrone*, Jena, Diederichs, 1919.

Iain Boyd Whyte, *Bruno Taut and the Architecture of Activism*, Cambridge, Cambridge University Press, 1982.

Colin Rowe, *The Architecture of Good Intentions*, London, Academy Editions, 1994.

Karsten Harries, *The Ethical Function of Architecture*, Cambridge, MA, MIT Press, 1997.

From *locus genii* to heart of the city

Art and Life, and the Building and Decoration of Cities: A Series of Lectures by Members of the Arts and Crafts Exhibition Society, Delivered at the Fifth Exhibition of the Society in 1896, London, Percival, 1897.

Charles Robert Ashbee, *Where the Great City Stands. A Study in the New Civics*, London, Essex House Press, 1917.

J. Tyrwhitt, J. L. Sert and E. N. Rogers (eds) *Congrès Internationaux d'Architecture Moderne, The Heart of the City: Towards the Humanisation of Urban Life*, London, Lund Humphries, 1951.

Sigfried Giedion, *Architecture, You and Me: The Diary of a Development*, Cambridge, MA, Harvard University Press, 1958.

Dietmaer Kamper and Christoph Wilf (eds) *Das Heilige: Seine Spur in der Moderne*, Frankfurt am Main, Athenaeum, 1987.

Straight or crooked streets?

George R. and Christiane Crasemann Collins, *Camillo Sitte and the Birth of Modern City Planning*, London, Phaidon, 1965.

Brian Ladd, *Urban Planning and Civil Order in Germany*, Cambridge, MA, Harvard University Press, 1990.

Michael Monninger, *Vom Ornament zum Nationalkunstwerk: Zur Kunst- und Architekturtheorie Camillo Sittes*, Braunschweig/Wiesbaden, Vieweg, 1998.

Anthony Vidler, *Warped Space: Art, Architecture and Anxiety in Modern Culture*, Cambridge, MA, MIT Press, 2000.

David Frisby, *Cityscapes of Modernity: Critical Explorations*, Cambridge, Polity, 2001.

August Endell: the spirit and the beauty of the city

August Endell, *Die Schönheit der großen Stadt*, Stuttgart, Strecker & Schröder, 1908.

Wilhelm Worringer, *Abstraktion und Einfühlung: Ein Beitrag zur Stilpsychologie*, Munich, Piper, 1908; English edition as *Abstraction and Empathy: A Contribution to the Psychology of Style*, trans. Michael Bullock, London, Routledge and Kegan Paul, 1953.

Tilmann Buddensieg, 'Zur Frühzeit von August Endell. Seine Münchener Briefe and Kurt Breysig', in Justus Mueller und Werner Spies (eds) *Festschrift für Eduart Trier zum 60. Geburtstag* (Berlin, Gebr. Mann, 1981).

Fritz Neumeyer, *Mies van der Rohe: The Artless Word*, Cambridge, MA, MIT Press, 1991.

Embodying the spirit of the metropolis

M. Rapsilber, 'Das Werk Alfred Messels', and Fritz Stahl, 'Alfred Messel', *Sonderhefte der Berliner Architekturwelt*, vols 1 and 2, Berlin, Wasmuth, 1911.

Karl Scheffler, *Die Architektur der Großstadt*, Berlin, Bruno Cassirer, 1913.

Simone Ladwig-Winters, *Wertheim: Geschichte eines Warenhauses*, Berlin, be.bra verlag, 1997.

Brian Ladd, *The Ghosts of Berlin: Confronting German History in the Urban Landscape*, Chicago, University of Chicago Press, 1998.

Geoffrey Crossick and Serge Jaumain (eds) *Cathedrals of Consumption: The European Department Store 1850–1939*, Aldershot, Ashgate, 1999.

The Hamburg Bismarck as city crown and national monument

Karl Scheffler, *Moderne Baukunst*, Berlin, Julius Bard, 1907.

Thomas Nipperdey, 'Nationalidee und Nationaldenkmal in Deutschland im 19. Jahrhundert,' *Historische Zeitschrift*, vol. 206 (June 1968), 529–85.

Ekkehard Mai and Stephan Waetzoldt, *Kunstverwaltung, Bau- und Denkmal Politik im Kaiserreich*, Berlin, Gebr. Mann, 1981, 277–314.

Eric Hobsbawm and Terence Ranger, *The Invention of Tradition*, Cambridge, Cambridge University Press, 1983.

David Boswell and Jessica Evans (eds) *Representing the Nation*, London and New York, Routledge, 1999.

The lantern and the glass

Le Corbusier, *New World of Space*, New York, Reynal & Hitchcock, 1948.

Joseph Rykwert, *The Idea of a Town*, Cambridge, MA, MIT Press, 1976.

Michael Raeburn and Victoria Wilson (eds) *Le Corbusier, Architect of the Century*, Exhibition Catalogue, London, Arts Council of Great Britain, 1987.

Maurice Merleau-Ponty, *The Phenomenology of Perception*, London, Routledge, 1989.

Le Corbusier, *Precisions on the Present State of Architecture and City Planning*, trans. Edith Schreiber Aujame, Cambridge, MA, MIT Press, 1991.

William Rubin, *Picasso and Braque: Pioneering Cubism*, Exhibition Catalogue, New York, Museum of Modern Art, 1989.

Le Corbusier and Pierre Jeanneret, *Œuvre Complète, 1910–1929*, 14th edition, Zurich, Éditions d'Architecture, 1995.

Transcendent modernity in British urban reconstruction

Ioan Gwilym Gibbon, *Reconstruction and Town and Country Planning*, London, Architect & Building News, 1942.

Charles B. Purdom, *How Should we Rebuild London?*, London, Dent, 1945.

Andrew Boyd and Colin Penn (eds) *Homes for the People*, London, Elek, 1946.

Richard Sheppard, *Building for the People*, London, George Allen & Unwin, 1948.

Frederick Gibberd, *Town Design*, London, Architectural Press, 1953.

Percy Johnson-Marshall, *Rebuilding Cities*, Edinburgh, Edinburgh University Press, 1966.

Privet: theologies of privacy in some Modernist urbanism

Evelyn Underhill, *Mysticism: The Nature and Development of Spiritual Consciousness*, London, Methuen, 1911.

H. V. Morton, *In Search of England*, London, Methuen, 1928.

Charles Williams, *The Image of the City and Other Essays*, Oxford, Oxford University Press, 1958.

Christopher Alexander and Serge Chermayeff, *Community and Privacy: Toward a new Architecture of Humanism*, Garden City, NY, Doubleday, 1963.

Gillian Rose, *The Broken Middle: Out of Our Ancient Society*, Oxford, Blackwell, 1992.

Rudolf Schwarz

Rudolf Schwarz, *Vom Bau der Kirche* (1938), second edition, Heidelberg, Schneider, 1947.

Rudolf Schwarz, *Von der Bebauung der Erde*, Heidelberg, Schneider, 1949.

Wolfgang Pehnt, *Bewohnte Bilder: Rudolf Schwarz 1897–1961*, Ostfildern, Hatje, 1997.

Rudolf Stegers, *Räume der Wandlung: Wände und Wege, Studien zum Werk von Rudolf Schwarz*, Braunschweig, Vieweg, 2000.

Hans-Georg Lippert, *Historismus und Kulturkritik: Der Kölner Dom 1920–1960*, Cologne, Verlag Kölner Dom, 2001.

Index